Reconnecting Marketing to Markets

W9-BEZ-930

Reconnecting Marketing to Markets

Edited by

Luis Araujo

John Finch and

Hans Kjellberg

OXFORD
UNIVERSITY PRESS

OXFORD
UNIVERSITY PRESS

Great Clarendon Street, Oxford OX2 6DP

Oxford University Press is a department of the University of Oxford.
It furthers the University's objective of excellence in research, scholarship,
and education by publishing worldwide in

Oxford New York

Auckland Cape Town Dar es Salaam Hong Kong Karachi
Kuala Lumpur Madrid Melbourne Mexico City Nairobi
New Delhi Shanghai Taipei Toronto

With offices in

Argentina Austria Brazil Chile Czech Republic France Greece
Guatemala Hungary Italy Japan Poland Portugal Singapore
South Korea Switzerland Thailand Turkey Ukraine Vietnam

Oxford is a registered trade mark of Oxford University Press
in the UK and in certain other countries

Published in the United States
by Oxford University Press Inc., New York

© Oxford University Press, 2010

The moral rights of the authors have been asserted
Database right Oxford University Press (maker)

First published 2010

All rights reserved. No part of this publication may be reproduced,
stored in a retrieval system, or transmitted, in any form or by any means,
without the prior permission in writing of Oxford University Press,
or as expressly permitted by law, or under terms agreed with the appropriate
reprographics rights organization. Enquiries concerning reproduction
outside the scope of the above should be sent to the Rights Department,
Oxford University Press, at the address above

You must not circulate this book in any other binding or cover
and you must impose the same condition on any acquirer

British Library Cataloguing in Publication Data

Data available

Library of Congress Cataloging in Publication Data

Data available

Typeset by SPI Publisher Services, Pondicherry, India
Printed in Great Britain
on acid-free paper by
MPG Books Group, Bodmin and King's Lynn

ISBN 978–0–19–957806–1 (Hbk.)
       978–0–19–957807–8 (Pbk.)

1 3 5 7 9 10 8 6 4 2

■ FOREWORD

Marketing is an activity and process in a market context. Thus most people will agree that marketing and markets are connected, both in theory and in practice. However, the title of this book, 'Reconnecting Marketing to Markets', suggests that not only has there been a disconnection in academic research sometime in the past but also that the editors and authors entertain ideas about a possible, timely, and worthwhile reconnection. The problem, it is argued, is that not enough attention is paid in academic research to how real markets are constructed, shaped, reshaped, stabilized, and changed over time. In the vocabulary used, markets are 'performed' in practice, and are not a priori defined as implied by marketing theories. Marketing has an important performative role in shaping markets. Efforts to understand this role will help to reconnect research on marketing to research on markets. How knowledge about marketing and markets developed in academia affects marketing practices and shapes markets thus becomes a major research question.

Market governance for products and services has become increasingly important and changed in character over the last few years. There are many examples of this. Deregulation of public services and transformation of centrally planned economies to market economies are efforts to create markets. Globalization of markets and 'convergence' of markets change market boundaries. 'Market orientation' refers to ideas of how a firm should relate more effectively to the market. 'Outsourcing' transfers some activities from the firm to suppliers. Much is thus at stake, both from a business and a societal perspective, to understand how markets are performed and the role of marketing in these performations. Academic research should help to provide such knowledge.

However, the disconnection between marketing and markets in academic research makes this more difficult to achieve. Why has this, somewhat surprising, disconnection happened? I believe there are three reasons. First, there is a *disconnection between academic disciplines*, especially between marketing and economics, and also between marketing and other subfields of business studies as well as between economics and sociology. A second reason is that *dominant research methodologies* in marketing and economics are inappropriate to conduct performative studies. Third, the dominating *conceptualization of marketing* as marketing management, rather than as a societal process enabling economic exchange, restricts marketing to specific seller activities and the market to a collection of buyers.

If we go back to the early stages of academic marketing research, the most important approaches, hopefully well known to marketing scholars even today, were the functional, commodity, institutional, and regional 'schools of marketing' (cf. Sheth et al. 1988). They focused on analysing marketing as aspects of structure, process, and effectiveness of markets. It was about society rather than about individual firms, and the distribution of goods was of primary importance. Until the 1960s, the academic subject of marketing in Sweden dealt with the economy of distribution ('distributionsekonomi'). Early marketing scholars to an important extent had a research background in economics.

The functionalist approach developed by Wroe Alderson in the 1950s connected marketing and markets using a systems perspective. Interaction within and between organized behaviour systems in markets linked heterogeneous supply to heterogeneous demand across several production levels. The year before he died, Alderson in 1964 co-published a book, *Planning and Problem Solving in Marketing*, together with a young colleague, Paul Green (Alderson and Green 1964). With the benefit of hindsight, this book captures, as I see it, a significant moment of change from a focus on marketing and markets using a broad societal perspective to a focus on marketing as a managerial activity, and research in marketing as application of quantitative techniques and model building. Paul Green, with a strong background in statistics, had an important role in this development. Research in marketing and economics became less and less connected. Marketing specialized on the marketing function in the firm whereas economics focused on the neoclassical, 'arm's length' market model.

Research in marketing became less preoccupied by the market as a phenomenon in its own right. The early interest in the overall functioning of markets and the role of marketing in this faded away. The market became the hunting ground for sellers to search out their target groups in competition with other sellers armed with their own marketing mix weapons, derived from the theory of monopolistic competition (cf. Chamberlin 1933). The dominating streams of marketing research became oriented to marketing management and buyer behaviour. In marketing textbooks, the market was mostly defined as a set of actual and potential buyers. There are of course exceptions. A major example is marketing research with a business network perspective on markets, to which the editors of this book have contributed.

Obviously, there is a connection between marketing and markets in the economic theories of imperfect competition that might be reflected in practice and contribute to the performative role of marketing. In the basic Industrial Organization (IO) model there is a feedback loop, rarely travelled though, from market conduct (aspects of marketing) to market structure (Scherer 1970). Mediated by public policy dimensions, such as competition laws, there is also a connection between market structure and marketing. The

IO model also includes a set of basic conditions (such as technology), which, as exogenous variables, affect market structure.

However, to understand how markets are performed, practice in real markets need to be studied, not just relations in a model or association between variables found in empirical research. The authors in this book have turned to sociological and organizational studies focusing on practice and performativity. These methodological approaches are linked to Science and Technology Studies (STS) and the related Actor-Network Theory (ANT) that have become increasingly applied to economic and business phenomena, thus becoming a new branch of Economic Sociology.

To give an idea about the content of the book and the nature of the approach to reconnect marketing and markets, I will refer to issues discussed in the ten chapters. Chapters are identified by the surnames of the authors. The book reports on the practice/performativity connections between marketing and market for a variety of markets, such as markets for DIY tools, food, air travel, clothing, petrol, and services. Exchanges in the markets studied concern what the editors refer to as mundane products and services. The plea for recognition of heterogeneity and complexity of such markets is certainly matched by the book's contents.

Evidence that *marketing practices shape and reshape markets* is presented and discussed in most of the chapters. Markets relate production and consumption (use), not just seller and buyer (Shove and Araujo). Use of material devices in retail marketing partly constitute and, over time, reshape markets (Cochoy). Implementation of marketing strategies serves to configure buyers as market agents (Hagberg) and to shape differentiated market practices (Finch and Geiger). Qualification experiments mobilizing different forms of expertise, data, and devices connect market participants (Dubuisson-Quellier). Buyers organize competition and influence the development of alternative exchange practices (Reverdy). Hybrid Fair Trade markets are co-constructed as an interaction between concepts and practices (Neyland and Simakova). Calculation of exchange practices in interaction between policy makers and a trade association influence the development of a differentiated market for public services (Fries). Implementation of competition law reshapes market boundaries (Kjellberg).

A common theme across the chapters is the role of *materiality and devices* in market practice. It is the use of products in their socio-material context, not the purchase of the products that performs markets. There is a dynamic, interacting, and evolving relationship between users and products (Shove and Araujo). Retailers' use of material devices as an aspect of marketing partly constitutes the market (Cochoy). Different modes of exchange evolved in the development of e-commerce that needed development of new devices to move buyers to different transaction points (Hagberg).

Measurements, sometimes related to devices, are important to understand market performance. Performance metrics help to shape markets because they assist in *calculation*, for example accounting practices when retailing strategies change (Azimont and Araujo). Various market research measures during product development processes influence product formulations, interactions within the firm, and the definition of consumers (Dubuisson-Quellier). Use of different price reference indexes when markets are re-regulated affect competition (Reverdy).

The performative role of *political actors* such as government agencies, trade associations, and NGOs is an important aspect of the performation of markets. Politics and marketing are intertwined. Deregulation of monopoly markets affects price structure and development of contractual forms for exchange (Reverdy). Certification of Fair Trade products by NGOs is important for the definition and differentiation of Fair Trade Markets (Neyland and Simakova). Trade associations influence new government policies for the marketization of public services (Fries). Implementation of competition law in a court case leads to changes in market conduct and to a redefinition of products and market boundaries (Kjellberg).

To account for and understand the performative role of *theories*, often in conflict with each other, is of central importance. In the application of competition law, microeconomic theory (IO) prevailed, but was somewhat reinterpreted in performing the market (Kjellberg). Market theories that treat the purchase of objects in isolation from their use is opposed to market theories emphasizing the dynamic relationship between users and products in their socio-material contexts (Shove and Araujo). Deregulation, based on microeconomic theory, did not result in competition as envisaged by perfect competition models (Reverdy).

I have suggested three reasons for the disconnection between marketing and market studies. For a reconnection the research approach needs to be interdisciplinary, use methods that are able to describe complex processes, and define marketing practices in broader terms than those portrayed in marketing management textbooks. This is a challenging task and a tall order for marketing research. But an increasing number of researchers are brave enough to venture into such a process.

Lars-Gunnar Mattsson
Professor Emeritus, Stockholm School of Economics

■ CONTENTS

■ ACKNOWLEDGEMENTS

The genesis of this book lies in many discussions, activities, and projects organized by the Market Studies group, a special interest group within the broader IMP (Industrial Marketing and Purchasing) community. The group has organized special tracks at the IMP annual conferences starting in Copenhagen in 2004. This led to a number of publications as well as a special issue in *Marketing Theory* on 'Market Practices and Forms' (Vol. 8, No. 1, 2008). Workshops at Euromed in Marseille, University College Dublin, the University of Southern Denmark, and the University of Strathclyde provided excellent opportunities to develop ideas and led to a number of further initiatives including this volume.

The editors are very grateful to colleagues in the Market Studies group for their support and for entrusting us to carry the torch for this project. In particular, we would like to mention Rob Spencer, Damien McLoughlin, Torben Damgaard, Claes-Fredrik Helgesson, Debbie Harrison, Lars Huemer, Thomas Ritter, Diego Rinallo, Franck Cochoy, Enrico Baraldi, Susi Geiger, Per Andersson, and Finn Wynstra for their support over the last few years. Outside the group, we thank friends and colleagues within IMP for their support of our various initiatives. We also owe a debt of gratitude to Lars-Gunnar Mattsson and Michel Callon for reading the whole manuscript and providing a preface and a commentary, respectively.

We are particularly grateful to the reviewers who helped us bring the individual chapters towards completion. We carved up the editorial work amongst the three of us and enlisted the help of two anonymous reviewers for each chapter. Our reviewers provided extensive comments on earlier drafts and engaged constructively and patiently with the authors and editors throughout the whole process. Thanks also to Geoff Easton, Susi Geiger, and Claes-Fredrik Helgesson for providing feedback on drafts of our introduction and conclusions. We also acknowledge the Telegraph Media Group for permission to reproduce the article, 'Ryanair sued by passengers over cancelled flight', in chapter 6. Finally, we acknowledge the help and support from the Oxford University Press, namely David Musson and Emma Lambert.

Luis Araujo, John Finch, and Hans Kjellberg

◾ LIST OF FIGURES

■ LIST OF TABLES

■ LIST OF CONTRIBUTORS

Luis Araujo is a Professor of Industrial Marketing at Lancaster University Management School. His research interests and publications are in the area of business markets, namely the boundaries of the firm and product-service systems. His recent work focuses on a practice-based approach to the study of markets.

Frank Azimont is Professor of Marketing at EMLYON Business School (France). His research examines market practices where manufacturers and retailers are involved in the business of fast-moving consumer goods. His current work investigates categorization, calculative and metrological practices, and performance definitions.

Michel Callon is a Professor of Sociology at the École Nationale Supérieure des Mines de Paris and a researcher at the Centre de Sociologie de l'Innovation. He works on the sociology of markets and the study of technical democracy, and he is completing a research with Vololona Rabeharisoa on European patients' organizations. He has recently published *Market Devices* (with Yuval Millo and Fabian Muniesa) and *Acting in an Uncertain World* (with Pierre Lascoumes and Yannick Barthe).

Franck Cochoy is Professor of Sociology at the Université de Toulouse II and member of the CERTOP-CNRS, France. He is also a Visiting Professor at the University of Gothenburg. His past and present research is focused on the human and technical mediations that frame the relation between supply and demand.

Sophie Dubuisson-Quellier is a Researcher at the Centre de Sociologie des Organisations (Sciences Po-CNRS) in Paris. She has been working on the sociology of markets, analysing the role of devices and actors in market mediation. Her current research investigates governance of consumer behaviour by firms, social movements, and the state.

John Finch is a Professor of Marketing at the University of Strathclyde. His research interests focus on the adaption of products and services in and around market spaces. His current research includes marketing and sales in industrial chemistry, how actors undertake business networking, and how standards contribute to making goods and services marketable.

Liv Fries is a PhD candidate in Management at the Stockholm School of Economics and the Stockholm Centre for Organizational Research (SCORE). Her research interests concern the organization of markets, the role of associations in the economy, and the organization of internal and external communication. Her thesis is an ethnographic study of a Swedish business association.

Susi Geiger is Senior Lecturer in Marketing at the Smurfit School of Business, University College Dublin. Her research considers market interfaces both in business-to-business and business-to-consumer markets, with specific emphasis on the sales function. Her academic work is widely published in a range of international journals and has been recognized with a number of awards.

Johan Hagberg is a Senior Lecturer in Marketing at the School of Business, Economics, and Law, University of Gothenburg. His research examines market practices in the field of retailing and his current work investigates the practices of retail store management and consumer logistics.

Hans Kjellberg is Associate Professor of Marketing at the Stockholm School of Economics. His research interests concern economic organizing in general and the shaping of markets in particular. Current research projects include how marketing practices contribute to shape mundane markets and how investment bank experts help shape the financial markets.

Lars-Gunnar Mattsson is Professor Emeritus at the Stockholm School of Economics. His research deals with marketing, internationalization, and distribution from a business network perspective. Currently, he works on the temporality of business practices to understand the dynamics of firms and markets, especially in globalization processes.

Daniel Neyland is a Senior Lecturer in Organization, Work and Technology at Lancaster University Management School. His research covers a broad array of issues focused around science and technology. In particular, he is interested in governance, accountability, security, marketing, order, disorder, resistance, ethics, and inequality. Empirically, his research engages ethnographically with CCTV systems, airports and biometrics, traffic management, waste management, Fair Trade, and neglected diseases.

Thomas Reverdy is Assistant Professor in Sociology and Organization Theory at the University Pierre-Mendès-France in Grenoble. His research examines institutional and organizational change concerning markets, energy, and environmental issues in industry. His current work investigates purchasing practices.

Elizabeth Shove is Professor of Sociology at Lancaster University and holds a Fellowship in the ESRC Climate Change Leadership programme. Her research concerns everyday practices, mundane technologies, and ordinary consumption. She is the author of *Comfort, Cleanliness and Convenience: Infrastructures of Consumption* (with Bas van Vliet and Heather Chappells), and *The Design of Everyday Life* (with Matt Watson, Martin Hand, and Jack Ingram). She has recently edited *Comfort in a Lower Carbon Society* (with Heather Chappells and Loren Lutzenhiser) and *Time, Consumption and Everyday Life* (with Frank Trentmann and Rick Wilk).

Elena Simakova is Lecturer in Innovation at the University of Exeter Business School. Her research broadly concerns the organizational practices of the construction of credible accounts of innovation in the context of market relations, with particular interest in developing an ethnographic perspective on marketing knowledge. Her current work focuses on the politics of emerging technologies at the university–industry–policy interface and its publics.

Reconnecting marketing to markets

An introduction

LUIS ARAUJO, JOHN FINCH, AND HANS KJELLBERG

Marketing produces markets—not only, nor on its own, but still. This is the simple statement that unites the contributions of this edited volume. The chapters that follow seek to explore, in various ways, the character and limits of marketing's capacity to produce markets. By doing so, the chapters provide powerful illustrations of the statement that marketing produces markets and also of its deceptive simplicity. First, there is no stable set of practices or ideas that we can unequivocally call 'marketing'; what counts or should count as 'marketing' depends on local contingencies and changes over time. Second, the processes of 'producing' markets are complex and many marketing efforts partake; hence, the outcome rarely takes on the shape intended as part of any one effort. Third, 'markets' regularly take on a wide variety of forms; there is thus no single outcome of productive marketing work.

These observations about the role of marketing in the production of markets are the outcome of detailed empirical inquiries by researchers from a variety of disciplines, brought together by a common interest in understanding markets. The genesis of this book can be traced in part to novel sources of inspiration for studying marketing and markets, and in part to dissatisfaction with the prevailing conceptualizations of markets and market processes in marketing and elsewhere.[1] The remainder of this introduction will develop these two inspirations for exploring the relation between marketing and markets, and in so doing explicate some of the fundamental ideas that inform the contributions to this volume.

Markets in marketing thought

Why have marketers' activities in producing markets received so little attention within the marketing discipline? Simply put, the marketing discipline has tended to represent markets as passive backgrounds, against which market-ers have got on with the serious business of organizing sellers' exchanges with buyers, for instance by developing cognitive profiles and typologies of buyers, or designing schemes for customer relationship management. In fact, the once mandatory summaries of microeconomic principles have all but disappeared from marketing textbooks, which either fail to mention what markets are or simply define them as 'collections of buyers'. We argue that this is far from satisfactory and suggest that the marketing discipline is well positioned to contribute to developing theories about markets. Specifically, we bring marketers' activities to the foreground, illustrating how we can study such activities empirically and analyse them as instances of producing markets.

The current state of affairs, regarding markets and marketing, is well summarized by Venkatesh et al. (2006: 252): 'Paradoxically, the term market is everywhere and nowhere in our literature.' We trace this paradox to the late 1960s and early 1970s, when the discipline of marketing engaged in a fierce debate over its purposes and aims (Araujo and Kjellberg 2009; Bagozzi 2009). The triumph of the broadened concept of marketing pioneered by Kotler and Levy (1969) meant that marketing became a set of portable management technologies deployable in markets and non-markets alike. A new paradigm emerged anchoring the discipline in a generic notion of exchange, typically understood from the perspective of a marketing manager, broken free from its attachments to markets (Kotler 1972; Hunt 1976). Bagozzi (1975: 39) described marketing as 'the discipline of exchange behaviour', and marketing management as a 'function of universal applicability'. Subsequent generations of students were taught the generic concept of exchange as a foundational dogma (Shaw and Jones 2005).

Hence, markets are 'everywhere' because they are idealized settings or environments in which exchanges happen, but 'nowhere' because for market-ers, marketing works in and through discrete exchanges conducted against what is typically regarded as a static market backcloth (for an exception, see Rosa et al. 1999). The interest in exchange, which itself has ebbed and flowed (see Bagozzi 2009), has further been hampered by being under the direction of narrow economic motives and seller interests. But even social exchange theory, for all its focus on the parties that make exchanges and the occasional reference to networks, takes us no nearer an understanding of markets and instead leads to an ill-defined sociality of exchange (see Hagberg, this volume).

To make sense of the paradox of markets being 'everywhere and nowhere', we need to revisit marketing theory in its earlier incarnation, prior to those programmatic debates that gripped the discipline in the late 1960s and early 1970s. The nascent marketing literature could draw upon the price theory of neoclassical economics, perhaps augmented by the then faintly exotic new field of information economics (Snehota 2004). This price theory envisaged a universal market in which numerous and impersonal monetized exchanges overcame temporary imperfections, created by the efforts of marketing managers and advertising professionals amongst others.

At the same time, much of the early work in marketing was devoted to careful empirical studies of markets and their functioning, viz. the enabling role of distribution in market-making (Bartels 1962). Alderson (1965) contested the view of markets as homogeneous settings, characterized by perfect information and cleared by prices, and introduced the notion of perfectly heterogeneous markets where differentiated segments of demand met corresponding segments of supply.[2] Perfectly heterogeneous markets in the real world would never be wholly cleared and the role of marketing was to investigate these breaks and propose remedial actions. The remit of marketing theory until the mid-1960s can be exemplified by these two crisp quotes:

- 'The primary observable phenomenon for any theory of marketing is the hard practical fact of the market' (McInnes 1964: 52)
- 'A theory of marketing explains how markets work' (Alderson 1965: 23).

The evolution in marketing theory, leading to the emergence of the broadened concept of marketing and the incipient interest in exchange, marked a shift from a concern with markets as institutions to a focus on the management of exchanges from a one-sided, supply perspective (Snehota 2004). Markets became mere collections of actual and potential buyers of goods and deserving of no more than a one-sentence definition in textbooks (Sissors 1966; Barnhill and Lawson 1980; Samli and Bahn 1992). Beside their neglect of markets, the generic concept of marketing and the foundational notion of exchange also served to displace what counted as marketing. By conceiving of marketing as a set of management techniques for regulating the timing, level, and character of demand (or some other form of patronage), a number of important practices that marketers regularly engage in typically fell outside marketing proper. Witness, for example, the many boundary struggles that have sprung out of efforts to define the proper domain of marketing, e.g. between marketing and strategy, logistics, sales, and customer support. Moreover, the potential consequences of marketing activities for markets were largely ignored (but see Arndt 1979; Stidsen 1979).

The claim that the theorization of markets is grossly under-developed is hardly confined to marketing. North (1977: 710) remarked that: '...it is a peculiar fact that the literature of economics and economic history contains so little discussion of the central institution that underlies neoclassical economics—the market.' Loasby (1999: 112) commented: 'It seems clear that what is called "market theory" tells us rather little about markets...Markets are much too important, and much too amenable to economic analysis, to be treated as primitives.' More recently, Jackson (2007: 235) reiterated the same point: 'Markets have always been central to economics, yet they remain strangely ill-defined and amorphous.'

We can trace further the reasons for the curious absence of marketing theory about marketers' activities in producing markets. If narrow marketing drew on the neoclassical economists' price theory, in lieu of richer explanations of markets, broadened marketing with its generic approach to exchange, bears a striking resemblance to the classical economic sociologists' antipathy to markets (Parsons and Smelser 1956) and the attempt by some contemporary anthropologists to dissolve the notion of markets into broader systems of value (Miller 2002). The attempts by Bagozzi (1975, 2000, 2009) to construct a foundational platform for an all-encompassing notion of marketing exchanges follow in the same vein.

With few exceptions, the rekindling of economic sociology initiated by Granovetter (1985) also left the neoclassical economists' notion of the market untouched. The so-called embeddedness approach attempts to correct the deficiencies of *homo economicus* by enriching its qualities (e.g. passions, interests) and infusing it with values beyond utilitarianism and calculation. Sociologists had implicitly assumed that markets were unsuitable objects of study, accepting the economists' presumption that social relations could only play a disruptive and frictional role in market processes (Granovetter 1985: 504). In contrast to neoclassical economics, the embeddedness approach regards social relations as helping to achieve efficient economic outcomes rather than causing friction (Granovetter 2005). While a core of market behaviour outside society is typically recognized, certain types of exchanges are suggested to benefit from being embedded in an appropriate social structure (Uzzi 1997). Thus, market actors, for example, can calculate the utility of developing particular types of social relations in order to achieve useful economic outcomes (Biggart and Castanias 2001). Similarly, actors may trust information that flows through well-developed social networks more than information obtained through impersonal sources (Granovetter 2005). In short, healthy social structures help achieve economic prosperity (Biggart and Castanias 2001; Barry and Slater 2002). However, as Krippner (2002: 776) noted: 'The basic intuition that markets are socially embedded—while containing an important insight—has led economic sociologists to take the market for granted. As a result, economic sociology has done scarcely better than economics in elaborating the concept of the market as a theoretical object in its own right.'

The under-elaborated image of markets is further underscored by the debate about the scope and limits of markets and the fear that market principles are penetrating every nook and cranny of social life (Slater and Tonkiss 2001). Market triumphalism is seen as crowding out a variety of forms of exchange by ever-more powerful market systems invading traditional non-market spaces, mostly in developing economies, as well as occupying the terrain left by a retreating public sector in advanced economies.[3] Apart from the issue of whether markets actually are displacing all other forms of economic activity in both advanced and developing economies (Williams 2004), there is a surprising similarity in how both market triumphalists and market sceptics conceive the market. Typically, both camps hark back to a unitary view of the market mechanism as portrayed by the neoclassical ideal. This conceptual agreement, which is convenient for ideological debate, has contributed to further cement a conception of markets, which arguably does little to promote increased understanding of how 'really existing' markets work (Boyer 1997). Further, the role of marketing in the construction and spread of markets has largely been left unstudied by both enthusiasts and opponents of markets, who either portray marketing as a neutral tool or as a prime mover (Kjellberg 2008). In both cases, a strong correlation between marketing and markets is assumed.

These observations concerning the domain of marketing, the conceptualization of markets, and the under-theorized link between marketing and markets provide a background for this volume's objective to reconnect the marketing discipline to the study of markets, its original remit. In the next section, we present a set of inspirations for the kind of connection we are pursuing.

Starting points for studying markets as practical accomplishments

In order to develop our argument that marketing produces markets, we suggest that markets are plastic phenomena that emerge from organizing, a process in which the marketing discipline plays a role among others. Hence, marketers who are interested in how marketing produces markets should take into account a wide range of practices including regulatory efforts, scientific work, strategic action, and ordinary acts of making do, such as the production and distribution circuits that early marketing theorists concerned themselves with (Araujo 2007). Consequently, the character of marketing and its role in shaping markets needs further elaboration. Four premises, or conceptual starting points, provide inspiration to the contributions collected in this volume: (*a*) markets are practical outcomes; (*b*) marketing knowledge is performative; (*c*) market exchanges require framing; and (*d*) market agents are hybrid collectives.

First, markets are practical outcomes. Our attempt at reconnecting marketing to markets is not an argument for Aldersonian revivalism adding to the long list of retro-tendencies in marketing (cf. Brown 2007). Nevertheless, we retain one important principle from Alderson and Cox (1948): markets are not the spontaneous, self-organizing collections of dyadic exchanges portrayed in marketing textbooks. On the contrary, a great deal of expertise and organization goes into setting up and maintaining markets as ongoing ways of organizing. Much of this work is, to coin a phrase, infrastructural; it resides '... in a naturalised background, as ordinary and unremarkable to us as daylight, trees and dirt' (Edwards 2003: 185). But of course, infrastructure exists and develops over time, can be highly valuable, has speculative qualities, can turn out differently to the intentions of its installers and contributors, can accumulate, and requires considerable maintenance. Alderson and Cox (1948: 148) expressed a similar idea in these terms:

Little thought (perhaps none) is given to the fact [...] that someone has to exert great effort continuously if there is to be the intricate organization required to inform potential buyers and sellers, to bring them together in the actual negotiation of a transaction, and to make it possible for them to carry out all transactions negotiated.

Inspired by sociological approaches developed to study the production of science and technology (e.g. Latour and Woolgar 1979; Latour 1987), we suggest that markets are practical outcomes of organizing efforts. As such, they are always 'in the making' rather than 'ready-made' (Latour 1987). This has important implications for our attempts to study them. Frameworks that characterize markets as 'entities' are handicapped at the outset; markets take on a wide variety of forms and no stable set of dimensions captures their essence. This directs attention to how 'really existing' markets (Boyer 1997) are constructed as skilful accomplishments and to what types of socio-technical arrangements are required to construct different market forms (see Cochoy, this volume). The economy, as Mitchell (2008: 1120) puts it, should be seen as series of competing projects to establish calculative spaces based upon socio-technical regimes involving a variety of devices including organization, measurement, representation, and rules. Many efforts are thus continuously made to shape markets according to particular templates (see the chapters by Kjellberg and Reverdy, this volume).

Second, theories about economic organizing are performative (Callon 1998a). Theoretical ideas can acquire the form and status of templates through debate in organized forums such as buyer and seller interest groups, regulatory inquiries, and reports. As templates, they do not only represent markets but also affect how markets work. Such effects can result from ideas 'invading' actors' mindsets and discussions (producing self-fulfilling or self-defeating prophecies), becoming linked to incentives or disincentives to action (altering the responses of involved actors), or becoming inscribed into devices with which market actors engage (thus changing the concrete situations that actors are required to deal with) (Callon 2007a). However, there are no inevitable effects that follow from actors adopting a particular set of ideas. Ideas spread by being translated, implying that as they spread they also change (Latour 1986). For this reason, it is difficult to know *à priori* which ideas influence economic organizing or whence such ideas come.

Formalized theories from scientific disciplines like economics and management are possible sources (Cochoy 1998; MacKenzie 2003; MacKenzie and Millo 2003; Kjellberg, this volume), but so is local and much less formal expertise (Kjellberg 2001; Rinallo and Golfetto 2006). As Callon (2009*a*) argues, the elaboration of expert knowledge plays an important role in causing markets to exist as both objects of representation and intervention. This knowledge and these representations result from the development of forms of expertise and professional knowledge, involving a variety of academic disciplines ranging from economics to management studies and the social sciences at large (Law and Urry 2004). A focus on expertise and professional knowledge does not imply that technologies of government achieve their intended effects (Reverdy, this volume) or that they succeed in making up docile agents (confer Rose 1999; Skålén et al. 2008). On the contrary, attempts at governing economic life are riddled with tensions between different interests and forms of expertise and display porous boundaries between experts and users (Neyland and Simakova, this volume).

To summarize, the ideas, models, techniques, methods, and professional practices related to the economy do not simply describe it but actively perform and shape the economy (Porter 2008). The question, then, is how and to what extent marketing contributes?

Third, the contributions to this volume are interested in establishing what makes economic exchanges viable and how economic agencies are configured. Contrary to conventional marketing theory, generic exchange is here neither regarded as a foundational concept nor confused with markets. Exchanges are events, some of which take place within and/or contribute to configuring markets (Loasby 1999: 107). Our inspiration is Callon's observation (1998*b*) that a host of actors for different reasons engage in extricating economic exchanges from the mass of social relations and place them in a frame of calculation. These framing processes require considerable investment in both social and material arrangements and are never completely successful (Finch and Geiger, this volume). Rather, actors produce framings and overflows, or in more conventional terms, externalities. For Callon, actors' processes of framing rely on a variety of practices that construct spaces of calculability (Azimont and Araujo, this volume); but the making of spaces of calculability is never immune to external interferences and one form of framing is always liable to be contested and overturned by another. Typically, economic exchanges are subject to many different such efforts (from authorities, sellers, buyers, NGOs, etc.), which are often visible, articulated, and contested. This suggests that markets are characterized by multiplicity and that the outcome of any one framing effort is always fragile, partial, and temporary (Kjellberg and Helgesson 2006; Dubuisson-Quellier, this volume). In summary, rather than dissolve economic exchange into a generic notion of exchange, we are concerned with how the realm of the economy is rendered visible as a distinctive set of practices.

Fourth, and closely connected to the idea that exchanges have to be framed as economic, market agents are understood as hybrid collectives (Callon and Law 1995). The argument that economic actions are embedded in social structures (Granovetter 1985) militates against under- and over-socialized conceptions of economic agency by situating economic action in ongoing networks of social relations. However, it does not take into account the material elements that typically form an important part of the make-up of economic agents. As such, it can be said to suffer from under-materialization (Kjellberg 2001: 16–18; see also Caliskan and Callon 2009). Within marketing, the notion of the extended self (Belk 1988) has highlighted the import of possessions, primarily their symbolic contribution to consumers' sense of self. When taking an interest in the practical organizing of markets, however, it is primarily the literal extension of self that comes to the fore (Shove and Araujo, this volume). Several authors have pointed at the import of mediating devices on the capacities of economic agents, for instance their calculative capabilities and practices (Hutchins 1995; Power 2004). From this perspective, action in and around markets is undertaken by materially heterogeneous collectives that need to be kept together in order to perform as expected (Andersson et al. 2008; Hagberg, this volume; Fries, this volume). This directs attention to the practical interactions through which others come to treat a collective of heterogeneous elements as one (actor). In focus here are 'the ways of operating', *metis* (de Certeau 1984); the ways in which associations are forged between entities in specific situations.

Taken together, these four starting points suggest ways in which the marketing discipline can come to regard markets once more as important phenomena, to be the focus of theorizing, researching, and practice rather than passive backgrounds. We expect markets to be produced and diffused through the interactions of many actors, to be shaped, negotiated, and contested rather than designed and implemented, providing both surprises and opportunities. The many actors who participate in producing markets engage in diverse practices, which are often obscure to others, opaque even upon reflection, and never wholly determining of particular organizing initiatives. At the very least, we suggest that the role and contribution of marketing to this process of shaping markets needs further elaboration.

Finally, our starting points bring attention to an issue that has been curiously neglected in most discussions about markets and marketing, namely, what kinds of markets do we want? We neither assume that marketing is central to the construction of markets nor are we committed to a view of unfettered markets as the default mode of economic coordination. Our interest in 'really existing markets' draws attention to the virtues as well as the limitations of markets and recognizes that their scope and mode of functioning is ultimately a political choice (Lindblom 2001; Nelson 2002; Wensley 2009). In an effort to summarize the contributions of this volume, we will return to these issues in our concluding discussion.

Outline of the chapters

In chapter 1, Shove and Araujo consider the role of materiality in mundane consumption. The chapter argues that reducing markets to mental spaces requiring quasi-semiotic analysis, and consumption to a question of decoding signifiers and constructing identities, hardly covers all aspects of consumption. Mundane, everyday consumption should be understood as inextricably linked to actors' engagements in practices. It is the requirements of practice rather than personal taste or choice that explain mundane consumption. Products can be viewed as materialized understandings, incorporating know-how relevant for specific practices. Successful consumption requires learning and the acquisition of skills and competencies. The boundaries between production and consumption are often blurred and dynamic, with products having the capacity to shift the distribution of skills and competencies required to accomplish particular projects. Material objects thus acquire value through and because of their role in accomplishing particular practices and projects.

In chapter 2, Cochoy explores how retail professionals use *fencing* and *branding* as strategies to organize marketplaces, provocatively likening consumers to cattle. More specifically, he addresses how marketers attribute a *place* to property rights while simultaneously allowing for the *physical circulation* of goods and exchanges. Cochoy shows how material devices, such as shop windows, packaging, and counters, are used to erect boundaries and to mediate between the parties on each side. With the advent of self-service, fencing and branding become ever more prominent with material devices circumscribing a space into which customers and goods can enter. Once inside, their interaction is organized using baskets, carts, signs, shelves, etc. all the way up to the checkout counter. The organizing does not stop there; it continues into forecourts with parking spaces for cars and carts, and symbols of commercial identity. These arrangements are central to the shaping of markets; they enable the seemingly free actions of autonomous agents through a tight framing of their behaviours.

The role of material devices is also addressed by Hagberg in chapter 3. Hagberg questions the notion of dyadic exchanges as the building blocks of markets since this assumes the pre-existence of fully formed agencies (buyers and sellers). Instead, he suggests that market agencies are constituted, negotiated, and argued over during the very acts of exchange. Hagberg shows how a Swedish consumer electronics retailer pursued different retail formats as a result of varyingly successful attempts at configuring customer behaviour. Starting as a Web-based retailer, the company tried to configure the customer as an 'e-commerce-literate' agent, willing to accept its proposed payment and delivery methods. This was only partially successful and purchase options multiplied, with customers being allowed to place postal orders and visit warehouses doubling up as retail stores. For each new option, the company had to configure a different type of customer and produce a set of devices (e.g. paper-based catalogues, web portals, store layouts) that channelled them to different transaction points.

In chapter 4, Dubuisson-Quellier examines the process of reaching workable agreements to accomplish exchange. Based on a study of product development in the food sector, she highlights tensions in products being simultaneously directed at mass markets whilst eliciting idiosyncratic consumer responses as far as taste is concerned. The study demonstrates how different functional areas within the food producer mobilize various forms of expertise, data, and metrological devices to sustain divergent qualifications of the product and its intended target market. The alignment between product characteristics and intended consumers is constantly in flux and there is no requirement for a consensual agreement on quality for the project to proceed and a product to reach the shelves. This suggests that the process of qualifying goods is more intricate, multifaceted, and contested than originally understood. Furthermore, there is no definitive qualification needed in order for exchanges to take place, only a series of local and provisional qualifications of products and consumers.

In chapter 5, Azimont and Araujo show how representations help perform markets. They examine how organizational roles and performance metrics configured calculative agencies as a fuel retailer shifted from product to category management. Under product management, the aim of retail operations was to produce an absolute margin to cover fuel distribution costs. The performance of stores was broken down to the product level using metrics such as volume, sales, and profit margins. These indicators governed product assortment decisions, with high-performing suppliers being awarded more shelf space, time for joint planning, etc. Market research data showing that many customers did not buy fuel triggered a move to category management and disentangled retail from fuel sales. Category managers became responsible for purchasing and marketing an entire product category. As a result, performance indicators that had previously been kept apart were combined in a total margin metric. This change, in turn, reorganized internal relationships within the company, reconfigured its relationships with suppliers, and changed the ways the company related to its markets.

In chapter 6, Finch and Geiger employ Galison's notion of *trading zones* (1997) to examine how incommensurabilities between supplier and buyer worlds can be bridged, and transactions accomplished between parties with different material, cultural, and interpretive backgrounds. The authors elaborate on the characteristics of four types of trading zone—enforced, subversive, fractionated, and interlanguage—involving different types of boundary work from the buyer and seller sides, and illustrate each of these zones with empirical examples. In Galison's original argument, trading zones develop as actors develop contact languages, but Finch and Geiger focus on situations where exchanges are difficult because buyers and sellers share little in common as far as their normal practices of producing, using, and exchanging goods and services. Exchange is a tempting possibility but can also be an area of contest, for instance, in the design of a coffee shop or in the language used to buy and sell coffee.

In chapter 7 by Fries, the link between politics and markets is explored. Fries draws on an ethnographic study of a federation of Swedish trade associations for the service sectors. The chapter explores practices related to the lobbying department of the federation and how these practices provide actors with capacities to act in relation to both politics and markets. Lobbyists advise member firms on how to 'behave' as representatives of the collective; marketing a firm is different from marketing a collective of firms. By combining actors, roles, and organizational identities, as well as by providing knowledge about political processes, the federation assists its members by presenting itself as a political actor. By acquiring particular forms of expertise (e.g. public procurement), the federation inserts itself as the mediator of practices involving its members and their customers. Finally, by promoting interactions with the political world, the federation encourages its members to become more reflexive about the possibilities for shaping the conditions under which they conduct their business.

The markets and politics theme is also present in chapter 8, where Reverdy discusses the deregulation of the European natural gas market. Reverdy explores the consequences of bringing new types of market devices into play in a market where a layer of devices is already in place. The encounters between these market devices result in competition, but not of the kind envisaged in the economic models that underpinned deregulation. Instead, competition takes place between alternative transaction practices employing different market devices, for example regulated tariffs vs. (free) market pricing; gas index vs. oil index; and calls for tenders vs. private contracts. The study shows how regulatory changes both interfere with established practices and threaten to introduce new asymmetries into a market by weakening some actors' capabilities for calculation. Finally, it raises questions about the prospects of a neoclassical market template ever being realized through regulatory scripting.

The realization of ideal markets resurfaces in chapter 9, where Kjellberg draws attention to the different templates that help to shape markets. The chapter follows a protracted controversy concerning the SAS EuroBonus frequent flyer programme in Sweden. This program was controversial from its inception: politicians, rival airlines, and major customers opposed Euro-Bonus with reference to regulations on benefit taxation, competition, and bribery. Despite this, SAS successfully lobbied to exempt frequent flyer programmes from taxation. Rival airlines subsequently complained to the competition authority, triggering a legal controversy about market abuse. Kjellberg suggests that loyalty programmes like EuroBonus are devices that carry statements about markets and that their proliferation depends on producing the necessary environment. Since the competition authority sought to realize a different version of the market from SAS, a performation struggle ensued (Callon 2007a). Over the course of a decade, this struggle resulted in temporary stabilizations of the market as the two parties alternately succeeded in making the other comply with their preferred version.

In chapter 10, Neyland and Simakova deconstruct Fair Trade retailing by asking what counts as 'Fair' and 'Trade'. They examine the co-construction of concepts and practices of Fair Trade clothing through an empirical study of UK firms and organizations. Practices related to Fair Trading are studied as hybrid fora proposing new forms of associations between producers, consumers, goods, and the world at large. Rather than following the standard marketing approach of launching a product into the world, Fair Traders attempt to launch an ethically superior world into their products. Neyland and Simakova identify three ways in which economic agents attempt to build Fair Trade clothing markets: (*a*) building a niche within the clothing market; (*b*) competing in the mainstream clothing market; and (*c*) opting out of markets altogether by focusing on charity. These communities seek to perform three different but related kinds of Fair Trade. Several of the actors involved had strong opinions about rival versions of Fair Trade and engaged in boundary work to clarify points of difference and superiority, according to their value judgements on what constitutes ethical trade.

■ NOTES

1. The sense of dissatisfaction with the state of marketing theory has been in evidence for the last decade, if not longer. The edited volumes by Brownlie et al. (1999) and Håkansson et al. (2004) contain prominent expressions of this dissatisfaction.

2. For a discussion on the sources of influence for this approach, see Alderson and Cox (1948). See also Wooliscroft et al. (2006) for a broader discussion of influences on Alderson's work.

3. See e.g. Michael Sandel's 'Markets and Morals', 1st Reith Lecture, British Broadcasting Corporation, 9 June 2009 (available at: http://www.bbc.co.uk/programmes/b00kt7sh, accessed on 01/03/2010).

1 Consumption, materiality, and markets

ELIZABETH SHOVE AND LUIS ARAUJO

Introduction

This chapter examines the role of material objects in shaping the structures of ordinary, everyday consumption. Our starting point is that, while the acquisition and possession of goods have long been recognized as markers of social position and identity, the role of materiality in consumption has largely been neglected by those seeking to understand the making of markets and the dynamics of demand.

In developing this position we integrate developments in anthropology (Miller 1997) and in the sociology of science and technology (Latour 1992). In these fields it is widely recognized that material objects play a key role in the construction of social orders and, more specifically, in the processes that constitute the behaviours, institutions and, more generally, objects that are qualified as 'economic' in a particular socio-temporal context (Caliskan and Callon 2009). Slater (2002a, 2002b) provides a comprehensive discussion on how materiality features in the discourse of economics and cultural studies arguing against the object-sign distinction. Cochoy (2007c, 2008a, 2009) examines the role of objects in configuring shopping in mass retail environments. However, the role of material objects in constructing and reproducing everyday consumption has received less attention (Watson 2008).

Gronow and Warde (2001: 3) observe that whilst the analysis of highly visible and conspicuous consumption is well developed, a focus on such activities may paint a misleading picture if other, equally important, forms of consumption require different forms of explanation. Gronow and Warde (2001: 4) coin the term 'ordinary consumption' to refer to those items and practices which are neither visible nor special, and require little or no deliberate decision making. These forms of consumption are '...pressingly mundane and embedded in typically inconspicuous socio-technical systems and routines' (Watson and Shove 2008: 70).

Attending to ordinary consumption requires a focus on mundane, everyday routine practices and the practical contexts in which material objects are appropriated and used. Whereas a variety of theories of practice focus on the routine character of everyday life (see e.g. Giddens 1984), there is a dearth of approaches that address the role of material objects, infrastructures, and products in the (re)production of social life (Shove and Pantzar 2005; Pinch and Swedberg 2008), or in the configuration of need, demand, and design.

The aim of this chapter is to explore ordinary consumption as embedded in the routine character of social life and to highlight the role of material objects, or 'stuff' as Molotch (2005) termed it, as constitutive of practices. Taking a practice perspective on ordinary consumption requires a view of consumers as active and creative practitioners who reproduce and transform the relationship between material objects and practices. More than that, taking practices as the central point of enquiry provides a fresh way of conceptualizing the relation between material objects and the emergence, persistence, and disappearance of social practices.

The chapter is structured as follows: in the first section, we focus on the role of materiality in consumption, treating consumption as post-purchase activity. Next, we examine theories of practice that take materiality seriously with reference to examples from an empirical study of Do-It-Yourself (DIY) projects. In the third section, we draw again on these examples to explain how material objects play a role in the formation of more complex projects bringing together multiple practices. In the fourth section, we extract a number of implications on how a practice-based approach can be used to offer new insights on consumption, before offering a set of conclusions and suggestions for further research.

Consumption and materiality

The term consumption, as deployed in the marketing literature, is often used as synonymous with the acquisition of goods through market exchanges. Alderson (1965: 144) noted that consumer behaviour '... is not a theory of consumption but of consumer buying. [...] The immediate interest of the marketing specialist is in the act of purchasing which takes a saleable item off the market. It has been said before that consumer purchase serves as the sink for goods.' Four decades later, Grönroos (2006: 319) complained that consumption is a 'black box' for goods marketers and what happens after the purchase is outside their scope of interest.

Consumer research has been heavily influenced by developments in cultural studies, a field in which material objects are also typically viewed as carriers and mediators of meaning (Slater 2002a, 2002b). The focus is on the symbolic experience of possession and the circuits through which meanings are produced and diffused (Levy 1959; McCracken 1986; Arnould and Thompson

2005). The suggestion is that the dematerialized objects contribute symbolically to an individual's extended sense of self and identity (Belk 1988, 2009). By extension, markets become 'symbolically malleable entities [...] structured by a logic that can be grasped through quasi-semiotic analysis' (Slater 2002b: 75).

The neglect of materiality is hardly confined to marketing. Harré (2002), for example, classifies material objects as things that can be understood in relation to their role in the practical and expressive components of social order. However, he believes an overwhelming case can be made for the primacy of the expressive: '. . . there is nothing else to social life but symbolic exchanges and the joint construction and management of meaning, including the meaning of bits of stuff' (Harré 2002: 32). Trentmann (2009) remarks that historical studies of consumption have been dominated by shopping, conspicuous consumption, and tended to view objects as 'bundles of meaning'.

As we mentioned earlier, symbolic aspects have their place, but exclusive emphasis on them results in a partial understanding of consumption. By contrast, those who write about ordinary consumption are more concerned with the appropriation of goods within and as part of accomplishing specific practices than with discrete acts of purchase (Warde 2005). The remainder of this section will address the issue of materiality and the appropriation of objects in contexts of usage.

The role of materiality in social theory is far from clear. Preda (1999: 348) argues that many contemporary variants of social theory regard objects as being of marginal relevance in explaining the workings of social order—'they are neither inside nor outside of social order'. For Latour (1996: 235), objects appear in social theory in three modes: as invisible and faithful tools, as determining infrastructures, and as projection screens. As tools, they faithfully reproduce the intentions of their users without adding or taking anything away from those intentions. As infrastructures, objects provide a material base on which an autonomous social world can subsequently take shape. As screens, objects project social status and play a role as markers in games of distinction.

Latour (1992) made a cogent argument for the role of material objects in constituting and reproducing social order. Social ties and the concept of social order need to be rethought from top to bottom once the role of artefacts—the 'missing masses'—is added. There should be no a priori distinction between the social and material and any course of action '. . . will rarely consist of human-to-human connections [...] or object-to-object connections, but will probably zigzag from one to another' (Latour 2005: 75).

Reckwitz (2002a: 196) sees Latour's position as a critique of the '. . . reduction of social order to dematerialised symbolic orders and of the material to objects of interpretation'. For Latour, artefacts or things are necessary participants in social practices, just as humans are. They are not just interpreted but applied, used, and maintained, and must be understood in their materiality.

Taking objects and their materiality seriously has important implications for our understanding of ordinary consumption. To begin with, it calls for a notion of active consumers with particular sets of skills and competencies and it regards value as something that is only ever realized through incorporating objects into practices.

The notion of the passive consumer, expressing preferences through discrete purchases, is aptly caricatured by Langlois and Cosgel (1999: 107):

> ... the consumer is important but inactive. Pareto is supposed to have said that we do not need the consumer at all so long as he leaves us a snapshot of his preferences.

The notion of the active consumer has been pursued from a number of angles. A recent trend in marketing theory regards consumers as co-creators of value during the consumption process (see e.g. Prahalad and Ramaswamy 2000, 2004; Vargo and Lusch 2004). These developments stand in stark contrast to traditional notions of consumers as using up the value created for them by production processes (Ramírez 1999) or as 'value sinks' (Normann 2001).

The new service-dominant logic advocated by Vargo and Lusch (2004: 6) regards '...value defined by and co-created with the consumer rather than embedded in the output'. Products are seen as one type of resource alongside others such as information, social encounters, infrastructures, and so on. But these conceptual moves continue to display a partial account of materiality, reducing products to mere '...platforms or appliances in providing benefits [...] best viewed as distribution mechanisms for services...' (Vargo and Lusch 2004: 9). Earlier, Kotler (1980: 352) defined a product as '...simply the packaging of a problem-solving service'.

The active consumer, or more accurately, the 'user' has figured more prominently in the literature on innovation. Whereas representations of customers as co-creators of value (Lusch et al. 2007) are comparatively recent, efforts to conceptualize the role of users in innovation have been making steady progress for the last three decades. In business markets, the studies of Von Hippel (1988, 2005) were instrumental in challenging the notion that innovation was the preserve of manufacturers whilst users were passive recipients of finished goods. Concepts such as lead-users (Von Hippel 1986), 'user toolkits' for innovation (Von Hippel and Katz 2002), and user communities (Franke and Shah 2003) were put forward as ways to describe how manufacturers capitalize on rich user knowledge during innovation processes.

A parallel demand turn took place in other fields, notably in the sociology of science and technology (Oudshoorn and Pinch 2003) and business history (Yates 2006). Bijker (1995) defines technological frames as the elements that influence the attribution of meaning to artefacts. These elements comprise ideas (e.g. current theories), practices (e.g. users' routines), rules, and material objects (e.g. testing procedures) and their interaction within relevant social groups. Interpretative flexibility refers to the early phases of the development of an artefact when multiple and often conflicting interpretations of its uses are permissible, before stabilization and closure set in.

Woolgar (1991) provides an alternative view on the interaction between users and designers through the lens of usability trials for a new personal computer. In usability trials, what constitutes the machine or the user is resolved through a process of interaction in which they mutually elaborate on each other (Woolgar 1991: 68). Product development is conceptualized as a continuous struggle to configure the user, to construct from multiple standpoints a realistic picture of 'what users are like' in interaction with the artefact.

Akrich (1992, 1995) and Akrich and Latour (1992) use the notion of a script to conceptualize the interaction between designers and users. Technical artefacts embody particular representations of users and their roles in particular frameworks of action (cf. Molotch 2005). Description is the retrieval of a script from a scenario and is the opposite of inscription—designers inscribe, users de-scribe. As designers inscribe, they also prescribe since they conceive prototypical users as embodying specific skills. Users may or may not subscribe to those prescriptions. Indeed, the gap between prescription and subscription which leaves room for negotiation and the agency of users. However, as Oudshoorn and Pinch (2003) note, the processes that account for users' accommodation or resistance to their representations by designers is left largely unexplored in this approach.

Much of the work on users is concerned with how producers mobilize users' knowledge and skills for innovation and much less with how innovations are appropriated into users' practices. The work of Silverstone et al. (1992), Silverstone (1994), and Lie and Sørensen (1996) constitute exceptions to this trend. Silverstone et al. (1992) coined the term domestication to denote the process through which artefacts are inserted into everyday life. Domestication is a process involving several transactions between technological artefacts and their users. First, a technological object must be transferred and transformed into an artefact with significance and meaning for its user. This phase is termed appropriation. Next comes objectification, where the artefact is displayed or aligned with other artefacts, which reveal aesthetic and cognitive meanings for its user. The third phase is incorporation, where the artefact is embedded into everyday use through its insertion into the routines of the user. These are all individual transformations, as the meaning and significance of an artefact are dependent on the individual and the particular contexts in which it is situated. The final phase, conversion, orients the artefact within more externally understood and commensurable meanings. The domestication approach has the advantage of moving the locus of user–producer interaction to the broader networks of practices in which users are embedded.

An artefact has no grounded meaning for users until it is appropriated and aligned with existing practices and other artefacts.

In summary, the notion of the user has traditionally been deployed in relation to situations where producers seek to capitalize on user knowledge for innovation purposes. Recent developments have pushed this line of thought further and have drawn attention to how users appropriate innovations and the contexts of usage. However, these representations of use and users are typically bounded, assuming the existence of a human actor on the one hand and a singular material object—that which is used—on the other. There are good reasons to focus on the interaction between user and artefact but such efforts are typically cut short (e.g. temporally specific, concentrating on one moment in a longer history), taking for granted processes involved in shaping the practice into which specific moments of 'use' belong, and overlooking the extent to which the user and that which is used are jointly implicated in the reproduction of practice. In the next section, we introduce a practice-based approach and show how this promises to provide an alternative perspective on the relation between materiality and ordinary consumption.

Practices and projects

Practice approaches generally conceive of the social as a field of interwoven practices anchored in habit, routine, shared understandings, and embodied skills (de Certeau 1984; Bourdieu 1992). Reckwitz (2002*b*: 249) distinguishes between 'practice' (praxis) as a way of doing and 'a practice' (praktik) implying '...a routinised type of behaviour which consists of several elements, interconnected to one another: forms of bodily activity, forms of mental activity, "things" and their use, a background knowledge in the form of understanding, know how, states of emotion and motivational knowledge'. Similarly, Schatzki (2001: 3) defines practices as '...embodied, materially mediated arrays and shared meanings'.

Traditional approaches to practice have tended to highlight their routine character and to overlook the constitutive role of objects and infrastructures in shaping and transforming those routines. And yet, the notion that material objects are implicated in the reproduction of everyday practice is important in a number of ways (Reckwitz 2002*a*: 213). If social order is localized in practices for which human bodies, minds, and artefacts are the necessary components, there is room for accommodating both interaction between human agents as well as interaction between human agents and material artefacts. Furthermore, social change presupposes a series of possible transformations in the constituent elements of practices from cultural codes to skills embodied in individual bodies and minds as well as artefacts and their relationships to other components. In short, as Shove and Pantzar (2005: 45) remark: '. . . practices involve the active integration of materials, meanings and forms of competence.'

A practice approach enables us to reframe consumption as well as the relationship between users and material objects. Warde (2005: 137) consequently defines consumption as '. . . as a process whereby agents engage in appropriation and appreciation, whether for utilitarian, expressive or contemplative purposes, of goods, services, performances, information or ambience, whether purchased or not, over which the agent has some degree of discretion'.

This definition has a number of implications; first, consumption is subsumed to practices, figuring as a moment within a practice rather than a practice itself, as Holt (1995) sees it. Secondly, material objects are appropriated, deployed, and consumed within practices. Warde (2005: 137) uses the example of motoring and what is consumed in the sense of using up or wearing out (e.g. petrol, tyres, the vehicle itself) to exemplify this point. Thirdly, similarities and differences in consumption across groups of people may signal ways through which practices are organized rather than the outcomes of choices based on individual motives. Thus practices generate wants and needs, as particular objects become defining components of practices and partake in their performances. As Shove and Pantzar (2005) show in their study of Nordic walking, practices emerge through particular forms of consumer–producer interaction and, in this context, the relations between materials, meanings, and forms of competence are critical.

Taking an example from a study of Do-It-Yourself (DIY) or home renovation we can illustrate the relationship between materials, meanings, and forms of competence (Shove et al. 2007; Watson and Shove 2008). The market for DIY products is well developed in most Western economies and it includes a variety of items that enable consumers to tackle a number of tasks from relatively small projects (e.g. putting up a book shelf) to more complex undertakings (e.g. renovating a bathroom), hitherto seen as the preserve of skilled trades (e.g. plumbers). DIY has a number of interesting characteristics (Shove et al. 2007). It straddles conventional divides such as work and leisure, production and consumption. It is also an example where the effective performance of a practice depends upon the effective integration of practitioner skills and competencies and the engagement of materials and tools. The evolving relation between tools and skills is important for both the professional and the enthusiast DIY markets, and for the detail of who does what.

If we open up any ordinary domestic tool box, personal collections of hammers, screwdrivers, plumbing fittings, half tins of varnish, etc. are all outcomes of very specific forms of 'consumption'. These items have been acquired as part of accomplishing DIY projects, the realization of which typically requires ownership of and the capacity to use a range of closely related artefacts. The use of a spanner goes hand in hand with the use of a tap washer and a nut: none being useful without the other—or at least not if the project is that of fixing a dripping tap. As this small example indicates, moments of use are positioned in a stream of doing, and that stream typically entails the active appropriation of multiple tools and materials. Items are not appropriated and used alone. Accordingly, relations of use should be conceptualized not only in terms of 'the user' as a human agent, and the artefact (the non-human), but also in terms of the 'families' of non-humans to which the artefact in question is related.

This example also draws attention to other crucial processes to do with the dynamic interaction between user and product. What is it to use a spanner together with a nut and washer? What is entailed in using a paint brush and a tin of varnish? For those who have no skill or experience in plumbing at all, nuts and washers are just so much metal and rubber. In effect, these products only acquire value when in the hands of someone with a requisite level of competence and with a project in view. By implication, use has something to do with the relation between the artefact and the skills of the potential user. But this is not as simple as it might at first seem.

Consider another mundane artefact: a tin of varnish. Ten or fifteen years ago, it took quite some talent and experience to varnish a door and achieve a professional finish with no drips or tears. The tin of varnish and the door made quite stringent demands of the 'user'. This is no longer the case, or at least not in quite the same way. Varnishes can now be bought that are 'non-drip'; that are touch dry in 20 minutes and that almost know how to go on the door itself. In other words, forms of competence previously embodied in human beings have been transferred to the contents of the tin. This skilling of the product, along with the de- or re-skilling of the user changes the human–non-human distribution of competence, and in so doing reconfigures the nature of the practice itself.

Now that effective varnishing is something that many can do, there is less need to call in a professional decorator. Though this is a limited example, the varnish tin provides an important reminder of the role of material goods and infrastructures in structuring requisite skills, in shaping their allocation, and in consequently configuring divisions of labour in society.

This is to take the analysis of 'user' relations much further than is normally the case: by implication, the user-relations entailed in painting are about more than ergonomics, personal desire, or symbolic appeal. As represented here, the precise configuration of 'using' is bound up with and, in a sense, reproductive of more extensive systems of social order, with questions of who does what, and with how those 'doings' are managed and organized.

There are other aspects to consider in regard to the relation between product, project, and the path or career of the 'user'. The social geographer,

Allen Pred (1977, 1981, 1983) has sought to conceptualize the relation between an individual career (in terms of the skills and experiences accumulated along the way, and what these mean for closing down and opening up future opportunities) and the development and success of more institutional projects which might include the goals and ambitions of an organization, a family, or perhaps a whole society. While his is a solidly 'social' account in which there is little or no reference to material culture, these concepts of personal and collective trajectory are potentially relevant in analysing the ways in which products are appropriated in and as part of emerging systems of practice.

Again the theme of competence is central. To return to the tool box studies, it was clear that household collections had different histories: many tools were handed down through the generations, others arrived as gifts; some items were in regular use, others so unfamiliar that their function was currently unknown. People encountered these bits of material culture at different moments in their own lives and because of this the relative value or utility of specific items differed widely.

As already mentioned plumbing fittings are just so much metal to those who have no ability to fit them together and/or no need to do so either. The utility quotient of a tool box was therefore intimately related to the competences and ambitions of its owner. More importantly, levels of competence and ambition were typically cumulative: in tackling one project—such as building a small cupboard or fitting a shelf—householders learned new skills, becoming more or less adept at cutting wood to shape, drilling holes to correct depth, and so on. Along the way they also necessarily acquired the drill and saw. With these elements now in place, future projects came into view in ways that would have been previously unimaginable. One project often leads to another though it is important to notice that such sequences might also end in failure and defeat, thereby bringing a DIY career to a sudden halt. In this setting, user–object relations are genuinely dynamic, one enactment having the effect of redefining the terms of future such relations, and potentially extending the range of new tools and materials with which a user-interaction is sought. Sometimes the tool leads the way. For example, one interviewee talked about getting an angle grinder for the first time. Having acquired this device, he went about looking for things to grind! More commonly, projects such as that of moving a radiator or redecorating a room—that is, projects which entail complex relations between many materials and which are the outcome of intersecting practices—were the meaningful point of reference (Shove et al. 2007).

In Pred's terms, practitioners' careers unfold, punctuated by the accomplishment (or not) of specific projects. These projects involve combinations of different practices. In figuring out how such practices evolve and how people are effectively 'recruited to them', it is, it seems, important to pay attention to the hardware involved and, more significant still, to the dynamic intersection of competence-and-stuff. There is thus a material dimension both to the careers of individual practitioners and consequently also to the formation (or not) of the projects in which they are willing and able to engage.

In summary, regarding consumption as a moment in a practice and practices as involving the active integration of material objects, meanings, and skills, provides an alternative view of looking at the relationship between objects and their users. As our empirical example illustrated, the intersection between materials and objects is more dynamic and more indeterminate than that featured in simpler notions of users as primarily concerned with appropriation of objects into stabilized practices or as users implied, invoked, or involved in processes of innovation.

Consumption and markets

There are a number of important implications for the study of markets stemming from a concern with ordinary consumption seen as moments in streams of practice. In this section we focus on the relations between production and consumption, on notions of value that follow from a practice-based approach, and on the implications of moving from analysing single artefacts to the active integration of multiple artefacts in practices.

The first implication is that, since material objects play an active role in the distribution of competencies, they indirectly influence structures of production and consumption. If we see consumption as the result of engagement in practices, we can reframe the notion of the consumer as actively involved in problem-solving activities. Consumption requires not just choices, time, and monetary budgets but critically, skills and competencies (Langlois and Cosgel 1999). Developing these skills and competencies is thus for consumers a matter of acquiring routinized understandings of the skills that relate goods to their uses.

Markets become essentially ways of discovering how to relate production to consumption, of (provisionally) matching the structure of skills and competencies on the consumption side to the products and services that producers can offer. In this context, material objects can be seen as 'materialised understandings' or forms of incorporation of know-how within practices (Reckwitz 2002a: 212). As the DIY case reminds us, consumers and producers are involved in the constitution and reproduction of practices. In addition, the successful accomplishment of practices requires specific forms of consumption (Shove and Pantzar 2005).

Objects have important consequences for the accomplishment of practices and for linking the structures of production and consumption. But, as we suggested earlier, seeing practices as the active integration of meanings, skills, and objects means that these relationships are never stable: they co-evolve over time. The DIY example we used earlier illustrates how these configurations co-evolved and as a result the structures of production and consumption altered. Innovations such as non-drip varnish or quick-fit plumbing, for example, incorporate particular understandings of the competencies and skills of users and redraw the boundaries between professionals (e.g. painters, plumbers) and DIY enthusiasts (Watson and Shove 2008). Similarly, the evolution of household spaces, such as the kitchen, are not just the result of technological innovations associated with new or improved gadgets but are closely linked to the accomplishment of particular practices and the meanings attached to and the technologies that support such practices (Hand and Shove 2004).

Gjøen and Hård (2002: 278) remark that users actively learn through practice and use, and in so doing redefine both the role of artefacts and of themselves in the process. In this sense, there is not just a process of delegation of qualities from humans to objects but also counter-delegation and re-delegation of attributes between humans and artefacts. In short, objects can transform practices and redefine what they and their users are about. By extension, the boundaries between consumption and production shift both as a result of the distribution of competencies amongst producers and consumers and also as a result of how practices evolve (Langlois and Cosgel 1999).

The second implication for understanding markets concerns the creation and appropriation of value that has so preoccupied marketing theorists in recent years (see e.g. Payne et al. 2008). The current consensus is that there is no value realized until an offering, product, and/or service is consumed. A design and production orientation purportedly views value as something that is added to physical products during the production process and is captured at the point of sale in terms of value-in-exchange or price. The alternative logic argues that value can only be created with and determined by the user in the 'consumption' process and through use or what is referred to as value-in-use. In this sense, value-creation occurs either in direct interaction between a consumer and a producer or is mediated by a material object, seen as a distribution mechanism for service provision (Lusch and Vargo 2006: 284). In short, value is always co-created with the consumer. These developments raise interesting questions about the value of material objects and the role of consumption in determining value. To this we add the point that consumption is, in turn, occasioned by practice.

By any standards, the 'value' of a material artefact is a slippery concept, being variously related to its emotional or symbolic significance, its use or exchange value, its value in specific contexts and circumstances, its durability, its centrality to specific projects or practices, to name but a few possible readings (Miller 2008*a*; Caliskan and Callon 2009). However they are framed, contrasting interpretations of value carry with them specific assumptions about the positioning of the artefact(s) in question with respect to the relation and relative significance of human and non-human actors (consumers, producers, and designers, other artefacts, infrastructures).

The contention that value is created during the consumption process is plausible but at the same time partly at odds with the view that product designers' key contribution is to 'add value'. Designers frequently define and justify their role in these terms, and in ways that take objects to have certain inherent qualities, the details of which can be modified and enhanced through design (Molotch 2005). These features, sometimes to do with brand positioning statements, sometimes ergonomics, or aesthetics, are routinely conceived to become properties of the object: hence a pair of scissors is beautifully designed to fit the hand or it is not. Likewise, the possibility of increasing the price of something like a set of kitchen knives or an ice cream scoop by design is typically interpreted to mean that the designer adds some magic, something which serves to distinguish the designer artefact from others. Industrial product designers routinely make claims about the nature and the potential value of this 'magic' ingredient each and every time they ply their trade (Tharp 2002).

In social theory, the notion that objects have inherent qualities is much more questionable. Authors from Csíkszentmihályi and Rochberg-Halton (1981) to Appadurai (1986) and Miller (1997, 2008*b*) have devoted themselves to cataloguing and describing the 'social lives' of things, documenting the active attribution of value and the fluctuating fortunes of individual artefacts and entire classes of goods within the fluid and contested world of goods. As others also notice (Strasser 2000), things flip in and out of categories: being for a moment objects of desire and then turning into rubbish and sometimes back again. Far from taking value to be somehow embedded in the artefact, such approaches emphasize the social organization of meaning and significance. To some extent, they take consumers to be 'creators of value' during but also before and after the consumption process. This can take generic and specific forms. Generically, entire classes of once highly valued objects can fall out of favour; at a more personal level, objects given as gifts can acquire sentimental value that far exceeds their value in the market. Put simply, theories of this kind deny the concept of inherent value and instead provide ways of analysing the processes of its construction. While product designers might have a part to play in this process, theirs is not the only role.

It is important to recognize that attributions of value are not entirely symbolic. While the vast literature on branding (see e.g. Stern 2006) emphasizes the production of signifiers and the calibration of meanings sensitive enough to separate one toothpaste from another or to locate styles of shoes as emblematic of youth, age, or sophistication—there are also much more pragmatic senses in which objects acquire and lose value through and because of their role in accomplishing specific practices or projects. In other words, value has often to do with the relation between a potential consumer/user, his/her ambitions, and talents, and the affordances of the material artefact itself. Defined like this, value is not simply a matter of social, symbolic negotiation (Caliskan and Callon 2009). It is also an outcome of a rather wider set of considerations, including those of skill, ambition, and project. In such situations, other material artefacts often come into view. As we have seen, plumbing fittings are infinitely more valuable if the person who wants to use them also has the correct spanner to hand.

The kinds of value at stake here have to do not so much with the artefact itself as with its role in the more or less effective accomplishment of a social practice the realization of which is, itself, something that is valued. This brings us to a number of still broader questions regarding the relation between objects and practices.

So far, we have tacitly assumed that achieving things like fixing a dripping tap requires certain products (washer, spanner) and competences to combine them in the right order and in the right way to achieve an outcome. This account locates the material artefact as a 'tool' and as a condition for the effective accomplishment of a practice. But it is also possible that material artefacts have a more active role, themselves configuring or as others have put it, 'scripting' the practice itself (Akrich and Latour 1992).

With this idea the 'designer' comes back into view, not as a figure capable of injecting value into products but as someone implicated in shaping the limits and possibilities of future 'use', and with that of shaping the practices into which and in relation to which material goods have significance, status, and meaning. This is immediately evident in relation to the design of something like a cruise ship. As Korkman (2006) explains, the distribution of space within the ship conditions the enactment and reproduction of practices like those of dining together, sleeping, or playing. Like it or not, the ship's interior permits and also precludes specific ways of spending time, building some practices into the experience of 'cruising' and ruling others out. Something similar applies to isolated artefacts like a chair, the form of which configures the body, demands posture, and reproduces specific concepts and meanings of comfort (Cranz 2000).

In this interpretation of the relation between consumer, producer, and objects, values of one kind or another are better understood as being co-produced, yes, partly by the designer and also by the consumer-user who actively appropriates and more or less faithfully enacts the 'inscribed' practice. Fulton Suri's picture book (*Thoughtless Acts?* (2005)) provides a catchy reminder of the consumer-users' creativity: using pencils to pin up hair; sitting and leaning on objects designed with other uses in mind; and actively customizing things to serve new and apparently unintended purposes. The point though is that such creativity is itself bounded by the artefacts involved; by others, necessary in support (or by their absence); and by the social order and organizations of the projects and practices being pursued.

We have argued earlier that the notion of a user, or of an active consumer, has the virtue of introducing an element of creative engagement, also implying particular embodied skills and competences; however, this somewhat individualistic framing downplays the dynamics of engagement with practices. As indicated above, individual users do not relate to individual objects in isolation. Instead, practices such as DIY involve the integration of a variety of materials, tools, and skills in the pursuit of specific projects. In other words, single goods exist in evolving networks or ecology of other goods and practices require the active integration of these various artefacts (Pantzar 1997). From this perspective, a 'choice' such as using a car for the daily commute to work should be understood as entrenched in a system of interconnected routines and norms rather than a statement of individual preference.

De Wit et al. (2002) and Geels (2006) illustrate how the use of multiple technologies in particular sites such as offices and factories requires interactions and exchanges amongst different artefacts. These exchanges result not just in the coordinated use of artefacts but also in the extension of their functional characteristics, including the transfer of functional characteristics across artefacts. By implication, the sites in which specific practices are typically enacted involve the use of multiple artefacts, the necessary coordination of which can result in particular location-specific innovations—De Wit et al. (2002) use the term innovation junctions to refer to such sites. Hand and Shove (2004) argue that homes and offices should not be regarded merely as places where practices are co-located and intersect, but as 'orchestrating concepts' and ecosystems with their own transformation potential. Thus the office, in De Wit et al.'s example (2002: 51), is both the emergent outcome of interactions amongst multiple technologies and an 'orchestrating concept' that becomes the subject of analysis and intervention by reflexive actors pondering on the potential for coordinating multiple technologies.

Lastly, the role of objects should also be seen in the context of moulding the temporal structure of practices and consumption (Shove et al. 2009). In the DIY example, the dynamic interaction between practitioner competence and material objects is central to the understanding of how practices are reproduced and transformed. DIY practitioners reasoned in terms of projects and cumulative trajectories of skill development, moving on to tackle bigger and more difficult projects as their repertoire of tools and requisite skills grew larger. Projects became the temporal unit around which doings and consuming are organized, influencing the careers of DIY practitioners, the shape of emergent projects, and future patterns of demand. This has implications for how producers might think about product innovations and how they might support evolving practices, and the careers of the consumer-user-practitioners who keep those practices alive.

Conclusions

This chapter addressed the role of materiality in ordinary consumption and its implications for our understanding of markets. Our key argument is that consumer goods, in their materiality, play an active role in constituting, sustaining, and transforming practices. This argument has implications for the social division of labour, the structures of production and consumption, innovation, and for how these processes are conceptualized and understood.

The approach we followed contrasts with marketing approaches that equate consumption with purchase, emphasize possession rather than use, and regard consumer goods as dispensers of pre-packaged benefits or mere projection screens for an extended self. The attention to users and the demand side turn have made important contributions to our understanding of the ways artefacts are appropriated in practical contexts. A practice approach, however, pays closer attention to how objects and practices interact and co-evolve. Rather than focusing on the relationship between single artefacts and users, a practice approach suggests a wider concern with the distribution of competencies between humans and non-humans, and how different types of artefacts interact in sets of interrelated practices.

Consumers and producers are involved in the successful accomplishment of practices which require specific forms of consumption (Shove and Pantzar 2005). If we regard consumption as dependent on knowledge, experience, and skills, we can interpret the role of objects as agents linking production and consumption, and carrying with them possibilities for reshaping this relationship. But, in saying that practices are co-produced by consumers and producers, we need to pinpoint the contribution of producers to the constitution and reproduction of situated practices. This contribution may involve close forms of interaction, as in services requiring direct contact between consumers and producers, or it may rely on more distant, mediated forms of interaction, namely, through the provision of material goods.

We also addressed the issue of value and how it is produced and consumed. We rejected notions that value is inherent in material objects or in the meanings they evoke. Instead, we proposed a notion of value as dependent on how objects are used and coordinated within practices. The career or biography of objects is important but so are the careers of practices and the forms of consumption that they entail. The value of goods changes as a result of the ways in which they are (provisionally) stabilized within particular configurations of meanings and skills.

Finally, we have touched briefly on the role of designers as mediators between producers and users, standing at the intersection of the 'soft' sensibilities of meanings culled from art and culture and the 'harder' facts of materials and production (Molotch 2005). Designers do not inject value into objects but they play an important role in shaping future uses and scripting particular types of practices. The argument we pursued opens up a number of interesting questions about the role of designers in giving form and function to material objects and to the practices in which these are embedded, as well as their interactions with other disciplines, namely, marketing.

As Slater (2002*b*: 101) remarks, marketing practitioners spend a great deal of time thinking about objects and the structures that stabilize and destabilize their meaning within a broader set of competitive and consumption relations. Designers are equally concerned with what keeps the role and meanings of objects 'interactively stabilised', as well as what makes that stabilization break down (Molotch 2005: 2). At present, we have little understanding of how varying concerns about purchase and use intersect in the everyday work of professionals such as marketers and designers, how these interactions unfold over time, and how they influence the way markets operate. If we are to acquire further insights into how the material world interacts with ordinary consumption, we need a better account of how mediators, such as marketing and design, intervene in the worlds of production and consumption, and how specific practices and associated patterns of demand emerge, persist, change, and disappear.

2 Reconnecting marketing to 'market-things'

How grocery equipment drove modern consumption (*Progressive Grocer*, 1929–1959)

FRANCK COCHOY

The argument of this book is that for some reasons marketing has lost its connection to markets. Marketers may object that even if their connection to 'markets at large' may be open to question, they are at least closely connected to consumers—their *raison d'être*—ever since the emergence of the marketing concept at the end of the fifties. But the consumers to whom marketers are connected are the consumers as marketing describes them. To use one of Bruno Latour's (1999: 252) and Barbara Czarniawska's favourite images (2008: 78), the marketing scholar who claims to be capable of explaining consumption by using the textbook version of consumers is like Baron von Munchausen claiming to be able to fly by pulling his boot-straps. Surprisingly, however, this does not mean that the Baron will never fly. In the marketing case, by means of the hard, tedious, and continuous work of 'market making' (Araujo 2007), marketers succeeded in having some consumers acting out this consumer-version, as if the dreamed reflections of them produced by marketing were true. In other words, these consumers accepted, consciously or not, to pull the Baron's bootstraps with him, and thus made him fly (Cochoy 1998). To put it differently, the marketer-Baron flew thanks to the performative character of the sciences that describe the economy. Drawing on Austin's distinction (1961) between constative and performative utterances, Callon and others have nicely shown that what market sciences say is often neither true nor false (their statements are not constative). Indeed, the world they refer to is not 'discovered' but rather 'made' through its very enunciation with the discrete contribution of the public (marketing statements are performative).[1]

But even with the magic of his performative bootstraps, the marketer-Baron never flew very high, very long, or very far, since these bootstraps are elastic, thin, and fragile: they cannot be pulled very strongly and efficiently without being broken. As Judith Butler (2010) recently noted, 'errancy and failure can and do enter into these performative circuits that we find in economic theory, popular discourse, journalism, and public policy'. This particularly applies to the marketing field. Thus, while acknowledging the performativity of market segmentations, Patricia Sunderland and Rita Denny (2010) also point at their failure: 'while consumer segmentations as abstractions are real, and thus as objects, as things, as reifications have a Latourian life and material agency of their own, in the practice of their use these schemas are also infiltrated by the messiness of human life'. The project of the present book, calling for a reconnection of marketing to markets, implicitly acknowledges this partial failure of the performativity of marketing. If Michel Callon (1998a) promoted the performativity approach to markets he also acknowledged that market theories do not have any automatic effects on market practices (Callon 2007a). In other words, performative knowledge is a kind of frame that, like any other frame, faces overflows (Callon 1998b) and even experiences 'misfires' (Callon 2010). And it is precisely the work of field marketers, rather than marketing theorists, to help marketing ideas become performative again; to reconnect marketing to markets.

Curiously enough, the more marketing textbooks are connected to consumers, the more these books forget what consumers are connected to. It is as if the partial redefinition of marketing as consumer research, focusing on one type of actor in the market picture (i.e. the consumer), led marketing to lose its privileged position between supply and demand, and thus neglect many other elements that contribute to shape markets and consumer behaviour. As Johan Hagberg notices (chapter 3, this volume), there is not just the buyer and the seller but also several mediations, many other actors and actants in between. In this chapter, I would like to bring these actors and actants back into the picture by positioning distributive practices at the centre of the marketing stage. As we will see, the agencies that make markets work are not only autonomous manufacturers and consumers, nor only market analysts and marketing theories, but also the distribution process, the distributive equipments, and the 'distributed agency' that make consumers move, goods flow, and supply side actors make money. In other words, I propose to study consumption without studying consumers directly (Cochoy 2010). The idea is that sometimes we may paradoxically get a better understanding of consumption by moving away from consumers and consumer research, and instead study marketing as the 'breeding and channelling' of customers. To make my point, I will push the metaphor a little bit further: consumers may be better described as cattle than as human beings. In line with this provocative metaphor, I suggest that one may better appreciate what frames the moves of cow-like consumers by attending to farm equipments and cowboy techniques rather than by trying to explore the cows' sociology and psychology through sophisticated market surveys and laboratory experiments.[2]

The cattle metaphor emerges from the fundamental dilemma that marketers face in their daily activity: how is it possible to attribute a *place* to property rights, while simultaneously facilitating their exchange and thus their *physical circulation*?[3] The two major generic solutions invented to solve this dilemma—fences and brands—were developed for the management of the cattle market, that is, the market which contributed to forge the American nation, its culture, as well as its economy (Peñaloza 2000).[4] Barbed wire was first designed to quickly, cheaply, and continuously reconfigure the limits of the American cattle in the prairie as an extensive, moving, and transitory property (Razac 2000).[5] Branding derives from the marking of the very same cattle with a 'branding iron', a practice introduced to promptly, inexpensively, and permanently trace the origin of merchandise, either to avoid its theft or loss or to promote and follow up property rights on the market 'within' or 'beyond wires' (Thoenig and Waldman 2005). While flexible fences help to gather and keep the goods in a given place so that they can be sold, clear brands help to trace/market them in the open/outer space. Bringing together these two stories and solutions (which are somehow 'two sides of the same cow') helps to understand that marketing (as practice rather than as theory) is all about property and space management—it is a matter of territory and technology, rather than abstract models and sophisticated psychology. In other words, marketing is a matter of market-things (Cochoy 2007*b*) more than a matter of 'market thinking'. In short, the situated aspect of markets is about 'fencing' and 'branding' goods.

In this chapter, I want to focus on this dynamic of fencing and branding.[6] I will show that this dynamic, far from being restricted to the rural world, has been shaping mundane marketplaces for a long time. In order to do so, I propose to shift from the prairie to the city, from cattle to retail management. My argument rests on a systematic reading of the trade journal *Progressive Grocer* (over the period 1929–59). This journal, launched in 1922 in the wake of the modernist rhetoric of the Progressive Era, presents itself as a professional magazine oriented towards small independent grocers. It shows to these professionals several ways to modernize their stores. The choice of such a field may seem surprising, since apart from a few exceptions (Monod 1996; Deutsch 2001; Leymonerie 2006), the history of distribution has neglected small retailing outlets in favour of department stores (Tamilia 2005), chain stores (Haas 1979; Seth 2001), and supermarkets (Bowlby 2001; Grand-clément 2008). However, it seems as if the historians of distribution embraced a little bit too fast the vision of Zola's great novel, *The Ladies' Delight*, which describes the ancient store as an immobile world, irremediably condemned by the modernity it refuses to accept. Yet, small stores did not remain immobile (Monod 1996); far from resisting, they often anticipated the competition of the new forms of distribution. Moreover, modernist grocers played a distinctive role in reconfiguring the material settings of ordinary consumption, thus ending up refining the identity of the consumer herself.

After presenting the ANT-driven methodology the chapter rests on, I will focus on the spatial aspects of the transformations of the retail business in grocery stores, which all rest on fencing and branding strategies. These strategies, heavily connected with market devices and varied marketing actors (Azimont and Araujo 2007; Callon et al. 2007), begin with the drawing of limits but also identity signs between the street and the shop, then between the consumer and the product by means of packaging. They go further with the technical *agencement* (Callon 2005) of the circulation of people and things in the commercial arena by means of turnstiles, shopping carts, metallic rails, and dividing bars on checkout counters with conveyor belts. The same strategies contributed to reshape and replace the shops themselves, with new signs (brands) at the heart of parking lots (fences). As we will see, all these transformations contributed to reshape not only the retail outlets but also consumer behaviour.

Method: an ANT visual archaeology of commerce

This chapter relies on a longitudinal reading of one trade journal to account for the evolution of commerce.[7] One may object that this renders the research very fragile: it is common knowledge that the media distorts reality, selects some elements, forgets others, etc. This type of criticism relies on the assumption that the world is divided in two parts: reality on one side, and its cultural construction on the other, with the former being directly accessible without the help of the latter.

Inspired by actor-network theory (ANT) this chapter relies on a different assumption. Reality is not the starting point, but rather the result of a long process of translation, inscription, and re-inscription of the world at stake, which selects some elements, articulates, and circulates them, so that the world may be transported, translated, and re-presented (Latour and Woolgar 1979; Latour 1995). In this respect, the media is just one actor among many others that produce accounts of reality. As Barbara Czarniawska (2010) recently showed, the media work very hard to arrange (rather than construct) facts that fit with their objectives: they select, sort, stage, outline, and hide the many elements they collect, produce, and transform. I have addressed this issue elsewhere, showing how *Progressive Grocer*, in playing on the 'before'/'after' rhetoric, managed to present an experimental state of commerce as its present state, and thus succeeded in convincing grocers that their contemporary shops actually belonged to the past. Yet, this is not to say that reality is only 'constructed', a pure effect of discourse. Discourses and matter of facts are closely articulated: 'les faits sont faits', as Latour (1993: 18) nicely puts it. Facts are both 'facts' ('faits' as a noun) and 'done' ('faits' as a verb). In *Progressive Grocer*, new ways of grocery trading are not invented, but articulated, by means of a clever selection and combination of facts and speculative arguments.

In this chapter, the idea that facts and discourses are produced at the same time is taken as a reason not to address the issue of the 'truthfulness' of *Progressive Grocer*. The idea is to share the point of view of the actors, to see commerce as *Progressive Grocer* presented it to them. My argument is that we have no better means to share the experience of the US grocery business evolution than to look at the 'arranged' views presented in the journal that the grocers themselves used to get an idea of the national state of their business.

But is it possible to trace the evolution of grocery retailing through the systematic reading of *Progressive Grocer* over our reference period (1929–59)? While I argue that the magazine is enough to account for the evolution of the grocery business, it may be 'too much', too large a source for the single researcher. Fortunately, the ANT approach proved useful for overcoming this second difficulty, as well. When I arrived in Berkeley for three weeks of fieldwork, I had already decided to study *Progressive Grocer* (based on a suggestion from a trusted colleague). I knew the library had it, but I had never seen it, and I did not know what I would find inside.

Given my time constraints and what I found in the journal, I soon realized that it made more sense, both temporally and intellectually, to focus on images rather than texts. *Progressive Grocer* is full of pictures, drawings, and ads that parallel, illustrate, and supplement the articles about new ways to handle the grocery business. Privileging pictorial elements became for me both a means to browse the journal faster and to pursue a historical approach defined elsewhere as 'archaeology of present times' (Cochoy 2008*b*). In relying on written documents, classic historiography accounts for meanings and thoughts that drive history, but in doing so it tends to neglect the material and 'mute' elements that sometimes and in some settings (like markets) play a major role. Thus, supplementing the historical stance with an archaeological one, analyzing what is shown besides what is said, was a way of achieving symmetry between objects and people (Callon 1986).

My decision to focus on pictorial elements would not have been feasible without a number of additional devices. The researcher and the grocer belong to the same world; they share similar constraints and resources. What they may do depends on the tools they have (or do not have). Just as grocers can make more money with proper shelves, cash registers, and shopping carts, researchers can do more (and hopefully better) research with ad hoc office

Figure 2.1. NLRF Library at Berkeley, USA, and home office in Toulouse, France

equipment. Indeed, the intellectual work is as material as the world it refers to, especially when conducted in a library and when dealing with distribution: libraries and food stores share many of the same elements, such as shelves, trolleys, checking counters, scanners, etc.

In the upper left part of Figure 2.1, we see three carts full of *Progressive Grocer* volumes. These carts carry part of the thousands of pages I turned during my busy weeks at the NLRF library. Working chronologically, I book-marked elements that fit my research interests. After marking a series of volumes, I moved them to the location shown in the upper right part of Figure 2.1. I placed them on the floor, in front of the armchair where I sat, bent down, opened the volume at the bookmarked pages, kept it open with my feet, and photographed the selected pages. The large windows and the sunny climate in California helped me take pictures without flash, and thus get good and usable ones. The place was not only sunny but also very quiet and empty, reducing my embarrassment: bare feet proved to be the most efficient way to keep the volumes open! By means of the sun, the privacy, the camera, and my ape-like behaviour, I could systematically collect an archive of more than 2,500 pictures.

The success of the work also depended on many secondary but indispensable devices that can be seen in the left lower part of Figure 2.1. The additional battery in the charger saved my project since my camera could not work a full day. I used the palm pilot to organize my time and take short notes and the laptop to empty the memory card of the camera, sketch some 'emergent' analyses, check the quality of the pictures, and organize them. For the latter, the external numerical keypad proved helpful, allowing me to quickly rename thousands of photographs by their issue number, month, and page (see the code 'yyyy, mm, ppp-ppp' used in the present text). Even the voice recorder in the foreground was a salvation. Obviously, I could not use it to interview anyone, but it worked perfectly as a jukebox helping me overcome the tedious character of my work! Last but not least, the main and most useful tool was my dear camera, which also allowed me to represent this collection of research tools. A major advantage of digital photography, apart from the superior picture quality compared to photocopies, is its ability to transform kilograms of data into files that you can easily bring with you and study.

Back in France, technical devices once again played an important role in improving my research abilities and my productivity. By manipulating computerized images rather than hard copies, I could copy the same items into different directories, and thus create as many thematic archives as I wanted. Inside these directories, the elements were listed in chronological order, giving a quick longitudinal access to each of the transformations I was interested in. A 'photo browser' software compatible with my triple screen office computer (lower right part of Figure 2.1) proved extraordinarily useful to make sense of the data. With its 'dual screen' feature, I could navigate (on the centre screen) in the list of photo-files and see the full size pictures at the same time (on the left screen). I could also edit a chosen picture in one click, since the browser provides direct access to a (famous) photo editing software. In the latter, I sometimes used a virtual transparent marker to outline elements that were of particular interest (especially in pictures of text). With this access to the material, and by means of the third screen in portrait mode on the right for my word processor, I could simultaneously analyse the pictures, develop my arguments, take notes, organize my ideas, and finally write my research account. The remaining part of this chapter is one particular outcome of this ANT-type methodology, that is, a methodology where practical tools and equipments cannot be separated from the analytical frameworks and intellectual constructs they feed and shape. Just like in the field in question, as we will see, 'market-thoughts' could not have evolved without the whole array of silent but powerful 'market-things' that drove them.

Interlocking: boxes on shelves, shelves in stores, etc.

The modernization of the grocery business relies on two opposite processes: a process of interlocking (objects) and a process of fluxing (goods and people). Both processes are closely connected to the fencing and branding games discussed in the introduction.

The history of the modern grocery business may be presented as a story of interlocked boxes. The packaging boxes are interlocked in the store box. Moreover, the two types of boxes share some common characteristics: they are both enclosures aimed at protecting the property of the shop and the integrity of the products; they are also marking spaces, presenting themselves as surfaces on which one may display the identity of the owner as well as the nature and origin of their contents (see Figure 2.2).

The game of boxes sets up a double and subtle transition from traditional counter service to self-service. The first transition begins outside with a first transparent enclosure—the shop window—that suggests the importance of the display (note the heroic pyramids of cans on the left in Figure 2.2!), and it goes on, inside the shop, with the introduction of window cases that replay and prolong the shop window logic at the heart of the commercial outlet (see the right-hand side of Figure 2.2). This furniture generalizes the visual access of clients to products that were naked before, but also hidden in opaque containers, or moved out of sight, behind the counter. This (re-)fencing of products behind shop windows and window cases corresponds to the

Figure 2.2. *Progressive Grocer*, 1931, 04, 24–5; 1930, 01, 29

introduction in 1927 of the new strategy of 'open display' (1930, 06, 22–23). This strategy was energetically pursued by *Progressive Grocer* during the 1930s. It consists in proposing to grocers a rearrangement of commercial enclosures: the barrier (of the counter) is reduced and relegated to the back of the sales area and replaced by a new logic of enclosure (with window furniture and large shop windows).[8] With windows, interior or exterior, the idea is not yet to physically remove commercial borders; it is rather to authorize the cognitive transgression of these borders: the shop window is to the grocer what barbed wire is to the breeding sector; it presents itself as a means to prevent undesirable moves, like escapes or intrusions. Moreover, the shop window offers to clients the possibility to 'touch with their eyes' what is not yet directly accessible to them. In doing so, open display preserves traditional grocery retailing (the vendor's mediation remains necessary) while modernizing it at the same time (the direct and visual choice of products becomes possible). Open display thus presents itself as an ambiguous modernization tool: as we may understand it today, it is both an 'alternative to' and a 'step towards' self-service.

The second transition goes on inside the shop, with cans playing the leading roles (see Figure 2.3). These cans helped actors of the time to understand that the shop window and window cases may be redundant. Of course, in the advertising of Blue Ribbon malt reproduced in Figure 2.3 (left side), the cans are still very shy; most of them show up behind the counter, aligned with the routine of a traditional sale mediated by the grocer. The ad thus anticipates that most of the professional clients it targets still behave in this way. In order to seduce them, it may thus be wiser not to break too many

Figure 2.3. *Progressive Grocer*, 1929, 08, 51; 1930, 09, 86–7

of their habits. Yet, a closer look at the same ad reveals that the cans already display their propensity not only to pile up without the help of shelves (as fencing devices) but also to present their content by themselves, to talk at the same time or in the place of the grocer (as branding devices). So, in accordance with their better ability for display (disposition and exhibition), cans may stealthily slide from the mute background of shelves to the talkative foreground of the counter. In doing so, they may relegate the grocer to an intermediary position, between the old counter service and the self-service to come.[9]

This evolution was later reinforced by the introduction of merchandizing techniques like the 'Monarch way' (see Figure 2.3, right). This display device proposes to move one step further. It suggests jumping the barrier of the counter and using other fences—low tables—so that cans become more accessible. In doing so, it suggests a subtle and discrete shift towards self-service. The Monarch way attempts to convince grocers that cans are not only stackable like Blue Ribbon showed but that they also can be left to the direct handling of consumers, without any material (cans are solid) or sanitary risks (cans are airtight). The standardized size and the flat top of metallic cans lend themselves to the construction game much better than the diverse jars, boxes, and packages that preceded or followed them. Their cylindrical shape and their modest size encourage their handling. This double affordance of cans for stacking and handling provoked a considerable craze among grocers, who started constructing 'mass displays'. These impressive pyramids of cans that invaded grocery stores were supported by can-food merchants (1929, 08, 6–7), can manufacturers (1947, 10, 102), and display contests (1939, 07, 117).

The examples of Blue Ribbon and Monarch Way still show that the actors involved in this development moved very cautiously. Blue Ribbon tried to promote a modest compromise between open display and counter service for cans. Monarch was as careful, but placed its caution elsewhere: it invented an astute device aimed at exhibiting a sample of the good being promoted in a glass container to encourage the sale of the same good placed in the cans—'See It in Glass, Buy It in Tin'. This device reminds us to what extent the acceptance of masked products under opaque packaging was far from obvious at that time (Strasser 1989). The Monarch way replayed the strategy of the invisible fence of the shop window at the level of the product itself, in order to show customers that the opaque cans really contain what they also mask. This suggests that cans, rather than hiding products, actually may show them better and differently. As a consequence of their aptitude to function as a scriptural space, which is both descriptive and contractual, cans may lead consumers to substitute the promise of a brand that engages its name and its responsibility in the long term for the advice of a self-interested grocer. Eventually, cans accelerated and perfected this evolution by means of a final property: their ability to function as a temporal barrier slowing down the course of time.[10] Through their ability to better preserve products, cans reconfigured competition both spatially and temporally: together with cans, more remote or older products may successfully compete against fresh, local ones. In this way, cans contributed to the disappearance of fragmented markets of old times and to the unification of the American mass market (Tedlow 1990); they contributed to the replacement of naked products controlled by the shopkeeper by branded products promoted by manufacturers' advertisements (Grandclément 2008); they led grocers to engage in negotiations with their suppliers, and eventually to gradually rearrange the whole point of sale.[11]

The interlocking of fencing and branding devices

The putting up of can pyramids and their migration beyond shop windows and counters is part of a reconfiguration of the commercial space as a whole. In order to retrace the dynamic of this reconfiguration and describe its components, I propose to first freeze on the photograph of a 1941 shop (see Figure 2.4).

NEW STORES   A rail around checkout counters in the Fisher Grocery
(Continued)   in Springfield, Ill., helps control basket carriers. As shop-
               pers exit, empty carriers go under rail, ready for re-use.

Figure 2.4. *Progressive Grocer*, 1941, 07, 64–5

This shop provides a good illustration of the spatial and technical organization of groceries just after the open display period, at the very beginning of the self-service era: the counter has disappeared; checkout counters have been introduced at the shop entry; the customer area is occupied by shelves and furniture in 'island' shape; the 'basket carriers' have made their appearance;[12] this whole system is channelled by turnstiles and rails, which were soon supplemented or replaced with 'magic doors' (Cochoy 2010).

Even if deprived of any human presence, the shop looks quite cluttered, hampered by traffic problems. Here is the main difficulty: is it possible to let consumers free while channelling their freedom at the same time? Is it possible to arrange things so that customers may circulate easily and everywhere to buy more, without allowing them to leave before paying or with the carts they borrowed? Once again, the solving of such difficulties included the setting up of discrete asymmetrical barriers at the periphery of the shop. At the entry, the turnstile channels customers like a rotating dam, which reconciles the contradictory properties of fences and flows. From fences the turnstile borrows its arms in order to sequence the entries and prevent exits. From flows, the same turnstile borrows its continuous movement facilitating people's entry. At the exit, a very discreet rail—which echoes the separating and organizing power of the barbed wire (hopefully without the jagged edges!)—intervenes to effectuate the decoupling of each customer-cart collective. Only one element in this collective may slide under the fence and remain in the commercial circuit, while the other is channelled out—with their arms full—on the other side.

The enclosing, sorting, and channelling logic of clientele, far from stopping at the periphery of the commercial fence, rather penetrates its very heart. The occupation of the commercial space by gondolas and 'islands' draws a course that one may follow in order to (re)view almost all the commercial supply; all the more so since the latterly is largely open to consumers' sight.[13] Later on came some other devices for a 'flexible fencing' of supply, like vertically adjustable shelves and laterally mobile separations between the products. In the very same way that the barbed wire of the past favoured the quick reconfiguration of the enclosures to fit the size and the movement of the products involved, these devices helped the continuous adjustment of the products to the flow and choice of customers (Cochoy 2010).[14] Moreover, everything is organized so that one may go from one enclosure to another, not only from the outside to the inside of the shop but also, once inside, from the fixed fences of the shelves, islands, and gondolas to the mobile fences of the shopping carts and automobiles, just as cowboys transferred cattle from one pen to another when ownership changed. However products and clients should not be confused. The latter, far from being passively submitted to the surrounding game of channelling, are also enrolled in the game of fencing and branding. They are invited to brand their property, at least figuratively, by placing the chosen items in the fence of the cart. Within the enclosure of the shop, the clientele is somewhat 'fenced-fencing': free to circulate while framed at the same time; led to fence the products while receiving the greatest freedom to do so.

The climax of this logic of transfer from one place to another (fences) and from one owner to another (brands) comes at the checkout stand. The successive improvements of this device were meant to overcome the difficulties of shifting from one place and identity to another. Here again, the problem was to reconcile the general flow of the traffic with the tight control of operations. The challenge was to manage the exact and exclusive attribution of baskets and products to their respective clients in spite of their faster and faster succession. This challenge was met by organizing the flow of goods and customers through checkout counters with rotating plates (1953, 02, 179; 1953, 05, 114) or conveyor belts (1950, 10, 220–1; 1953, 04, 162). However, the increased flow favoured by these devices soon led to a possible confusion between fluxing and sequencing customers...A simple little bar, fixed on a checkout counter with a conveyor belt, was suggested to overcome (or stage) the latter problem. This bar was meant to trace the limit between the purchases of different clients when checking out. While the conveyor belt supported the flow logic, the small bar helped to re-establish the order and discontinuity necessary to control it. In the ad for Zephyr (see Figure 2.5), the

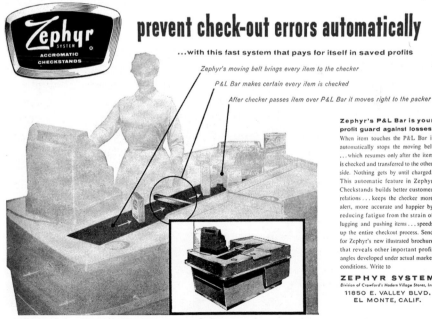

Figure 2.5. *Progressive Grocer*, 1955, 10, 229

commercial argument first and foremost targets the grocers. In order to convince them to buy the device, Zephyr praises the part (the bar) for the whole (the checkout counter with conveyor belt) and underlines, in large bold characters, that the former 'prevent[s] check-out errors automatically'. As a contemporary reader, I almost took this bar as the first occurrence of the small mobile fences we know today, that aim at delimiting the transitory property spaces between clients. But the Zephyr bar is different: it is a single fixed barrier aimed at supporting the cashier's calculation by stopping each moving product at the 'checkpoint' level, without stopping the belt (see Figure 2.5).

But, in the very same way that the preparation of orders was used as an argument to sell self-service and shopping carts to grocers while being aimed at clients (Cochoy 2010), the argument of preventing checkout errors also appears as an astute way of presenting, in 'grocer terms', a device that may also prevent property conflicts between customers. Such conflicts are also managed by means of a new type of mobile barrier that intervenes downstream in order to separate the purchases of two distinct customers at the exit of the checkout counter while preserving, like the previous solution, the continuous movement of the belt (see Figure 2.6).

With such devices, one discovers that the apt term 'mobile counter', used by Catherine Grandclément (2008) to describe shopping carts, also applies to checkout counters: while the shopping cart helps the chosen products to remain immobile (in relation to others) when the consumer moves, the conveyor belt helps the products to move while the consumer is immobile. The checkout counter is obviously a fencing place for products and a branding

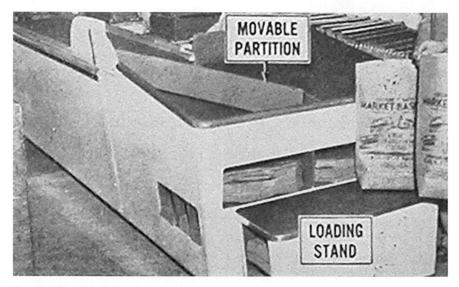

Figure 2.6. *Progressive Grocer*, 1951, 07, 84–5

device for property rights. The one does not go without the other: when products move from one fence to another (from the shelves to the cart, from the cart to the belt, from the belt to the bags, see the 'loading stand' arranged beyond the 'mobile fence' in Figure 2.6), they simultaneously pass from one brand (or name) to another, from one owner to another, from hand to hand (from the manufacturer to the grocer, from the grocer to the customer). Yet, the shift from one fence and one brand to another is far less radical than one may have thought, since professionals try for each transfer of property to preserve traces of the prior allotments, in the hope that customers will pay a later visit to the same circuit. Thus, the grocers' products carry the brands of their manufacturers, just like the consumers' bags will soon carry the brands of the grocers ('YOUR NAME GOES HERE', says the advertisement of the paper manufacturer to the grocers, see Figure 2.7).

Figure 2.7. *Progressive Grocer*, 1955, 12, 1

All in all, the interlocking dynamic of fences and brands that I have described follows the 'faire laissez-faire' logic I presented elsewhere (Cochoy 2007b, 2010). On the one hand, the progressive arrangement of self-service performs the liberal utopia of a fluid and free action of economic agents on the market ('laissez-faire'). On the other hand, and paradoxically, market professionals know well that such an utopia can only be achieved through very tight framing and control operations ('faire', i.e. make) by means of fluxing tools (conveyor belts), channelling equipment (rails, gondolas), and control agents (cashiers), or even by means of some interlocked devices that combine these three operations like the turnstiles, magic doors, and checkout counters. These arrangements are precisely aimed at 'faire laissez-faire'.

Changing the fences and adding a new brand

With the passing of time, the permanent redefinition of fences and brands that shape the grocery business ended up being redefined spatially but also morally. For a long while, small business remained small business, even if energetically modernized as we saw: if the furniture, décor, and supply of products were substantially renewed, it was to preserve the stability of the small shop, well established within its four walls, immobile on Main Street. But with the growing use of automobiles and the proliferation of other forms of commerce in suburbs (Longstreth 1999), streets became too narrow and too jammed for the parking of vehicles—hence the decision of some grocers to move elsewhere, to the periphery of cities (1946, 10, 54–5; 1953, 08, 48–52). With this relocalization of shops away from downtown, place became adjustable and could be valued differently.

As far as adjustment was concerned, the logic at work was that of the extension of fences, both outside and inside the shops. Inside the shops, the move was of course that of the growth of sales floors (1955, 02, 142–3). Outside, the new trend was to develop parking lots, those 'enclosures for cars' that progressively received the same planning care previously reserved to the shop as an 'enclosure for products and customers'. One cared for the setting of maps about parking facilities at the scale of a city (1956, 03, 62–3sq). One wondered about the 'best arrangement for parking areas' (1956, 05, 41) in the very same way that one until then had cared ad nauseam for the best store plan (Cochoy 2010).[15] One envisioned sharing parking lots between different businesses where space was scarce. And one measured the impact of parking lots on real estate value as well as business turnover (1956, 10, 160–3).

**Parking area
for shopping carts
saves time and money**

The new Supreme Market in South Weymouth, Mass. has many money saving features within its colorful walls, but the parking areas designated for shopping carts taken to automobiles have already paid their own way.

Wisely located throughout the parking lot with easily read signs, these locations have proved most successful in keeping carts from rolling loosely about the lot, and causing accidents and damage.

Designated employes make periodic trips through the lot and collect the carts which have been pre-collected by considerate customers.

MORE ▶

Figure 2.8. *Progressive Grocer*, 1958, 04, 100

Eventually, one also invented special parking places for the shopping carts (see Figure 2.8).[16]

But the most important aspect of these changes is probably the new way of valuing the point of sale, which once again joins together the brands and fences dynamics, combining their properties to defend and extend the grocery trade. The relegation of sales surfaces to the background of vast parking lots raised some problems concerning the identification of stores. It thus led to the invention of new devices to signal commercial identities: giant signs (brands) positioned at the top of tall masts placed in the middle of parking lots (fences) (see Figure 2.9).

The extension of the brands and fences dynamics outside the stores represents a turning point not only for the stores—since this move was accompanied by a shift in their size and identity—but also, significantly enough, for *Progressive Grocer*. Indeed, the magazine had no other choice now than to encourage and further the transformation, first by adopting a larger format in 1950 (fence) and then by adopting subtitles with larger and larger meanings (brand): *The magazine of mass food selling* in 1952, *The magazine of supermarkets and superettes* in 1953, *The magazine of supermarketing* in 1957. It is here that I have to stop: it is at this point that the grocery business and *Progressive Grocer* fuse with the modern supermarket.

BECAUSE their sign had to be erected a certain distance back from
the street to conform to a city ordinance, The Boys Market placed
this striking, shopping basket-shaped sign on their parking lot.

Figure 2.9. *Progressive Grocer*, 1956, 10, 172

Conclusions

My attempt to account for the modernization of US retail marketing by
looking at the arranged views presented in *Progressive Grocer* suggests that
this modernization depended to a considerable extent on the articulation
of a certain type of association. Rather than the embeddedness of economic
action in on-going social relations, emphasized by economic sociologists

(Granovetter 1985), it was its entanglement with the material world that came to the fore (Thomas 1991; Callon et al. 2002). In grocery stores, it would seem, markets are to an important extent staged by channelling goods and consumers. The fencing and branding strategies I have described contribute to this configuration of markets both by situating competition in time and space and by formatting individual consumer behaviour.

As to competition, *Progressive Grocer* shows that the magazine articulated competition between suppliers of competitive tools and strategies (brands, press, manufacturers of cans, shelves, checkout counters, shopping carts, etc.). Together with the magazine, these companies contributed to perform a fantastic laboratory of 'progressive' selling methods where we expected to find rigidity and gradual decline. Their tools and strategies contributed to reshape competition and, by extension, the market for groceries, by redrawing both temporal and spatial boundaries. Fencing strategies, like improved packaging and enlarged sales floors, extended product competition in time, space, and across categories. Branding strategies, like product labelling, promoted increased consumer-participation in the competitive process by reducing the direct mediation of the grocer.

As to the formatting of consumers, I argued at the outset of this chapter that its challenge and paradox was to understand consumption without directly studying consumers (Cochoy 2010). In a provocative manner, I have sought to develop consumer research without looking at the consumer, proposing a view of consumers that likens them to cattle. For surely, understanding cattle behaviour is better done by describing the technical organization of farming than by interviewing cows. This approach has helped me illustrate that consumption agency is distributed between the consumer, the brands, and the fences. The consumer is thus only one part of the picture. For instance, her behaviour is closely linked to the wires of her cart and to the packaged and branded products she fills it with. At this point, I can now distance myself from this provocative 'market-things' approach and acknowledge that there is (at least sometimes) a huge difference between a consumer and a cow. So how can we then characterize the relationship between consumers and market-things? Are objects merely extensions of selves, as Russel Belk (1988) proposed? Or is it the other way around: are selves the extensions of objects, as my account seems to suggest? Neither one nor the other; neither the consumer nor the technical equipment should be considered as the unique source of action. Rather, both of them should be seen as extensions of a complex and composite process that mixes the properties of human and technical agencies.

In this chapter, I have overemphasized the technical components of this process, in order to counterbalance the view that consumer behaviour is essentially an anthropological, social, and psychological affair. This is just a first step, which helps to understand what type of new knowledge and insights we may gain in moving away from the reductionist type of analysis that tends to confuse 'consumption' and 'consumer'. We now have of course to conduct a more subtle, balanced, and complete analysis; we have to be much more respectful of the remarkable knowledge and insights of consumer research (Cova and Cova 2009; MacInnis and Folkes 2010). The next challenge for ANT-driven consumer research is to reconnect technical and cultural agencies, STS, and consumer research, in order to study how market scenes and actors articulate devices and dispositions (Cochoy 2007a) that renew consumption and market behaviour.

■ NOTES

1. For a fascinating example of the performation of marketing ideas, see Liz Moor's study (2010) on social marketing in practice, which shows how social marketing ideas once ended up in producing an exhilarating segmentation of alcohol addicts into nine unbelievable segments ('Depressed drinker, de-stress drinker, re-bonding drinker, conformist drinker, community drinker, boredom drinker, macho drinker, hedonistic drinker, border dependents'). Another very nice example is that of how the 'minivan' product category was accepted in the car market (Rosa et al. 1999). This latter study shows that the performativity process, far from being unilateral (from market discourse to consumer behaviour) is rather bilateral and interactive: it crosses the 'stories' of both supply and demand about the product.

2. A metaphor can always become real: for a fascinating ethnography of how marketers commodity the Western culture during a stock and rodeo show, see Peñaloza (2000). Significantly, the author explains that in order to conduct her project, she needs to move away from the tradition of consumer-centred consumer research, and rather focus on a detailed study of marketers' activities. In doing so, she complements the argument of the present book and my chapter: while Peñaloza is interested in how marketers produce consumer culture, I focus on how marketing equipment shapes the physical moves of consumers.

3. As Araujo and Spring (2006: 800) put it, 'tradability is associated with the ability to define and attach property rights to tangible, material entities'.

4. I do not only refer to the Western and cowboy imagery, but more seriously to the unification of the American mass market (Tedlow 1990) and the later development of mass marketing, in which agricultural economics played a prominent role (Cochoy 1998).

5. I thank Catherine Grandclément for introducing me to the work of Olivier Razac.

6. This study is one result of a research mission to the University of California at Berkeley, 14 July to 8 August 2006. I thank Catherine Grandclément for the idea and the Education Abroad Program for funding the research. I am also very grateful to Jutta Wiemhoff, Martha Lucero (NRLF), Steve Mendoza (main library), and three other anonymous librarians at the Business/Economics Library and Environmental Design Library at Berkeley. Finally, I am indebted to David Vogel for his support, the Haas School of Business for its material help, and Carmen Tapia for her administrative assistance. I warmly thank *Progressive Grocer* for granting me the permission to reproduce the

images this publication rests upon. I am very grateful to Luis Araujo, Hans Kjellberg, and two anonymous reviewers for their remarks and suggestions. The present chapter is an updated and adapted version of a paper previously published in the French journal *Entreprises et histoire* (Cochoy 2008*b*). When writing it, I benefited from the material and intellectual support of the School of Business, Economics and Law, University of Gothenburg, Gothenburg, Sweden.

7. Other examples of works on consumer practices and culture that have drawn on the analysis of printed magazines include Hand and Shove (2004) and Rosa et al. (1999).

8. Even if transitory, the open display logic crossed the American borders; for instance, it was introduced in Sweden (see Kjellberg and Helgesson 2007*b*).

9. The same pictorial rhetoric is used in other advertisements: for example, 1929, 11, 127.

10. Here, we discover that 'market-things' contribute to shape market time as well as marketers and other organization specialists (Czarniawska 2004).

11. Of course, the mediation of cans is far from exclusive: their contribution to the transformation of commerce was accompanied and supported by the use of Cellophane, glass jars, cardboard packages, etc. For more details on these innovations, see Grandclément (2008) and Cochoy (2010).

12. The innovation was introduced in 1936 (Grandclément 2006; Cochoy 2009).

13. The importance of low furniture and tubular devices is crucial: these elements favour a maximum visual aperture, which is useful both for the consumer (for locating the products) and for the grocer (for the surveillance of the shop).

14. The analogy is not fortuitous: several manufacturers of commercial equipment of that time—shopping carts, turnstiles, metallic shelves—were specialists in metal equipment; see American Metal Products, Inc., American Wire Form Co., Boston Metal Products Corp., Lyon Metal Products Inc., or United Steel and Wire Co.

15. The presentation of ideal store maps was a recurrent theme in *Progressive Grocer* and the references I could quote are quite countless.

16. One even makes a reflexive use of parking lots as a commercial space for the sale of cars (1958, 08, 68).

Exchanging agencies

The case of NetOnNet

JOHAN HAGBERG

Introduction

This chapter reports on a study of an online retailer in Sweden.[1] I use this case to examine the adequacy of the exchange paradigm in marketing to explain how the nascent online retailer engaged with its customers over the first few years of its operations. The prominent place afforded to the exchange dyad in marketing theory is denoted by such terms as a 'foundational notion', 'the classic dyad', 'the basic marketing relationship', and 'the parent relationship of marketing' (Gummesson 2002; Bagozzi 2009). The picture below depicts clearly differentiated actors, a seller and a buyer, entering into an exchange (Figure 3.1).

Using the concept of exchange means that researchers need to attend to the necessary conditions for exchanges to take place. Among these conditions is the presence of two or more parties, units, agents, or actors (Alderson 1965; Kotler 1972; Håkansson and Prenkert 2004). These agents have been variously conceptualized as 'organized behaviour systems' (Alderson 1957, 1965): an organized set of interacting elements taking the form of human behaviour; social units 'consisting of one or more human actors' (Kotler 1972: 49); and social actors who 'may consist of salesmen, retailers, consumers, advertisers, and other conceptual entities found in marketing' (Bagozzi 1974: 78).

Kotler (1972: 49) introduced sharp distinctions between the 'social unit' on the selling side (called the marketer) and the buying side (called the market), as well as what was exchanged between them (social objects). This meant that marketing should be seen as separate from the market; the buyer should be clearly distinguished from the seller and exchange took place *between* them, but was initiated by the seller. In spite of some attempts to reorient marketing from the one-sided emphasis on the seller's activities towards a broader notion that would include buying activities (Kotler and Levy 1973), the emphasis on the seller's role is still apparent in marketing theory.

Over the years, a large number of critical accounts have challenged this approach, namely for its view of exchange as a set of discrete, serially independent transactions and the implicit assumption of atomistic buyers and sellers.

Figure 3.1. The classic conceptualization of exchange in marketing

Nevertheless, one issue that has been largely neglected is how actors participating in exchange are constituted.

An analysis of the exchange dyad cannot start from the assumption that the buyer and the seller arrive at the exchange fully configured. Instead, it seems likely that both buyers and sellers, as market agents, are shaped *by* the exchange process as much as they shape it. In other words, buyers and sellers are not pre-existing types endowed with essential traits. They emerge through the practices involved in situated exchange processes. In order to develop this notion, the study reported in this chapter applies the so-called practice-based approach to marketing (Araujo et al. 2008). This approach draws on insights from science and technology studies (STS) and actor-network theory (ANT) to explore market practices across a broad range of settings. This approach is particularly suited to study how actors emerge and take shape in concrete exchange situations.

The rest of the chapter is structured as follows: I start by introducing a practice-based approach to exchange in general terms, followed by a description of the methodology employed in the empirical study. Secondly, I introduce the NetOnNet case which describes the emergence of different modes of exchange related to different retail formats. In the third section, I examine the relationship between exchange and market agencies using the material from the NetOnNet case. Finally, a set of conclusions are drawn and some suggestions for further research are put forward.

The practice-based approach to exchange

In recent years, marketing researchers have developed a practice-based approach to marketing (Araujo 2007; Kjellberg and Helgesson 2007a; Araujo et al. 2008) calling for a reconsideration of the insights of earlier marketing theorists such as Alderson (1965) and McInnes (1964), according to whom markets were central to marketing theory. In this approach, 'Marketing can be understood as a distributed and heterogeneous set of agencies involved in the process of facilitating market exchange and constructing markets institutions' (Araujo 2007: 212). In the same vein, Andersson et al. (2008: 68) claimed that '...from a market practice perspective actors should be conceived as composites comprised of multiple acting entities'. Greater knowledge of market actors can thus be obtained by paying closer attention '...to the concrete actions undertaken by those involved in the buying and selling of goods and services, and the rules and tools employed by them as part of concrete exchange situations' (Andersson et al. 2008: 68).

Kjellberg and Helgesson (2007*b*) explored the co-constitution of modes of exchange, objects of exchange, and agents of exchange. They used the term 'mode of exchange' (borrowed from Lie 1992) to refer to '...the specific combination of practices that together produce an economic exchange' (Kjellberg and Helgesson 2007*b*: 863). Employing Czarniawska's (2004) notion of action nets, Kjellberg and Helgesson compared three modes of exchange: (*a*) full service exchange, (*b*) self-service exchange, and (*c*) distance exchange. They demonstrate how the introduction of a self-service mode of exchange involved a gradual reconfiguration of stores, retailers, customers, and goods. During this reconfiguration, self-service as a mode of exchange also underwent changes and, in the process, 'blurred the boundaries between the initially distinct modes of exchange' (Ibid.: 875). Thus the configuration of modes, objects, and agents of exchange were intertwined.

The focus on the configuration of agents participating in exchange stems from a recognition that they are not predefined entities, but are shaped by the exchange process. Callon (2005, 2007*a*, 2009*a*) uses the term *agencement* to analyse the configuration of agents, showing that these configurations are shaped by a heterogeneous set of elements, involving humans as well as other entities such as tools, equipment, technical devices, etc. *Agencements* are thus arrangements of heterogeneous elements '...endowed with the capacity of acting in different ways depending on their configuration' (Callon 2007*a*: 320).

Two important implications follow from this approach. The first relates to the role of material devices in market exchanges (Callon and Muniesa 2005; Callon et al. 2007; Cochoy 2008*a*) and the assumption that: '...equipment matters: it changes the nature of the economic agent, of economic action, and of markets' (MacKenzie 2009: 13). The second implication follows the ANT-inspired notion '...that actors should not be seen as having fixed natures or fixed characteristics' (MacKenzie 2009: 22). Instead, the 'nature' or 'characteristics' of actors are outcomes depending on the entities and the relationships between the entities that constitute them.

Focusing on *agencements* means that agency

...is distributed in the sense that the capacity to exert agency resides not simply in human beings but in the *agencement*—those fixtures and fittings, material arrangements and devices which help furnish them with certain characteristics and enable them to act in particular environments. Different *agencements* produce different forms of action. Agency, rather than being a singular, universal and human-centred capacity, is distributed, plural and contingent upon particular socio-technical arrangements. Social agency does not have a unitary form. It varies with the forms of discourse, techniques and practices defining a given activity. (du Gay 2008: 50–1)

The study reported in this chapter concerns retailing, which has been chosen not only because it has proven fruitful for developing this approach (Kjellberg 2001; Azimont and Araujo 2007; Cochoy 2007*a*, 2008*a*; Kjellberg and Helgesson 2007*b*) but also because of its deceptive simplicity and taken-for-granted character. Retailing is often seen as the simplest form of exchange, involving individual consumers (in contrast to complex business-to-business exchanges) and packaged products (in contrast to more complex exchanges involving services or product–service combinations).

In order to analyse how these *agencements* evolve, we must consider not only the sellers' efforts to influence customers but customers' actions and reactions as well (Akrich 1992). In short, the 'selling side' as well as the 'buying side' are potentially involved in configuring these *agencements*. To explore exchange further, it is important to move beyond its idealized, pure versions, such as reciprocity, redistribution, or market forms (Appadurai 1986; Kjellberg and Helgesson 2007*b*; Caliskan and Callon 2009). This becomes particularly relevant when studying mundane marketing practices characterized by multiplicity (Coviello et al. 2002; Kjellberg and Helgesson 2006).

I use the terms *assemble* and *disassemble* to describe how *agencements* are configured and take shape during exchanges. These terms emphasize the hybrid and collective character of *agencements* and the notion that they have to be put together to acquire the capacity to act in specific situations. And, similarly, *agencements* have to be taken apart when they are no longer required to perform as collectives.

Method

The analysis presented in this section is based on a longitudinal case study of NetOnNet, a Swedish retailer of consumer electronics (previously reported in Hagberg 2008). The study lasted from 2001 to 2008, and was based on the methodological principles of ANT, namely 'follow the actors' (Latour 1987, 2005). Field material was collected from interviews with managers, newspaper articles, company documents, observations, and attending public presentations. The empirical material reported here is based on observations of the NetOnNet online web store and the NetOnNet bricks-and-mortar warehouse shop in Malmö, Sweden. Data concerning the web store consisted of field notes, screen downloads, documents from placing orders on the Web, and subsequent correspondence by e-mail, text messaging, and post. Observations of the web store were made during the period 25 September–18 October 2006. The warehouse shop in Malmö was visited on its opening day (3 November 2006) and field material was collected in the form of notes, photos, and artefacts.

The part of the study reported here concerns the way that different modes of exchange were developed. Inspired by Cochoy (2007*b*), the analysis was performed by comparing two different sites (web store and warehouse shop). It was guided by Cochoy's injunction (2007*b*: 111): 'Rather than looking for hidden backstage mechanisms behind the observed phenomena, rather than calling for some external knowledge in order to increase the understanding of the field ... try to begin simply from the surface of behaviours and things.'

Alternating modes of exchange

NetOnNet was founded in the city of Borås, in the western part of Sweden, in early 1999. The founders had previously worked in the consumer electronics business. The company was established in order to sell consumer electronics through the Internet. NetOnNet constructed its first website with the help of a local advertising agency using standard software. The site was kept on a third-party server and was connected to an e-commerce portal. Descriptive text, photographs, and prices of consumer electronic products were prominently displayed.

The NetOnNet web store was launched on 10 March 1999. The server was unable to handle the large number of visitors and crashed on the first day. The CEO of NetOnNet described the incident in a public speech a few years later. He said that on the morning of the opening day he was told that the server was too small, that it would take a day or two before it would be up and running again, and that all this was to be expected when launching a new web store. In his talk, he compared the website experience to opening a physical store, having thousands of people queuing outside but being unable to open the doors. The server was like a landlord who, when contacted, admitted he did not care much, but would probably be able to open up the doors the following day.

In the months and years that followed, NetOnNet made numerous efforts to transform the customers of their store-based competitors to online shoppers via their web store. Potential purchasers were solicited by advertising on Internet portals and newspapers. Visitors to the site could search for and pick products, place them in a virtual 'shopping cart', check out, and enter their personal information. The customer could choose home delivery or pick up their merchandise at a post office, with orders being paid for in cash on delivery.

After the disastrous opening day, the website was moved to another server, but long waiting times for visitors persisted for months due to limited capacity. Eventually, the web store's software platform was identified as an obstacle to handling visitors in an efficient and reliable manner. With the introduction of a new software platform with shorter response times, innovative functions were introduced, such as product comparisons, a technical glossary, and a membership registration procedure. An e-mail address and a phone number were posted on the site so that customers could call for assistance. In addition to transforming their web store, NetOnNet made efforts to attract customers by offering low prices and focusing their advertising on price.

Around the Christmas of 2000, many new customers found their way to the NetOnNet website and sales grew rapidly (Figure 3.2). The number of purchases was so high that NetOnNet found it increasingly difficult to deliver products on time. Customers were supposed to place their orders on the website and then wait for delivery but many refused to accept this. Some called customer service to confirm that their order had been received, creating a growing workload for the NetOnNet customer service department. Others wanted to come to the warehouse location and pick up their products thereby reducing their waiting time and shipping cost. After some hesitation, NetOnNet decided to allow for the latter procedure. It soon became clear that this led to disruptions caused by the conflict between customers picking up their products and the regular delivery of goods to customers. Although NetOnNet was able to handle their regular shipping commitments before Christmas, these incidents led to protracted negotiations with customers.

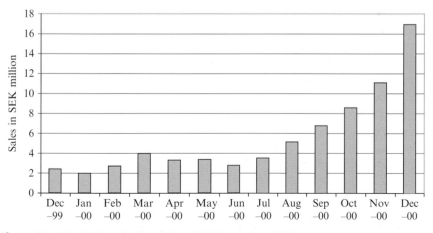

Figure 3.2. NetOnNet sales December 1999–December 2000

Source: NetOnNet Year-end Report 2000.

In April 2001, NetOnNet launched a direct selling operation from their central warehouse in Borås. They introduced this plan through advertisements in the local newspaper and a press release: 'This way we will reach everyone in the west of Sweden, whether they have a computer or not. However, this should not be compared to an "ordinary" store where products are unpacked' (NetOnNet press release 2001-04-20, my translation). With the help of computer terminals, it was now possible to search for products and to place an order on the premises. After completing the order and paying at a cash register, the customers could pick up their purchases at the loading dock. During the following months, experiments and negotiations with customers took place and continuous adjustments were made.

Subsequently, NetOnNet packaged the emerging solution into the notion of 'the warehouse shop' which was launched first in Borås, then in Ullared in 2002. This meant that from now on there was a dedicated warehouse for handling web store orders which was distinct from the warehouse shops. A catalogue was also trialled as a complement to both operations. In a press release NetOnNet announced that: 'We will be unique among consumer electronics retailers in combining a web store, warehouse shops, and catalogue ordering. The task of the catalogue is to provide deeper insight into the offerings of NetOnNet, and the reasons why we are able to offer such low prices' (NetOnNet press release 2002-10-10, my translation).

The catalogue contained instructions on how to shop from NetOnNet and presented five alternatives: Internet, telephone, fax, mail, or visiting a warehouse shop. Purchasing from the warehouse shop and the web store were presented in detail, using text instructions, pictures, and headlines such as 'This is how our warehouse shops work' and 'Self-service!' to describe the warehouse operation, and 'It's not hard to shop easily' and 'This is how you shop over the Internet', showing an eight-step process for purchasing over the Internet. One of the main purposes of the catalogue was that it should be distributed to visitors at the Ullared warehouse shop, a destination also housing Sweden's largest discount store, Gekås, and attracting a large number of visitors from all over Sweden. The shoppers were supposed to take the catalogue home and use it for placing subsequent orders via the Internet, telephone, or by returning the order forms included in the catalogue by fax or mail. The intention was to transform visitors to the warehouse shop into Internet customers, hence the detailed instructions on how to make purchases through the NetOnNet web store (Figure 3.3).

With the opening of the warehouse shops, customers were not forced to place orders through the web store before picking up their purchases from the warehouse. In fact, this procedure was later discontinued. As it turned out, some customers placed orders on the website to be picked up at the warehouse shop but never went to collect their goods. As the number of uncollected goods grew, requiring more and more storage space, ordering for later

Så här handlar du hos oss!

Internet:
På www.netonnet.se
finns ytterligare flera
tusen produkter. Här kan
du kolla senast uppdat-
erade prisuppgift samt
beställa varor.

Faxorder:
033-103 188
Använd gärna vår order-
talong som finns i slutet
av katalogen.

Telefonorder:
033-488 488
Här kan du även få
produktrådgivning av
vår kunniga personal.
Öppet vardagar kl. 9-17.

Lagershop:
I **Borås** och **Ullared**
(öppnas i november)
kan du handla direkt
från lagret. Läs mer på
nästa sida!

Brevorder:
Skicka din beställning till:
NetOnNet AB
Ordermottagningen
Bockasjögatan 12
504 30 Borås
Använd gärna vår
svars/ordertalong som
finns i slutet av katalogen.

Figure 3.3. Catalogue showing five ways to shop from NetOnNet

pickup was barred. Instead, customers who placed an order through the web store would have to wait for their purchases to be delivered to their homes or a post office branch. Otherwise, they had the option of going to the warehouse shop. In the warehouse shop, they were urged to use a computer terminal to search for products, but not for placing orders.

The two original warehouse shops were followed by a national rollout of warehouse shops, starting in Malmö in November 2006. A press release coinciding with the opening of the warehouse shop in Malmö declared: 'The combination of web store and warehouse shop will keep our costs down so that we will be able to sell at low prices. Self-service along with simple and modern facilities lets us reduce costs and keep the prices of our products really low.' (NetOnNet press release 2006-10-19, my translation). In the following two sections, the operations of the web store and the warehouse shop are examined in further detail.

PURCHASING SCENE I: THE WEB STORE

I visited the NetOnNet web store on 25 September 2006 in order to purchase a USB memory stick. The home page had a column on the left displaying different product categories, such as 'Car stereos', 'Mobile phones', and

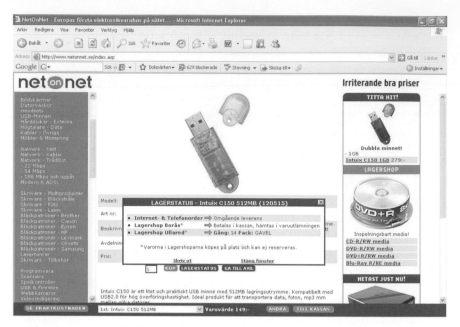

Figure 3.4. Intuix C150 512MB, showing product specification, product availability, and upgrade offer

'Stereos & Hi-Fi'. By scrolling around, I eventually found the category 'Computer accessories' and the subcategory 'USB memory sticks'. By clicking on the link, a picture and accompanying text displayed an Intuix C150 512MB memory stick for 149 SEK. The item could also be compared with the picture, description, and price of similar items. It was also possible to check the availability of the product for 'Internet and telephone orders' ('deliverable immediately') and at the warehouse shops in Borås ('to be paid at the counter, then collected at the goods collecting point') and Ullared ('located in Aisle: 14, Pigeonhole: Gable'). I was also informed that goods in the warehouse shops could only be bought in person and could not be reserved in advance (Figure 3.4).

Upon clicking on the product a picture of another USB memory stick appeared with 'Look here!' printed above it and 'Double memory!' below, being offered for 279 SEK. Clicking on the button showing 'Purchase' changed the scroll menu at the bottom of the page from displaying 'The shopping cart is empty!' to displaying '1 Intuix C150 512MB' and a purchase price of 149 SEK. Three buttons showed the alternatives: 'Display the delivery cost' (at the time of the purchase there was a campaign offering free delivery); 'Change (order)'; and 'To the counter'. By clicking on the button displaying 'To the counter', I was directed to a new page which read 'New customer' or 'Existing customer'. When choosing the alternative 'New customer' a prompt directed me to select either 'Private customer' or 'Business customer'. Upon choosing 'Private customer', I had to enter my first and last name, as well as create a password containing at least six letters and two numbers.

There was also a link to a description of 'Terms of Purchase'. After entering the required basic information, I clicked on 'Continue' and discovered that more information was required. Beyond name and country, the website now asked for address, e-mail, phone numbers (day and evening), and 'person number' (a ten-digit identity number assigned to a Swedish citizen for life). A button at the bottom of the page labelled 'Next' directed me to a checkout counter where the price of each item was displayed and where I could choose a method of payment and delivery. If I selected 'pick up at a post office', I could choose to be notified by mail or text message. Another button was linked to purchasing conditions, a second to 'log out', and a third indicated 'Next step'. A new screen now displayed my personal information and order details. There was also a 'opt in' box on the bottom of the page, where I was required to agree to the statement 'I hereby accept the purchasing conditions of NetOn-Net' in order to proceed and finalise the order.

Next, I was prompted to answer a set of questions relating to the NetOn-Net shopping experience ending with the traditional request for socio-demographics (gender, household size, age, and zip code) and an exhortation to 'Describe your total impression of the purchasing experience of NetOnNet' using at least fifty words. There was also an opt-in checkbox giving NetOnNet permission to anonymously publish customer responses on Pricerunner (www.pricerunner.com, a well-known price comparison site). After clicking on the button 'Finalize', I was switched back to the ordering window with a text stating that the order had been received; an order number was displayed, along with a message stating that a confirmation of the order would follow by e-mail. At the bottom of the web page the text now read anew: 'The shopping cart is empty!'

The order confirmation e-mail arrived immediately afterwards: 'Hello Johan Hagberg', it began, repeating information such as order number but also containing new references, such as a customer number. Again, the purchasing conditions were repeated in detail. The e-mail also stated that the order would be delivered within one to three days. As soon as the order was shipped, a notice of delivery would be sent by e-mail, including a package reference number and a link to the shipper's website, making it possible to track the package in transit. In the event I did not pick up the package, a fee of 395 SEK would be charged to cover delivery costs and other expenses. It was also stated that the order confirmation was automatically generated 'without manual verification', and, due to possible errors regarding price and time of delivery, NetOnNet reserved the right to make changes afterwards. The purchasing conditions referred to the Swedish law on distance selling, which includes the right to return goods within 14 days on the condition that the return includes the original packaging. The purchasing conditions also de-scribed the procedures for returning merchandise, such as filling out a form and contacting NetOnNet customer service or a post office, depending on the weight of the package.

On the evening of 26 September 2006, one day after the order was placed, a notice of delivery appeared in my e-mail: 'Hello Johan Hagberg. Today your order number 31643193 is leaving our warehouse with Posten [the Swedish national postal services]. Delivery will be made by the method you have selected: Post parcel. Method of payment chosen is cash on delivery.' The notice of delivery contained a package number, making it possible to trace the parcel on Posten's website.

On 27 September 2006 at 13.49, I received a text message: 'Your package from NetOnNet AB is now at GA-Kiosk, Tips o Grill, Lasarettsgatan 1, amount 149.00 SEK, State no 7737, Regards Posten' (the new reference number 7737 was added to the article number, customer number, order number, and shipment number used so far). Two days later another message was received: 'Reminder! Your package from NetOnNet AB, etc.' repeating the earlier information. On the following day I went to GA-Kiosk, Tips o Grill, Lasarettsgatan to retrieve the parcel.

I paid for the goods with a bank card and the clerk gave me a receipt and a paper with the delivery information. The goods had been shipped in a padded envelope listing the sender, receiver, and contents. Inside the envelope, there was a packing slip stating the purchasing conditions, a form to be filled out in the case of returns, and the long-awaited USB memory stick.

On 1 October 2006, an e-mail arrived from www.pricerunner.com with an invitation to evaluate the delivery along the same lines with the questionnaire I filled at the web store. After a final 'Thanks for your help', these responses could now be sorted, aggregated, and compared to what other customers had replied or will reply to the same set of questions about NetOnNet and its competitors. Despite the generic term 'price comparison services', prices were only one of many aspects of what this web service quantified and compared with competitors.

On 12 October 2006, a new e-mail arrived from NetOnNet with the subject line 'Did NetOnNet live up to your expectations?' By clicking on a link included in the e-mail I was directed to a web page entitled 'Re-shop experience'. A new set of questions with a number of statements were posed along with a scale ranging from '1 = do not agree' to '6 = agree completely' and the alternative 'don't know'. By filing the questionnaire, clicking on 'Send' (and not being in need of returning the product), this exchange had finally come to an end.

PURCHASING SCENE II: THE WAREHOUSE SHOP

Seven years had passed since the NetOnNet website opened. It was a cold morning on 3 November 2006, the opening day of the NetOnNet warehouse shop in Malmö. A few minutes before the doors opened, visitors began queuing outside. Some of them were already equipped with carts. There may have been many different reasons for visitors coming to the warehouse shop on the opening day, as there could have been many different ways for each of them to learn that a NetOnNet warehouse shop was opening in Malmö. One of the main promotional activities used by NetOnNet was a two-page advertisement in the local newspaper containing twenty-three product offers, a map of how to get to the shop, and hints on how to prepare for the opening: 'be there on time, bring a strong friend(!), be rested, and bring a lorry'. There were also ads and maps placed on the NetOnNet website announcing the Malmö warehouse shop opening. Whatever had brought them there, prospective visitors were standing in the cold waiting for the doors to open.

Anybody who wanted to make a purchase at the NetOnNet warehouse shop had to pass through the front door. Contrary to one of the episodes described earlier, where customers collected goods at the docks or entered the warehouse through the loading area during the Christmas rush, no one was waiting by the docks at the other end of the building. A sign proclaimed that these docks were intended for receiving goods only (Figures 3.5 and 3.6).

Furthermore, in contrast to the opening of the website on 10 March 1999, when, metaphorically speaking, the doors did not open with customers queuing outside, the doors did open this time. As visitors streamed in, the

Figure 3.5. Visitors queuing outside NetOnNet warehouse shop, waiting for the doors to open

Figure 3.6. The docks without customers queuing and a sign saying the docks are intended for receiving goods

NetOnNet CEO greeted the first visitors at the entrance (perhaps the CEO attended the opening to make sure the doors would actually open!). The queue soon disappeared and was replaced by a lighter but steady stream of visitors.

Further out in the parking lot, three people representing NetOnNet's main competitor El-Giganten were handing out flyers to visitors. One was a voucher offering a 100 SEK discount on purchases of at least 500 SEK in two El-Giganten stores in Malmö. The other was a price comparison of the products advertised by NetOnNet in celebration of the opening. It included prices for the same items at NetOnNet and El-Giganten suggesting that prices were lower at El-Giganten.

Close to the entrance, trolleys and shopping carts were lined up and a nearby sign stated: 'Don't forget the shopping cart! In our Warehouse Shop you have to search for and pick up the products you wish to purchase by yourself. In return, we offer you lower prices and all the help you need'. While a sign reminded the visitors to take a cart, there were also devices attached to the carts requiring a coin deposit in order to unlock one and thus providing a reminder to return it to its proper location when leaving (Figure 3.7).

To the right of the entrance, a large sign read 'Customer Service' and beneath it stated 'Installation, Upgrades, Exchanges, Service, Returns on

Figure 3.7. Don't forget the shopping cart!

approval'. Three clerks were standing behind counters, alternating between gazing at computer screens and serving customers. A queue number dispenser was attached to the wall and an electronic display read '00'. Two men and a woman were being served and no other visitors were queuing up at the time. Inside, past the entrance to the store, were two pairs of swinging gates. To their left more shopping carts were lined up under another sign saying 'Don't forget, etc.'

Passing the gates and walking a few metres further inside, visitors encountered the CEO handing out shopping bags similar to the blue or yellow ones found at IKEA but these were red and had a NetOnNet logo. As it turned out, these shopping bags were not for sale and were intended for use on the premises only.

The attention of visitors was caught by a slide show projected onto a big screen showing: 'This is how you shop in four simple steps.' The same steps were shown on signs hanging in many locations in the store: '1) Search—search for the product in the computer; 2) Note—note down the article number and location listed below the stock availability; 3) Pick up—pick up the merchandise from where it is located. Some products can be picked up at the goods collection desk directly after payment; and 4) Pay—pay at the counter. If you wish to pay on instalments, contact the information desk.'

Figure 3.8. Computer stations and displays showing four steps to making a purchase

Many customers were gathered around the information desk located below a sign reading 'Information: products, home delivery, instalments, and subscriptions'. Shelves, pallets, aisles, packaged products, and displays met the visitors throughout the facility. There were also numerous small information desks throughout the store with personnel standing behind them and whimsical signs above saying, 'I hope that someone wants to ask me for help!' Computer stations consisting of a terminal, a screen, a mouse, a keyboard, pencils, and notebooks were everywhere. Above them, signs described the four steps involved in making a purchase. The same steps were also displayed in the notebooks, which contained a table with nine rows of empty cells and columns labelled 'Product name', 'Article number', and 'Location' (Figure 3.8).

Some visitors used the computer stations to search for items, while others walked down the aisles scanning the shelves.

Another pattern can be identified in Figure 3.9: the aisle (Swedish: *Gång*) numbers. As with the web store, there was no shortage of numbers in the warehouse shop, but these were different numbers. Instead of customer, order, package, and retrieval numbers, there were numbers signposting the aisles and the shelf sections. There was some confusion since the aisles numbers ran from 1 through 10, then continued on from 14. It turned out that aisle numbers 11, 12, and 13 were located in a different place and their

Figure 3.9. Combining 'face-to-screen' and 'face-to-shelves'

signs were missing. At the top of this picture (Figure 3.9), a sign read 'Picture & Sound' (Swedish: *Bild & Ljud*). Why were these signs hanging there if everyone was searching for the location in the computer? Presumably, such signs were there for visitors who did not (or could not) use the website. In support of the assumption, the 'departments' in the warehouse shop (such as 'Picture & Sound', 'Household', and 'Bodycare') did not corre- spond to the 'departments' found on the web store menu. This picture also illustrates a specific limitation of self-service in this case: although required to pick up their own merchandise, visitors did not have access to the ware- house's upper shelves.

In a dedicated space in the warehouse shop, I found a racing track for radio-controlled cars. A couple of visitors were manoeuvring the cars while others watched. A bit further along, an area furnished with tables and chairs, soda vending machines and signs invited the visitors to 'Take a break! Here you can rest your legs, have something to drink, and let yourself be inspired by the latest technology'. At another location, two small and portable display counters featured manufacturers' representatives demonstrating products.

Employees circulated through the store ready to assist visitors whilst a few others staffed the information desks. Two employees were conspicuous in their security guard uniforms. Two other employees, wearing business suits

Figure 3.10.   Goods pickup placed at the opposite end of the building as compared to the docks for receiving goods

and earpieces, moved watchfully around the store. Many products' packaging had anti-theft devices attached to them to discourage shoplifting. Some especially valuable items were only available at a merchandise pick-up point. This counter was behind a window with a sign cbove it reading 'Goods pickup' (Swedish: *Varuutlämning*). An employee was leaning on his elbows, waited for customers to come and collect their goods. In comparison to the Christmas rush of 2000, this counter was hardly busy. The 'goods pickup' location was at the opposite end of the receiving dock, probably in order to separate different customer flows (Figure 3.10).

A moped was on display and a sign announced that it was the first prize in a contest open to those who had purchased goods valued at 500 SEK and above. In order to participate, a customer had to fill out a coupon with name, address, phone number, and e-mail as well as a check box reading 'Yes please! I very much would like to receive the NetOnNet newsletter'.

There was a long row of manned checkout lanes where one could pay by cash or credit card. A bin for the return of shopping bags was placed at the exit. On one occasion, three out of the four security guards stood next to the bin, probably in order to ensure the shopping bags were returned before visitors left the store. Purchases were placed in paper or plastic bags but customers were charged 2 SEK per bag. A receipt showed what had been bought and included such information as store hours, the warehouse shop's address, and the name of the cashier. In striking contrast to purchasing on the Web, where the terms of sale featured heavily, purchasing conditions were scarcely mentioned. Apart from three sentences explaining the warranty periods for different types of products, purchasing conditions were summarized in one sentence: 'There is a right to return the goods within 14 days when showing the receipt; the product must be unused and in its original packaging.' If someone was using a trolley or shopping cart, these could be returned in the parking lot. Customers exited the store at the same point they entered, as new visitors poured in. A large sign over the exit read: 'Thanks for your visit! We'll meet again soon—here or at www.netonnet.se.'

Discussion

From the empirical study I have identified five issues related to the seller–buyer exchange dyad. First, the agents participating in exchange are heterogeneous entities. Secondly, exchange processes require the assembling and disassembling of agencies depending on the mode of exchange. Thirdly, the question of whether exchange should be regarded as a discrete transaction or an episode in a relationship is examined. The fourth aspect concerns the mutual configuration of agents participating in exchanges, whereas the fifth relates to the configuration of agents who partake in different modes of exchange.

HETEROGENEOUS ENTITIES

The exchange settings described above were populated by a heterogeneous set of elements involving both humans and non-human entities. The retrieval of the parcel at the kiosk was the first face-to-face encounter between humans during the web store shopping process: might that specific encounter make this activity 'peculiarly human' (Kotler 1972: 49), thus placing it within the domain of marketing? What if the product had been ordered to be delivered to a residential mail box and the customer was not home when it was delivered? Would it still be peculiarly human? Would it still be a marketing activity? Indeed, there were humans involved in the scenes described, but also signs, computers, carts, bags, packages, shelves, pencils, notebooks, screens, telephones, faxes, pictures, and many other entities. Throughout the exchange episodes we can see the interaction of a combination of already existing materials (often there for multiple purposes, e.g. computers) as well as tailor-made devices dedicated to the specific mode of exchange (e.g. shopping bags). These entities (e.g. a visitor or a shopping cart) do not act as buyers by themselves but in combination. Taking this into account, the notion of 'self-service' may be misleading. Far from persons serving themselves, the involvement of other entities is of particular importance (see also du Gay 2004, 2008; Kjellberg and Helgesson 2007*b*; Cochoy 2009). Put differently, self-service is, among other things, dependent upon shelf service. In short, the notion that the actors behave as self-contained entities during exchange and that exchange is something that happens between them needs revising.

EXCHANGE: ASSEMBLING AND DISASSEMBLING *AGENCEMENTS*

Agencies such as buyers and sellers are assembled and disassembled during exchange. If that had not happened, the exchanges described above would not have taken place. During this assembling and disassembling some things are given away, some are taken, some are borrowed, and some are lent. In some parts of the process, the buyer had to subscribe to additional equipment during the exchange (Latour 2005), while other parts of the process relied on the buyer already having access to the necessary equipment. For example, access to a computer was a prerequisite for purchasing on the website, whereas in the warehouse shop computers were part of the equipment the buyers could subscribe to while shopping. In the web store, the computer was a part of the buyer's agency, whereas in the example of the warehouse shop the computer was a part of the seller's agency, to be disassembled and reassembled as part of the buyer during the exchange. In both cases, the computer enabled contact between the parties, thus being involved on both sides of the exchange.

How might one decide whether the shopping bag, plastic bag, name, address, trolley, sign, computer, receipt, or GA kiosk belong to the seller or buyer sides? If one were to put the buyer and the seller into two distinct groups, thus disassembling the *agencements*, it would be necessary to begin all over again in order to make exchange happen. Imagine stopping halfway through the description of the processes of the web store or the warehouse shop and drawing a line. On the left side, there is a seller. On the right side, there is a buyer. Then, one takes all these humans, devices, and pieces of equipment and places them on one of the sides, making them the 'pure' property of the seller or the buyer, respectively. If one succeeds in placing every single item on just one of these two sides, one would end up with two separate and distinct groups of entities (as in Figure 3.1). But then, how would they meet and recognize each other? Who would be the seller if nothing was sold? Who would be the buyer if nothing was bought? In order to render the exchanges possible, the assembling and disassembling of these *agencements* must take place.

The *agencements* are the *results* of preceding as well as concurrent assembling and disassembling. Therefore, it is necessary to focus on an issue pointed out by Andersson et al. (2008): new *agencements* are created from already existing ones. At the entrance of the warehouse shop, there were efforts aimed to prevent some assemblages from taking place (competitors standing outside exhorting prospective visitors to 'Go elsewhere!'), as well as efforts to promote other assemblages (Take a shopping cart!). There were also efforts to prevent disassemblings (newsletter registrations to enable further communication) as well as to enhance disassemblings (signs and bins urging visitors to return shopping bags). The assembling of new *agencements* can also build upon previous assemblages. For instance, the 'existing customer' entry for the web store means that this assembling can start with some modules of the *agencement* already in place.

The reiterations of the terms of sale when purchasing over the website, as compared with purchasing in the warehouse shop, means that the assembling of the *agencements* is also performed by others, not directly present at the exchange. In this case, the Swedish law on distance selling required the seller as well the buyer *agencements* to be assembled to some degree—by stating their rights and duties.

TRANSACTION OR RELATIONSHIP?

Should these exchanges be described as single transactions or episodes in a long-term relationship? There was a difference in the duration of the transactions: the warehouse shop procedure was completed in a single day, while the web store procedure extended over many days. Both were single transactions in the sense that goods changed hands and transactions were concluded. But there were also efforts to initiate a relationship. A contest in the warehouse shop was used to invite visitors to enter their e-mail addresses in order for them to receive future newsletters. Buyers could enter into an agreement to pay by instalments. Thus whether a given exchange is a single transaction or an episode in a relationship depends on what happens next.

There were numerous efforts made in the web store to collect information about the visitor, all of them far removed from the online anonymity suggested by Hoffman et al. (1999). Website visitors were encouraged to reveal their name, address, e-mail, phone number, gender, age, and household size, and state what made them visit the website, what caused them to buy, how satisfied they were, if they were first-time buyers, how often they purchase over the Web, when they expected delivery, how probable it was that they would purchase again, and whether they would recommend NetOnNet to a friend. The last question appeared three times during the process.

MUTUAL CONFIGURATION OF THE BUYER AND SELLER

Although there might be asymmetries between the capacities of the buyer and the seller, the configuration of the buyer *agencement* should not be seen as a one-way process orchestrated by the seller. This became obvious when customers acted differently from what NetOnNet anticipated: they called customer service to pick up their merchandise; they went to the warehouse and waited at the dock; they entered the building; or did not call for goods that they had ordered. All these activities are examples of how buyers participated in configuring the seller's *agencement*. This was also evident when buyers agreed to answer Pricerunner's questionnaire, assigning ratings to their shopping experience, sharing reviews, etc.

Another way of expressing the actions of the buyer upon which the configuration of the seller is dependent is in following instructions provided by the seller. The seller can only be sustained in these practices (such as offering low prices or providing assistance) as long as the visitors cooperate by following these instructions (e.g. providing information, searching for and picking up products). So 'lower prices', for example, was not something the seller could continue to provide unless buyers were prepared to cooperate with the seller's prescriptions, such as using a cart or taking goods from the shelves.

AGENCEMENTS AND DIFFERENT MODES OF EXCHANGE

Different modes of exchange require different buyer and seller *agencements*. Exchanging one *agencement* for another (such as a bricks-and-mortar store customer to a web store customer) requires the assembling of different sets of entities.

Different modes of exchange can also involve different limits, possibilities, and sequences of events for the *agencements*. In the warehouse shop, there was a volumetric constraint on how much could be put in a cart, or shopping bag, as well as how much could be carried through the doors in one visit. In the web store, the constraint consisted in the limit of the number of items (10) that could be placed in the virtual shopping cart at any one time, which could be easily overcome by putting in 10 at a time many times over. The web store also had a minimum and a maximum freight charge for each order.

In the warehouse shop, a cart or trolley had to be taken before beginning to shop, which required some planning if one wished to avoid starting all over again (e.g. choosing the proper carrying equipment after selecting the goods). In the case of the web store, the virtual shopping cart was placed on the screen irrespective of one having chosen a product or not (either saying 'The shopping cart is empty!' or displaying the product(s) chosen). The web shopping cart also tallied the total amount purchased, providing the online buyer with a different calculative ability compared to the warehouse shop buyer. There was also a difference regarding questions and answers on the web store and the warehouse shop. In the warehouse shop, visitors were encouraged to ask questions ('I hope that someone wants to ask me for help!'). Visitors to the web store, however, were prompted to *answer* questions rather than pose them.

Yet another issue concerned the order and sequence of shopping. Even though the visit to the web store began on the home page provided by NetOnNet, this need not be the case. In the warehouse shop, the visitor had to enter a specific doorway in order to become a customer, and then follow a route inside the warehouse shop. In the web store, visitors could come from anywhere (e.g. price comparison sites, blogs, or search engines) and go anywhere on the website, bypassing the home page and not following a specific mapped route (imagine customers suddenly popping up and/or suddenly disappearing from the aisles of the warehouse shop!). Online shopping is a matter of windows rather than doors. For all that, when it came to placing the order, there was a specific route to be followed in the web store which was more prescriptive than in the warehouse shop.

Comparing the *agencements* of different modes of exchange is not the same thing as looking for universal functions that 'must' occur in order to bring about the same effect. It is not a matter of using different means for producing the same agent, but rather taking into account that these *agencements* and their capabilities may differ. However, there were also efforts to combine and coordinate them, so that they would be capable of participating in different types of exchange. Warehouse shop visitors were handed catalogues presenting five forms of exchange: Internet, telephone, fax, mail, or visiting a warehouse shop. Visitors to the web store could see the availability of specific products in the warehouse shops. Visitors to the warehouse shop could sign up for newsletters linked to the web store. It was thus a matter of creating *agencements* capable of participating in different modes of exchange. But there were also efforts to keep apart *agencements*: for instance, the possibility of placing an order in the web store and then picking up the merchandise at the warehouse was removed. Apart from the blurring of boundaries between initially distinct modes of exchange noticed by Kjellberg and Helgesson (2007*b*), in NetOnNet there were also some efforts to bring together as well as keep apart different modes of exchange.

Conclusions

The marketing management approach builds upon a simplified version of actors, focusing mostly on humans, meaning that other entities have either been ignored or marginalized. Even though it has been acknowledged that actors are heterogeneous entities, there is a need for further studies showing how they are shaped in practice. This requires taking into consideration the wide range of entities participating in contemporary marketing activities, such as computers, scanners, and mobile phones, as well as those entities yet to come.

It is not that entities other than humans participating in marketing have been forgotten, but they have been analysed as instruments or functional objects under the singular control of humans. Some approaches, such as the service-dominant logic (SDL), push this asymmetry even further, by stressing the intangible aspects of contemporary markets. In contrast, the practice-based approach emphasizes their material character. According to SDL, material entities, such as goods, if involved in exchange at all, are subordinated—as assisting appliances, intermediaries, or distribution mechanisms for the provision of service (Vargo and Lusch 2004; Lusch and Vargo 2006)—to humans who intervene in the exchange of service (Vargo and Lusch 2006). This a priori division between different entities on the ground of their 'essential' characteristics should be resisted. In the epoch of the virtual, the fluid, and the intangible, there are paradoxically more reasons to look deeper into the materiality of markets. The selling and buying *agencements* analysed in this empirical case are indeed fluid, but this fluidity depends on a large number of solid entities (cf. Cochoy 2009). The concept of *agencement* provides a good starting point to examine how agents participating in exchange are constituted by a large variety of entities including computers, displays, humans, shopping carts, etc., as well as to study their contingent and temporary attachments. These entities deserve to be treated not just as tools in the hands of humans participating in marketing processes but as active participants in marketing.

Furthermore, there have been numerous debates about what the line connecting the buyer and seller in the typical exchange dyad represents: transactions, relationships, interactions? Different forms of exchange are often treated as polar opposites, for example transactional versus relational exchanges, or service versus goods exchanges. Another example of this approach to exchange is the assumption that 'actor type' determines the 'form of exchange', for example business-to-business exchange is seen as relational while business-to-consumer is seen as transactional. Such idealized versions of exchange become problematic when applied to actual exchanges. Empirical studies have revealed the plurality of marketing approaches among different types of firms (e.g. Coviello et al. 2002). As Kjellberg and Helgesson (2007*b*) have shown, there is no univocal relationship between agents and mode of exchange. As argued in this chapter, agents shape exchanges but exchanges also shape the agents that take part in exchanges.

Is it time to broaden the concept of marketing (Kotler and Levy 1969) once more? While the SDL stresses the evolution from one dominant logic (goods) to another (services), seeking to identify unifying *principles*, a practice-based approach calls for sensitivity to diversity and multiplicity by attending to situated *practices* (Kjellberg and Helgesson 2006). Marketing is not in need of broadening in the sense of seeking similarities across different sectors, places and times, or striving towards a unifying logic, whether service-dominant or otherwise. In order to reconnect marketing to markets, there is no need to ditch the concept of exchange, but rather to broaden it by analysing a larger variety of exchanges. There is also a pressing need to include a larger set of entities involved in exchanges. The concept of *agencement* is well-suited to meet these requirements. Rather than making a priori assumptions about what actors are, whether exchanges should be characterized as discrete trans-actions or events in ongoing relationships or, still, whether they are manifes-tations of a goods- or service-dominant logic, we should seek to convert these into worthy empirical questions.

■ NOTE

1. The writing of this chapter was financially supported by the Swedish Retail and Whole-sale Development Council and the University of Borås. I would like to thank Franck Cochoy, Barbara Czarniawska, two anonymous reviewers, and the editors of this volume for their helpful comments and suggestions.

4 Product tastes, consumer tastes

The plurality of qualifications in product development and marketing activities[1]

SOPHIE DUBUISSON-QUELLIER

Introduction

The new economic sociology literature recently proposed the need to pay greater attention to the relationship between market participants (Granovetter 1985; DiMaggio and Louch 1998; Fourcade 2007) and the coordination of economic action (Beckert 2002, 2009). Within economic sociology, some studies, inspired by the sociology of science, focus more specifically on the role of activities (Barrey et al. 2000; Cochoy and Dubuisson-Quellier 2000; Barrey 2007) and devices (MacKenzie 2006; Callon et al. 2007; Dubuisson-Quellier 2007) involved in market relations, rather than on the social or cultural embeddedness of economic action. These devices and activities aim at connecting market participants through equipped market mediations. These connections produce and involve qualification activities which make actors able to compare products either to singularize them (Karpik 2007) or to link them with other products.

This chapter focuses on the role of product development and marketing activities in shaping market relationships (Araujo 2007; Araujo et al. 2008). The development and marketing of mass consumer products involve various qualification processes: products have to be defined, tested, altered, and commercialized, and qualifications change as products evolve. These processes are recurrent and concern actors within the firm as well as outside partners. The R&D engineer, the marketing manager, the sales manager, the advertising agent, the salesperson and, finally, the consumer will all, in turn, attribute qualities to the products that are developed, sold, and consumed. Nothing predisposes these actors to share the same definition of a product's quality. Yet the product has to be able to circulate in the market space, from the supply side to the demand side, via all the mediators who contribute to shaping the encounter between the two. This coordination process implies temporary agreements between the actors about what is exchanged. In what I call an economy of judgements (Dubuisson-Quellier and Neuville 2003), many

definitions of product quality are produced throughout the product development and marketing processes. This suggests that there may be no need for
a consensual agreement on a product's quality for exchange to take place. It is
interesting to test this hypothesis in the case of food products. As mass
produced products, they are intended for a mass market but, as food products, they bring into play idiosyncratic and difficult to define tastes, open to
multiple qualifications (Fischler 1990).

The product development process involves building a representation of
consumers' tastes and preferences: I call this a representation of consumers.
This representation stems from the results of different activities within the
firm which aim at assessing consumers, testing products, and confronting
representations of consumers with product features. These activities rely on
different types of techniques, but they all contribute to the building up of
a qualification of consumers which may be used to design product features.
I call these activities local qualification of both consumers and products.

The purpose of this chapter is to supply an ethnographic perspective on these
different activities and to present their contribution to the marketing of food
products. My main argument is that these activities produce a proliferation of
qualifications of both products and consumers, which are essential to develop
and market products—even though they are not aligned with one another to
produce a unique, stable qualification. I will show that these different local and
temporary qualifications are necessary to make decisions about the product.
Qualification as a process of coordination between different departments
within a firm is more important than qualification aimed at stabilizing a
matching definition of consumers and products. This perspective on qualification allows us to see the final stage of marketing the product, namely the meeting
of a consumer and the product in a retail store (Dubuisson-Quellier 2006) as
another round of qualification, in which the consumer qualifies the product in
order to make his or her decision to buy it or not.

After presenting the theoretical framework of my approach in the first section,
I will highlight two of the different product development activities carried out by
a company, regarding the way they produce stabilized and negotiated qualifications of products and consumers. In the last section, I will show that this
production of qualifications is one of the core activities when marketing products. The analysis is based on an empirical study carried out in a French
manufacturer of cooked pork meat products: the Britham Company.[2]

From product development to product career

The first economic sociologist to highlight the role of marketing techniques
in the shaping of markets was Viviana Zelizer (1978). She described how

marketing techniques succeeded in removing the blockage of demand for life insurance by religious groups and allowed the development of an insurance industry in nineteenth-century America. The role of marketing in shaping markets has recently been rediscovered by economic sociologists inspired by science and technology studies (Cochoy 1998; Callon et al. 2002). These authors argue that marketing creates consumer attachment to goods and, in that way, stabilizes both consumers' preferences and product qualities through a singularized relationship between consumers and products. This argument is consistent with the core principles of the marketing discipline, namely, to define a project for the economic life of a product. This project must encompass the different components of the marketing mix, which gives specific directions on the selection of product, price, place, and promotion options (Kotler and Keller 2008). The marketing mix must reflect the market's structure and target particular segments of demand. The application of marketing techniques relies on assumptions about the preferences and profiles of specific market segments.

But, as Beckert (2009: 17) notices: '...to understand such attachments, market sociology needs a theory of preference formation.' One solution is to follow the performativity argument developed by actor network theorists, which states that most of the techniques and materials that intervene in the construction of markets perform the theories they incorporate (Callon 1998*b*). This argument suggests that marketing incorporates and performs a theory of preference formation which may produce the consumers' attachments that economic sociologists have identified 'in real settings'.

This explanation is unsatisfactory at the theoretical and empirical levels. As far as theory is concerned, recent developments in economic sociology emphasize two main aspects of value and worth in economic exchange. First, they show that many collective devices, conventions, and institutions are needed to organize singularized relationships between products and consumers based on stabilized commensurability between products' features (Karpik 2010). Secondly, they show how uncertainties (Beckert 1996) and the increasing complexity of firms' environments (Stark 2009) prevent companies from stabilizing their relationship with consumers. Furthermore, marketing theory has produced insights on the contribution of marketing practices to the production of market orders (see Araujo et al. 2008) and this provides an avenue for empirical studies of how marketing practices help frame consumer–product relationships.

In this chapter, I will study the marketing practices of a food company, Britham, through the different tasks and activities performed throughout the development of a number of products. Britham had an old plant that was bought in the early 1990s from a large food company specializing in ready-made food products.[3] This was considered a strategic activity for the firm as the plant produced *charcuterie*[4] products sold through supermarkets (*produits à la coupe*).[5] Britham employed 420 people in its different departments: sales, development, production, and marketing.[6] It produced roast ham, *pâtés*, and *saucissons*. When I conducted the field study, Britham was implementing ISO 9001 procedures on how to organize the product development process. I followed four product development processes.

The empirical study showed that the process of product development may not be interpreted as the construction of a singular, stabilized, and univocal relationship between products and consumers. Instead, the process produced several temporary definitions of both consumers' preferences and product features which were not always compatible. While going through the different stages of the development process, the product is given successive and temporary qualifications. However, these processes are not regarded by the firm as trial and error. Instead, they correspond to the succession of stages that products have to pass in order to be developed and marketed: the product career. These qualifications are temporary since they are the output of the process of coordination and validation amongst the firm's staff at every stage of the process, from the first idea to the sale through the distribution channel.

From measures of products and consumers to real confrontations

Product development activities stem from two main types of confrontation between products and consumers. The first confrontation is based on objective measures produced on both of them separately, whilst the second organizes the meeting of consumers and products.

ASSESSING CONSUMERS AND PRODUCTS THROUGH OBJECTIVE INDICATORS

The first activity is aimed at qualifying products and consumers in the development and marketing process, and relies on techniques that provide some objectification of both through measurements. Surveys based on samples of consumer panels and sensorial analysis tests are the most representative techniques of this category of qualification devices. The specificity of these techniques stems from their ability to produce quantitative information about consumers (e.g. composition of their shopping basket, age, and income) and products (e.g. market shares, salt content). This information can then easily be used in different departments of the firm, as it may circulate in reports and notes shared by a large number of people. These qualifications do not need to be interpreted or negotiated. Their limitation is that they produce a narrow definition of consumers and products, which can support only very limited interventions on product features.

Quantitative surveys of consumers may be produced by the marketing department of a company or by external parties such as professional agencies (e.g. advertising, merchandising, design).[7] They may assess several components of market demand (e.g. consumers' characteristics, modes of consumption). These approaches are based on the assumption that there is a wide heterogeneity of consumer behaviours. A generic knowledge of consumer behaviours is necessary before any form of data reduction or segmentation of demand can be carried out. The question of choosing discriminant variables is particularly relevant. The solution favoured by professionals—manufacturers and retailers—is to obtain a multitude of data on which a large number of indicators can be built. Thus market research agencies propose a variety of services, from the measurement of consumers' purchasing behaviours to the analysis of inter-brand competition. Measurements may concern either products (e.g. sales, market shares) or consumers (e.g. socio-demographics). The first type of data is used by companies to qualify the targeted population, the marketing objectives and, consequently, the type of offer to be developed, while the second type may help improve sales activation devices, track market shares, or other performance indicators. These different techniques produce a specific qualification of products by building up a database of their market performance.

The second qualification technique is more product-oriented. Like many others in the food industry, our food manufacturer uses a variety of tools to steer its production process based on the study of product characteristics. The qualification of food requires the use of specific metrological devices as in any industrial production system. The product has to be characterized physically but also in other respects, namely, its physico-chemical, bacteriological, and organoleptic attributes. Physico-chemical and bacteriological measurements are taken at the end of the production process by means of various instruments, in an internal laboratory dedicated to that purpose.[8] Sensorial analysis of the organoleptic dimensions of products is also a form of metrology, but one whose specificity lies in that the measuring instrument is the human palate. This means that people are trained to become a collective, calibrated instrument which can evaluate qualities such as sweetness, acidity, saltiness, the sensations of crunchiness or softness, the aspects of brightness or redness, and so on.

This technique is to an extent symmetrical to the measurements performed by professional agencies. As noted above, agencies use metrological tools to describe the consumer in minute detail, from the angle of her or his food consumption through objectifying characteristics (e.g. age, gender, occupation, consumption of packaged cooked meats per month and per product). Symmetrically, sensorial analysis applies a specific metrology to describe the product in just as much detail, from the angle of its objectified organoleptic characteristics (e.g. appearance, colour, touch, smell, flavour, texture).

The large companies in the food sector pay good money for customized market research reports and tailor-made sensorial analysis of their products. The agencies and institutes that provide these services also publish reports containing generic and partial findings which are more accessible to the small and medium sized enterprises in the sector. Britham belongs to this segment of the industry and makes heavy use of general market data contained in these secondary reports. At the same time, Britham mobilizes many other simpler and less objectifying devices. Their more diffuse and local use in the organization emphasizes the less general character of the statements produced by these tools.

By becoming available to all concerned, public data provides a general framework enabling the company to take decisions internally and in collaboration with its partners. Tests have the reliable and irrevocable character of codified, objective knowledge, circulating independently of its conditions of production. Hence, the use of publicly available data is uncontroversial and consensual. It may therefore be used as a starting point in the qualification of the product and consumer in a product development process involving several departments of Britham, by giving a general orientation on market positioning.

CONFRONTING CONSUMERS WITH PRODUCTS: REACTIONS AND ENGAGEMENTS

A second type of qualification activity aims at confronting consumers with products: focus groups are a good example of this type of activity. These tests are fairly well framed and designed to validate certain choices within a framework for formulating a product's characteristics.

The focus group is not designed as a test and differs from sensorial analysis in so far as it is neither a matter of calibrating consumers' tastes in order to build a tool to measure product characteristics nor a furtive and sometimes mute tasting at the point of sale. Here, consumers are asked to apply themselves, both to answer questions and voice their opinions on products by imagining episodes of everyday life (e.g. shopping in the supermarket, eating at home). They are also asked to account for behaviours which are not always verbalized or even rationalized. The weak framing of questions suggests extremely varied answers, not only from one consumer to the next but also for each of them, depending on the question. With this test, one rapidly gives up the idea of identifying a single rationality for the choice of products. The particularity of this encounter is clearly to show that various principles of consumers' rationality (e.g. price, length of the queue) are articulated to account for specific behaviours.[9] Ranking choice criteria is sometimes impossible, and some try to stick to them by over-rationalizing purchasing behaviours that may, in fact, be far more iterative or spontaneous.[10] This fact makes the analysis of focus group results difficult. It is not an easy matter to convert idiosyncratic and local judgements made by consumers into decisions about product development. For instance, how can one interpret participants' statements such as 'this terrine has no character' or 'this one is like cat food'? One characteristic of focus groups is that they show that qualifications of products made by consumers are neither stable nor objective, and are not easy to turn into managerial or technical decisions within the firm.

But the openness of the test is also its strong point, in so far as the list of characteristics tested is not stabilized during the test, even if the aim is very precise (e.g. to test consumers' reaction to an alteration in a recipe using more mushrooms). This openness facilitates the emergence of categories that consumers find more relevant: for example, in a test of reactions to a new label, consumers linked the colour of the label with its position in the product range ('this orange gives the impression of a bottom-of-the-range product'); while in another the product's texture was linked to the price ('there are whole food bits in this one, it must be more expensive'). In these tests, consumers make a connection between their tastes and their qualifications of the product. The advantage is that it shows the references they mobilize to produce a judgement. It thus highlights the fact that the terminology that consumers use to make judgements is not stable, thus leading to further testing. From this point of view, it is interesting to see that this terminology is broadly in line with that suggested by the offer: the product and its characteristics, and also the vocabulary and categories mobilized by the facilitator of the session. During the session, the marketing terms that she uses (e.g. 'fresh produce department', 'positioning in the range', 'loss-leader') are gradually taken up by the consumers who apply them directly for qualifying their tastes and the products (see Lezaun 2007). Furthermore, consumers are far more comfortable expressing an opinion during a collective discussion than in the answers they give individually. This situation reflects the effects of prescriptions at play in the construction of the relationship between consumers and products. The opinions of other consumers become resources on which their own qualification of products can be based. In other words, others' judgements help equip the judgement that each one produces. Even though the consumers may sometimes start with very different opinions on the products, the functioning of the focus group slowly turns into a coordination process which helps the facilitator write her report to Britham and produce a recommendation for the further development of the product.

These tests produce redefinitions of what those consumer competencies and product characteristics are: on the one hand, the consumer may change his/her opinion on the product (the product modifies the consumer). On the other hand the product may also be changed (the consumer modifies the product).

Relying on consumers' and products' spokespersons

The metrological devices described above can be seen as the construction of specific spokespersons for products and consumers. The notion of spokesperson in actor network theory refers to the idea that, in an innovation process, participants, data, or objects may stand in for or represent others (often users) who are absent from the process. These people or devices advocate options which are supposed to be preferred by those they represent (Akrich et al. 2002).The metrological devices used by Britham are specific in so far as they make it possible to give a quantitative description of products and consumers, producing objective (in the sense of definitive) qualifications of them. In this section I focus on other operations that place more emphasis on the subjectification of the qualifications produced, which are no longer detachable from the conditions and the people that produce them. These operations vary widely and engage a large set of market actors. Even within the firm, they can be mobilized at different levels: production, marketing, development, sales, quality, and top management.

I will present two examples of these processes of qualifying products and consumers. The first relies on the information reported by people in the firm who act as representatives of the consumer, either because their occupation enables them to have a specific assessment of demand (salespersons) or because they themselves are consumers (everybody in the company). The second type of process produces some information about the product and comes from people, within the firm, who claim to be specialists on particular features of the product (production managers). The qualifications produced through these processes are negotiated in meetings where decisions are taken.

'BECAUSE, WE KNOW THE CONSUMER': THE VOICE OF SALES STAFF AND FEEDBACK FROM THE MARKET

The first of these examples is 'feedback from the market', the voice that the sales representatives of the firm stand for. In the eyes of Britham, their close contact with customers (retailers) gives them legitimacy to feed information back to production and design on certain needs expressed somewhat diffusely by their customers (shops and supermarkets). As they spend more of their time in the field than inside the firm, they rarely have the opportunity to share their knowledge of the market. Organized events such as debriefings or consultations on particular issues are designed to harness this form of expertise, and to integrate it into approaches to the design and improvement of Britham's products. The qualifications of products and consumers resulting from these meetings can seldom be separated from the conditions and contexts in which they are formulated. For example, it is known in the firm that sales representatives are not equally skilled at assessing consumers' preferences. Thus some of their recommendations will be taken into account while others will be ignored. In some cases, the main focus will be on their expertise concerning consumers' needs (e.g. type of packaging, expectations regarding innovation), whereas in others, their feedback on consumers will also be taken into account (e.g. new food habits). This suggests that the mobilization of sales expertise within the company was weak. The main idea was to have an additional qualification of products and consumers at different stages when product formulation may still be underdetermined. The firm enables its sales representatives to put themselves, albeit temporarily, in the retailer's or the consumers' shoes, and thus highlight certain demand characteristics. It is clear that these qualifications cannot be detached from either the people (e.g. sales representative's skills, sales figures) or the conditions of their production (e.g. sales representative's sector, type of customers visited, location of the shops monitored). For this reason, the qualification produced by this type of process is the subject of intense negotiations during the meetings where decisions are made. For example, a sales representative explained that some of his customers reported that the colour of the slice of *saucisson* turned dark very quickly—something that customers regarded as suspect. Other people in the meeting (especially from the product development department) asked him who had said that, in what kind of shops, how long the *saucisson* had been on the shelf, how often it happened, what kind of light was used by the supermarket, and so on. The subjective dimension of this qualification made it contestable and not easily transferable from one situation to another. Nevertheless, it appears that this kind of qualification is used more often than objective ones. According to our interviewees, it is more useful when drastic decisions have to be made regarding product development.

'BECAUSE, I AM A CONSUMER': THE PROFESSIONAL AS A SPOKESPERSON FOR THE CONSUMER

Although market access puts sales representatives in a privileged position to express opinions on definitions of markets and products, they are not the only ones to be allowed to express a view on the subject. All other professionals in the firm are called upon regularly to give a voice to products and consumers. This principle has been institutionalized within the firm, as an hour-long product tasting session is organized daily at 10 a.m. for the heads of all the departments and the chief executive officer. This session has several objectives.

The first objective is quality control. The people who participate in the session eat a small piece of each type of product of the previous day's production (ham, cooked meats, cured meats, *saucisson*) to identify the main production defects before it is dispatched to customers. This control is random and its frequency varies depending on the products and the problems identified. Ham and other meats are sliced and presented on a plate placed on a table in Britham's cafeteria. The tasting is deliberately unassisted: participants take no notes, are not trained in tasting, and have no protocol to adhere to.[11] They start by examining the products, smell them, and finally taste them. Visual control is important because several faults in ham can be identified in this way—ranging from problems of the cut to an excess of salt—and may cause an entire batch to be stopped before being dispatched. The various defects identified are discussed, negotiated, qualified, and, in some cases, recorded. The process allows Britham to deal with specific and recurrent problems (such as visual defects in ham) or to progress in the development of a new product (such as defining the appropriate size of the mushroom pieces in a new pâté recipe).

The identification of defects and the incidents that caused them are fairly rare. Tasting sessions usually turn into an open exchange amongst the various people attending. This is a secondary aim of these sessions: organizing encounters around products between the various professionals in the firm usually involves the entire firm's managerial staff. Operatives and supervisors also take part but on a rotating basis. Interaction sometimes transcends the framework of the products themselves and focuses on other subjects. For example, these sessions are an opportunity for the procurement manager and the quality control manager to review the use of certain traceability tools, or for the head of management control to inform the scheduling manager of the new use for identification codes to monitor products during the production process, or for marketing and sales managers to discuss new marketing strategies. I even witnessed a session in which one of the participants brought in a rival product. Tasting it prompted interaction around the development of new pâté recipes, such as liver mousses, in an upmarket segment.

Discussions however remained very close to products when tasting was aimed at assessing the result of production tests. This was the third objective of these sessions. For instance, when a new ferment for dried sausage was tested, the production manager redefined the drying time. Tasting sessions were then aimed at verifying the homogeneity of dryness between the core and the outside of the sausage. In another session, the workshop managers presented tests for cooking terrines after they had switched to different containers (Britham had changed to another supplier of glass jars and had opted for a shallower model). The tests also made it possible to evaluate the impacts of this change on the distribution of fat and jelly after cooking. Finally, colleagues' opinions are usually sought when new recipes are tested. In this case, opinions can be expressed without the need to arrive at a decision, and various conflicting reactions can be expressed. The production manager then decides what to take into account, and carries on defining his or her recipe through trial and error.

On the other hand, in the case of a test organized according to the framework of a product design procedure, a report of the tasting session is drawn up, recording the results of the evaluation. This time the production manager has to account for a position common to the different participants or at least, a majority of them. The construction of the agreement may transcend the framework of the daily session. That is the case when an additional tasting session is organized to formalize an intermediate review for a product launch.

These examples enable us to identify a fourth type of objective. These tasting sessions are also platforms for the definition of products and consumers for whom they are intended. Apart from providing Britham's managers with a daily space for interaction and coordination, they also enable them to have a particular knowledge of the products manufactured. The tasting has few rules but a definite goal: participants express their opinions with a fairly precise aim, that is, to subsequently be able to intervene on, say, a production process, a purchasing policy, or a market positioning. Each participant can then choose to express any type of opinion, from the most technical (e.g. referring to processes or the recipe) to the most hedonic (e.g. relating to personal tastes and preferences). These daily meetings construct a local, collective, and incorporated knowledge of Britham's supply and the demand for which it is intended. Professionals express themselves either as product specialists ('I know that if we use bigger pieces of mushrooms in the preparation, it won't produce an homogeneous appearance' said the plant manager) or as consumers ('I don't like pâté jars with a cover plate on them, they look like cheap and low-quality products; I prefer jars with screw-on lids', said another participant), producing a subjective evaluation of the product or the market that the configuration of the session legitimizes.

Such expertise is not intended to be developed outside the collective;[12] on the contrary, it is only meaningful within this collective since it provides it with the means to constantly monitor and make adjustments between the taste of products and the knowledge of consumers. Moreover, it is not surprising—as evidenced by a small test organized by the quality control department—that individuals' aptitudes for evaluation emerge which cannot easily be transferred but which are operative in the framework within which they are developed.[13] The tasting sessions give rise to interactions which often leave lay observers in the dark. Where outsiders are no longer capable of differentiating between two hams, the participants can debate at length the causes and consequences of their texture. Thus every feature of a product, be it accidental or deliberately planned, is monitored and qualified by each panellist. The firm believes this knowledge is indispensable to the management of the adjustments between products and consumers. The tasting sessions are not summed up in a series of objective parameters, but are more loosely represented by a series of impressions that colleagues learn to share and define together, based on definitions of products and markets that remain specific the professional expertise of each of them. Moreover, the productive capacity of this knowledge lies in its provisional character: far from being definitive, it allows for the monitoring of product and market variations, and is continuously updated from one session and test to the next. The test becomes a moment of coordination between the different professions' definitions of the market and the products, in order to construct another definition which colleagues jointly produce.

Like the information feedback produced by the sales representatives, the daily tasting sessions allow the emergence of a definition of tastes and products, with each professional putting him or herself in the place of demand-side actors (customers or consumers) and speaking on their behalf. As described above, different activities are used and organized within the firm to produce local and temporary qualifications of products and consumers. Their purpose is not to produce a general and definitive qualification of the product or the market, but rather to allow different professionals to coordinate in order to make local decisions on the product development, production, or marketing.

Furthermore, it is interesting to see that these positions are adopted by many professionals within as well as outside the company. Retailers—Britham's customers—regularly produce definitions of the tastes of products and of consumers, while partners—such as advertising or communication agencies on which the firm can call occasionally—make up their own definitions of products and consumers. These qualifications are naturally linked to the field of intervention of each of these professionals. They take the relationship that they perceive, between the consumer and the product, to highlight the qualification that they want to uphold. For example, Britham equips itself with a device, the tasting session, which enables it to monitor the stability of the product over time and to identify and overcome organoleptic shortcomings. Each product is compared with the one from the day before or with the version prior to the change. The sales representatives have definitions aimed primarily at the customer's (the retailer's) satisfaction. The marketing communication agency puts forward a qualification that is closely linked to the image conveyed by the product; it will therefore discuss the *mises en scène* of the relationship between the product and the consumer that this representation is supposed to suggest. Yet the multiplication of spokespersons does not do away with opportunities for consumers or their representatives to talk directly. The firm also organizes activities aimed at capturing these voices.

Producing qualifications as a resource for developing and marketing products

As observed in our study of different product development and marketing activities, they all produce a series of qualifications about the product and about the consumers. Most of these qualifications are local and temporary; they are not uniform or univocal. Instead, they proliferate through different forms (objective and subjective) and circulate among wide or narrow collectives; they are hardly aligned. Although they do not produce a final definition of the product and the market, these activities are essential for developing and marketing products. They allow for coordination to be performed amongst the different participants in the collective involved in the development, production, marketing, retailing, purchase, and consumption of the product: in short, from the plant to the consumer.

QUALITIES OF CONSUMERS AND PRODUCTS: A DUAL DEFINITION OF TASTE

Notwithstanding the diversity of the tests and the actors they involve, a common characteristic is apparent, pertaining to the nature of what they produce within the production and market organizations. It appears that each of these tests contributes to redefining the product and the consumer, in order to produce a locally shared and adjusted qualification of both. They contribute in some way to testing a relationship between the two. The consumer's preferences are defined to test the characteristics of products. Conversely, a version of the product will make it possible to test consumer preferences. But the indeterminacy never concerns one of them for more than a moment, as the result of the test is an adjustment between characteristics of the product and definitions of the consumer. Hence, these activities not only aim at enabling products to evolve but they also very broadly re-qualify consumers themselves and the way in which they rely on certain characteristics of the product when they choose and judge them. The redefinition of products' characteristics is accompanied by a redefinition of the competencies mobilized by consumers to choose, buy, and judge products. It is a constant loop in which each change in either the products or consumers impacts on the other, that is, on the way of manufacturing the products and on the consumers' way of judging.

From this point of view, merchandizing operations, from point-of-sale tasting or advertising to the measurements of sales, are all tests contributing to this constant mutual adjustment between products and consumers. The encounters between the two, whether they are organized by the manufacturer or its partners, alter both the consumer's taste (through his/ her preferences and competencies) and the product (through its characteristics). Hence, they allow for the continuous mutual learning of consumers and products that underlies the constant adjustment between the two.[14]

The aim of these qualification activities is clearly the testing of the encounter between products and consumers. For example, in one case the result of a focus group helped to produce a new recipe for *terrine forestière* (mushroom terrine), with more pepper and mushrooms, and helped to reinforce the consumers' association of the name *terrine forestière* with the presence of these two ingredients. In another case, during a daily tasting session, Britham tested a product whose packaging had been altered. Colleagues talked about how jelly leaked out of the jar, and evaluated the appropriateness of sealing it. In this situation, the marketing manager pointed out that the product lost some of its character and became too much like *rillettes*;[15] the texture remained satisfactory but the seal on the jar was not appropriate. He noted that it was usually *rillettes* that were presented in sealed jars, whereas the product in question was supposed to be more upmarket. In this example, we see that taste is doubly re-qualified: through the product's characteristics, which are linked to flavours or linked to the choice of the packaging, and through the points of reference that consumers use to identify products and make comparisons.

We cannot but be struck by the diversity of tests and their capacity to produce and mobilize different qualifications, whose articulation is not self-evident. For instance, the definition of ham produced and mobilized in the framework of the tasting test focused on its stringiness and the absence or presence of holes due to the arrangement of muscle tissue is very different to that of a consumer tasting a product in the shop and having a hedonistic reaction ('it's nice', 'I don't like it').

Each test has its own particular autonomy, which is why it is important to understand the functioning of the test itself and the forms of closure to which tests lead.

THE IMPOSSIBLE ALIGNMENT OF THE QUALIFICATIONS PRODUCED . . .

I will now examine the possibility and conditions of alignment of these qualification activities. Are the actors trying to reach an agreement on the qualification of the market and products that can be defined in order to manufacture and trade products?

I will pause to consider what can be interpreted as attempted alignments. That is what the tasting session described above may appear to achieve. It is a time and a place when—as opposed to the other moments of product design which spawn a proliferation of definitions of the product and its consumers—a simplification may be made around a common definition of the product's and the consumers' tastes. The tasting session can be understood as a coordination and decision-making tool that is particularly useful for the development of food products. Yet this convergent construction of impressions is not easily achieved for all products. It seems to be more accessible in the case of hams and cured meats than for cooked pork meats. In the case of *pâté*, discussions are often laborious and many tests yield no common conclusion. Admittedly, at the time of my research, experiments on terrines were not subjected to quality control procedures during the product design phase.[16] The test was therefore not formalized as a step in the procedure and did not require a report to be written. For example, during a test, following a change in the container and the addition of a seal for a *pâté*, various managers talked about their impressions. The participants noted the poor distribution of mushrooms which were all at the centre of the terrine. The product was too much like a 'truffle recipe', which was not the intention. But the tasting produced disparate qualifications. The experiment led to no conclusion, no diagnosis, and no action. As is usually the case in these situations, associations were made with impressions related to known products, within the firm or in the market, so that the interactions could be consolidated and the collective knowledge of products updated. But for the experiment to result in a common qualification, it seems that the definition of a reference taste was missing, that is a commonly shared qualification serving as a reference for the qualification of the sample tested. The tasters were in a sense, less well equipped for this test.

Finally, the tasting session is aimed less at aligning qualifications of products than at producing a collective qualification that captures the memory of a definition of tastes of products and consumers, even if it is only temporary. This represents an additional qualification device, in the long series identified above. Likewise, certain devices which seem to reflect essentially a wish to align definitions actually fulfil a role similar to the other qualification devices. This is the case, for example, of the barometer from an organization devoted to promoting the meat industry from which Britham buys regularly. This technical centre has a panel of 100,000 individuals (for all product types) spread across several cities in France. The results of annual surveys on this panel are exploited for different cooked pork meats (e.g. cured meat and hams) in relation to different product categories (e.g. ham without rind, or with rind or fat).

The particularity of barometers is that they cross-compare the results of different types of experiment which are usually carried out and used in separate environments: tests on the physico-chemical characteristics generally produced by manufacturing; sensorial analyses for which the quality control department is responsible; and, finally, tests on the variables of the mix (packaging, price, product, promotion) carried out by marketing departments. The originality of these studies lies in the coupling of results of hedonic tests on products, with a more technical characterization, so that consumers' reactions to products can be linked to production variables. First, the technical characterizations of products are defined (physico-chemical and organoleptic).[17] Consumers on the panel are successively presented with the different products in a category, and questioned on their willingness to buy and repurchase ('do you want to buy it again after tasting it?'). The latter question is supposed to measure how 'disappointing' the product can potentially be and to what extent it may not generate repeated purchases. The scores generated by consumers in these hedonic tests are cross-compared with the forms of more technical characterizations stemming from physico-chemical tests (e.g. level of lipids, proteins, carbohydrates, and pH) and organoleptic ones (by sensorial analysis). This barometer provides the manufacturer with two types of information: it indicates the positioning of Britham's products compared to rival products,[18] in terms of rank in consumers' preferences, and it makes it possible to obtain a physico-chemical and sensorial characterization of the product that obtains the best hedonic classification score. Obviously this tool is useful for marketing, in that it provides a description of what the manufacturer will retain as the market standard. The ham preferred by the panel is also described through the tools of physico-chemical and sensorial analyses. This characterization is also highly compatible with production management tools. This articulation enables a direct translation of the consumers' preferences into actionable levers for steering a production process. Here again, the purpose of this activity is not to produce an alignment, in so far as it does not reduce the different representations that emerge along the whole development process to one single figure. This is an additional activity, designed to equip the decision-making process, for both marketing and product development.

These two examples highlight the results of qualification: it helps in the coordination of competencies within the firm and it equips judgements in the decision-making process. No one would try to make all the qualifications produced the same, as there is no need for a single definition of the taste of products and consumers. When the experiments are articulated, it is not with the aim of aligning the qualifications that they produce. The goal is rather to take certain statements produced through some experiments, as references for future judgements. Consequently, the more general the character of these statements, that is, the more detachable they are from their conditions of production, the more they function as resources that can be shared by all to facilitate agreements. This means that the qualifications produced are different in terms of the size of the collective sharing them. The more objective the qualifications are, the bigger the collective sharing them will be. On the other hand, a very subjective, complex, and incorporated qualification would have only local legitimacy in the collective in which it has been produced. But this second type of qualification is essential to work on very specific and narrow features of the products or on very specific consumer judgements. Nevertheless, this mobilization of the results of another experiment serves as an input to the construction of further qualifications. In short, there is clearly a sequential series of experiments but not an alignment of their results.

... OR THE CONDITIONS OF CIRCULATION OF THE PRODUCT IN THE PRODUCTION AND MARKET SPHERES

The proliferation of these experiments nevertheless leaves unanswered the question of their collective outcome: under what conditions do these continuous processes of qualification make it possible to produce stabilized definitions of the characteristics of the demand and of products? Obviously, requalification cannot be a never-ending process working on the basis of the recurrent indeterminacy of qualifications. The firm has to sell a product whose characteristics are stable at that point in time. It is therefore necessary to understand the implications of these qualification experiments.

I saw that each experiment makes it possible to feed a particular decision-making process. The elements of decisions may be more or less formalized. They tend to be formalized when the test takes place in the framework of a procedure certified by the ISO 9001 standard. A review of the test is then an opportunity to draw up the list of actions to be undertaken. In other cases, as highlighted earlier, the qualifications produced remain informal interactions between colleagues. These examples show the importance of the test itself as a coordination tool for differing points of view or definitions of products and consumers which may be expressed within the firm, at different points in time. The experiment thus makes it possible to qualify both product and consumers locally and momentarily, with the aim of reaching an agreement between the various participants. The participants in the experiment and those whom they represent thus constitute the collective associated with this local redefinition. This passage, via a redefinition of the contents of the product and the market, is the condition on which the collective thus summoned can be involved.

It appears that each experiment leads to an agreement, the aim of which is the involvement of a collective adapted to the test. This collective may be composed of members of the firm, partners, customers, and/or consumers. As we have seen, merchandizing a product is an additional test which can also be exploited: it could be seen as a 'scaling up' experiment. While the tests produce collective local agreements, the question of their capacity to aggregate remains open. What is the result of this proliferation of all kinds of experiments, whose forms and outcomes are often incompatible? As noted above, there may be attempts not at alignment but rather at articulation amongst certain tests. This is the case for example of the barometer which relates physico-chemical to hedonic tests, and whose results can be used during a tasting session. The session may also mobilize results of consumption tests disseminated by consultancy firms. In such cases the idea is essentially to have references to support the judgement, and resources that can be shared by all, in test configurations where the possibility of the engagement of judgements is not left open and where no attempt is made to find a framework common to the different participants.

The objective is not to achieve an alignment for the purpose of broadly or definitively producing the twofold definition of the market and the product. It is not to ensure that all the actors involved on the supply side, market mediators, and the demand side are in tune around a single definition capable of federating the largest collective possible, from the producer to the consumer. It is because the collective concerned by the circulation of the product, from design to consumption, is plural and protean that the proliferation of experiments is necessary. In the final analysis, what emerges is the space of circulation of the product, similar to a large network stretching from the actors on the supply side to those on the demand side. In this network, temporary stabilization of the adjustment between a product and its market circulate, defining and redefining qualifications as products move along. If we were to take localized, cross-cutting views at various points, we would see widely different forms of such adjustments. At the stage of design, the adjustment is made between a planned product, which does not yet exist physically but is described by a production potential, and manufacturing choices, contacts with suppliers, a target market envisaged, and a particular representation of that market (e.g. current and prospective quantitative data on the consumption of products in this category, socio-economic data on consumption habits and food preferences). At the merchandizing stage, the indeterminacy is less strong, and the adjustment is made between a product whose physical characteristics are stabilized (ingredients, packaging, recipe, price, form of retailing) and consumers engaging their competencies in the production of a judgement.

Between the two, we find a multitude of adjustments. For example, the adjustment that makes it possible to define a specific promotion campaign with activities at the point of sale. The adjustment in this case is that between a physical product with various features (e.g. a recipe attached, an answer-coupon for winning a prize) and a definition of consumers (e.g. consumers looking for ideas for meals, who are playful and readily seduced by a product with which they are unfamiliar). In effect, the multiplication of experiments to test possible adjustments between products and consumers permits the proliferation of definitions of both of them. By making the experiments vary, the definitions to which they lead are made to vary together with the nature of the collective involved. The circulation of the product is possible only at the cost of a high level of instability concerning the very type of collective that a market is.

Conclusion

In this chapter I have focused on the multiplicity of qualification experiments that may be involved in the development and marketing of food products. For this purpose, I have described a variety of tests punctuating the trajectory of some products from the earliest design phases right down to its commercialization. In the latter phases, experiments are developed which feed back into a redefinition of the product, since new hypotheses become available on products and markets. This is clearly a process of constant and collective redefinition of the adjustments between products and consumers, through organized and repeated testing. The impact of these tests lies in (a) their capacity to redefine the profiles of the consumers for whom the products are intended, as these profiles can never be defined once and for all and must be re-specified regularly; and (b) their ability to temporarily stabilize the characteristics of products which will be made available to consumers. The specific nature of each test stems from the characteristics of the products and consumers tested.

Contrary to the networks described by the sociology of innovation (Callon et al. 2002), the product is not stabilized as soon as the operations of recruitment of all the human and non-human actors necessary for its definition are complete, because this recruitment is always provisional and is constantly being undone. There is thus no universal collective device (Callon and Muniesa 2005) but instead a large number of local devices and activities producing local and temporary qualifications of products and consumers that help the product to circulate but which cannot themselves circulate. Consumers are never captured once and for all. Hence, the implication of this constant redefinition lies in the possibility, through new products, of recovering consumers who may have turned away from existing products, rather than trying to capture them for good. Capturing consumers for good is impossible in a context where all the actors on the supply and demand sides are constantly doing and undoing attachments between products and consumers. From this perspective, the processes of developing and marketing products are ideal opportunities for observing the construction of markets and modes of exchange. It also produces insights on the role of the firm's organization in marketing products. The fact that the product development process does not emerge with a single qualification of consumers and products is not tantamount to saying that the process is chaotic or incoherent. On the contrary, the firm uses several solutions to regularly provide the product development process with procedures that allow the different people and departments to validate these temporary definitions of consumers and products. All these validation procedures make the process move from the first idea to the final product, even though all these successive decisions are not fully compatible in terms of the qualification of products and consumers.

■ NOTES

1. I am grateful to the editors of the book and to the two anonymous reviewers for their very consistent comments on previous versions of this chapter.

2. Britham is not the real name of the company.

3. Its turnover was 600 million French Francs in 1998 when the study was carried out.

4. *Charcuterie* can be broadly translated as 'prepared meat products'.

5. The type of food products loosely translated as 'bought loose', is very important to French supermarkets. Stocking this type of product (e.g. cheese, fish, meat, and *charcuterie*) is regarded as crucial to boost the turnover of stores.

6. The methodology involved several interviews with the different people in all the departments of the firm (thirty interviews), ethnographic observations of marketing briefs, internal product testing and meetings, and ethnographic observations of sales in a supermarket (the products of this company are exclusively sold by a vendor in supermarkets). I also held interviews with several partners of the company (e.g. a market research agency).

7. On market mediation and the diversity of the practices and professionals involved in mediation see Barrey et al. (2000).

8. These procedures are mandatory in terms of the legislation and regulations concerning food products.

9. Analysis of consumers' paths in a supermarket reveals the same type of result, as does the analysis of discourse on choices of products in that context (Dubuisson-Quellier 2006).

10. For example, a consumer first insisted that 'price is always the first criterion', and a few minutes later admitted that 'I like to treat myself every so often'.

11. The only tacit rule observed was avoiding coffee just before a session. A coffee break usually followed the tasting.

12. Note that the boundaries of this collective are shifting in so far as members may leave the firm, and the firm may recruit new staff. Nevertheless, the group clearly maintains a collective memory in the development of collective learning.

13. The quality control manager had organized a test that was closer to the tests carried out by a sensory analysis panel. This test showed that the participants had a real ability to detect and rate salty and sweet flavours (two characteristic flavours of ham), but little ability to detect the sour and bitter flavours in this type of product.

14. Food markets are characterized by a high rate of product renewal and a high level of consumer fickleness. Normally, these are described as exogenous characteristics of the sector. In fact, they are the direct result of forms of adjustment between products and consumers.

15. *Rillettes* is a meat preparation not unlike pâté, made to be spreadable on bread or toast.

16. The firm had yet to obtain its ISO 9001 certification in cooked cold meats.

17. Physico-chemical analysis relates to salt rate and pH; organoleptic analysis refers to sensorial analysis of texture, flavour, odours, and taste.

18. When the firm receives the summary document, the names of other products tested do not appear. The firm may however see how its product is positioned compared to rival products (classification based on the preferences expressed by consumers on the panel).

5 Governing firms, shaping markets

The role of calculative devices

FRANK AZIMONT AND LUIS ARAUJO

Introduction

This chapter focuses on the role of instruments such as formal organizational structures and performance metrics in relating a company to its markets. It follows in the wake of recent interest in the role of devices, understood as assemblages of material and discursive elements, in the construction of markets (Lascoumes and le Galès 2004; Muniesa et al. 2007). Specifically, we inquire into how a change in the performance regime of a company, from product to category management, came to alter the calculative capacities of its co-workers and how these changes affected both intra- and inter-organizational practices.

Our interest in these issues derives from the debate following the formulation of the performativity programme (Callon 1998a) and its acceptance of the economists' notion that the operation of markets relies on the existence of calculative agents (Callon 1998b, 1999; Caliskan and Callon 2009). This stirred sociologists and anthropologists into arguing that there is nothing special about calculativeness in markets. Miller (2002: 231), for example, suggested that markets rely on relatively simple calculations compared to other modes of exchange, since '...they reduce the concept of value to a quantitative instrument'. Miller called for a clear division between ideology and practice in economic life, contrasting the apparent simplification ushered in by numbers with the more complex and nuanced forms of calculation permeating exchanges. But Miller's argument denies any autonomy to the economic sphere and elides why particular types of calculative agencies emerge. On this issue, Callon (1998b) takes a radically different position from economics. Rather than assuming that agents are hard-wired to be calculative, he proposed turning calculative agencies into a topic for empirical inquiry by insisting that calculativeness is a practical accomplishment.

The research on calculation that followed has provided us with rich insights into the nature of markets. For example, Callon and Muniesa (2005) and Kjellberg and Helgesson (2006) demonstrate how markets are performed and shaped by multiple calculative agencies. Other contributions, namely, Kjellberg (2007) and Andersson et al. (2008) illustrate how the emergence of market agencies is closely associated with particular calculative tools. However, the interest in calculation has not been matched by an interest in how modes of calculation are deployed in efforts to govern economic life (Miller 2008). To put it differently, how do modes of calculation link up with, represent, and embody particular ideas about how economic life should be governed? One important way of linking calculation to ideas is to focus on the role of classification systems in constructing economic orders (Bowker and Star 2000). Classification systems are powerful yet often invisible technologies generating everyday categories that quickly disappear from view, inscribed in infrastructures and taken-for-granted routines. To date, few empirical studies have examined the interaction between calculation and classification systems. One notable exception is Sjögren and Helgesson (2007), who highlight the role played by classification devices in linking medical and pharmaceutical classifications to health care provision and economic value.

Our starting points are that calculativeness requires calculative tools and that there is an intricate relationship between what is measured and the tools deployed to measure it. These tools are not innocent devices that record an objective, external reality, but actively shape what they measure. Hence, calculative tools provided by economics and management disciplines, such as accounting and marketing, are of considerable importance to the actual calculations being performed by economic agents and, by extension, to how the *economy* is constituted. In this study we look at the way formal structures and performance metrics are deployed as devices to govern the way a company relates to its markets. Our empirical case reports on how the retail division of a petrol company moved from a product to a category management system. This shift implied a change in the set of metrics that the company used to evaluate its market performance. As we will show, these changes had important consequences for the company's strategic identity, its relationships with suppliers, and the markets in which it operates.

The chapter is structured as follows: in the next section we review the literature on the use of calculative devices to govern economic life. In the third section, we describe the methodology employed in our study before presenting the empirical case. This is followed by a discussion of our findings before offering concluding comments in the final section.

Calculation and governing the economy

We start this section by revisiting the relationship between the economy and the disciplines that address economic practices, including economics and management subjects. The key argument of the performativity programme is that economics, broadly construed, does not just describe how the economy functions (Callon 1998a). In essence, ideas, models, techniques, methods, and professional practices about the economy actively shape the nature of economic phenomena (Porter 2008). These ideas, models, techniques, methods, and professional practices are essential in constituting and rendering visible the subject domain of economics and management. To manage is to be able to establish a correspondence between the world 'out there' and the techniques of representation (e.g. lists, hierarchies, statistics) that abbreviate and condense the essential features of that world (Cooper 1992). In a similar vein, Czarniawska and Mouritsen (2009) regard management as a process of turning the complexity embodied in things and people, with the help of managerial technologies such as accounting inscriptions, into simplified quasi-objects that can be treated and acted upon as discrete and separate entities. Inscriptions, as Latour (1987) noted, abstract and summarize the main features of a phenomenon or object and transport them to a centre from which remote interventions can take place.

Foucault (1991) introduced the term governmentality to draw attention to the ways through which attempts at knowing and managing populations are embodied in particular types of thinking and acting. Governing, as Foucault (1991) argued, is not just about the legitimately constituted forms of economic or political power. It is also about structuring possible fields of actions through expert modes of intervention that should be analysed through the prism of government technologies or, '. . . the complex of mundane programs, calculations, techniques, apparatuses, documents and procedures through which authorities seek to embody and give effect to government ambitions' (Rose and Miller 1992: 175). The events and phenomena to which government applies must be rendered tractable through particular forms of information (e.g. numbers, graphs, spreadsheets) that can become stable, mobile, combinable, and comparable (Miller and Rose 1990: 7). Information must be able to re-present the world from which it is extracted in the sites where decisions about the world are taken (e.g. board rooms, managers' offices).

Calculation is thus central to the understanding of how economic entities are made visible and rendered governable. Calculation, in Callon's (1999) terms, designates the processes, which make possible the assignment of numbers (such as prices or rankings) to entities, an assignment which, in turn, endows these entities with relative stability and makes possible their circulation throughout society. As pointed out by Espeland and Stevens (1998), commensuration, or the transformation of different qualities into a common metric, is one important part of this process. Before calculation is possible, things must be placed in some kind of order to allow work to be done on them (Bowker and Star 2000). Classifications such as standards (e.g. quality certificates, accounting rules) place boundaries around objects and activities and render a degree of order to an otherwise chaotic world. Thus jobs, for example, are usually described, graded, ranked in some kind of hierarchy and pay scale for individuals to be able to situate their role and contribution to an organization. The formalization of an organizational structure is not just a passive representation but also an active process of constituting the organization as a bounded entity separate from its external environment (Cooper 1992).

Cochoy's notion of *qualculation* (2002, 2008*a*) stresses that calculations draw on qualitative and quantitative components, metrics as well as judgements. Defining the qualities of things is integral to their calculability. All measurement systems are made possible by calibration, understood as the creation and determination of quanta (Power 2004). The creation of quanta is a special case of metrology, which requires technical instruments to make phenomena standardized and measurable. This requires the establishment of frames, the decontextualization of objects, and the grouping and comparing of objects in the same frame. Once quanta are established, they can be subject to further calculative operations. In other words, measurement is based on classification systems that ignore purportedly irrelevant differences and reduce complexity.

Callon and Muniesa (2005: 1231) propose a broader view of calculation and one that is not confined to performing numerical operations. Instead, they suggest that calculation involves three distinct steps. First, entities must be detached from their contexts, classified, and ordered within a single space (e.g. a trading screen, a spreadsheet). Secondly, once ordered in that space, these entities can be compared, manipulated, and transformed according to particular rules (e.g. aggregating performance indicators at the product level to calculate performance at the store level). Thirdly, results such as a ranking of products or suppliers must be produced that both summarize and represent the entities in that calculative space.

The performative roles of both classification devices and calculation have long since been studied by accountants. Carruthers and Espeland (1991), for example, evoke the power of accounting tools and inscriptions (e.g. figures, charts, tables) in performing calculations. For Miller (2001), accounting represents an essential set of devices for acting upon individuals in an attempt to ensure that they behave in accordance with specific economic objectives. Accounting practices are regarded as contributing to both the make-up and the transformation of the entities they seek to represent.

Miller and O'Leary (2007) discuss the instruments that mediate between arenas and actors. Their purpose is to understand how artefacts, such as capital budgeting techniques, mediate between science, technology, and the economy. Miller and O'Leary invite further research on the ways instruments are used to mediate between the investment strategies and planning procedures of different entities. This call has been reinforced by Ahrens and Chapman (2007) who propose to look at management control numbers as resources for action and tools to advance managerial agendas.

For marketing scholars, we suggest, the theoretical agenda is broader than that featuring in the accounting literature. This literature has provided us with useful insights on how classification systems and modes of calculation transform the identities of producers and constitute them as calculable subjects. However, we lack a broader understanding of how calculative systems link organizations to their suppliers and markets (but see e.g. Håkansson and Lind 2004; Mouritsen and Thrane 2006). Accounting numbers, however important, are only one way to measure performance, and organizations deploy a variety of other performance metrics at different levels of aggregation (e.g. store, region, nation) and with different foci (e.g. benchmarking internal units against each other, evaluating suppliers). Similarly, we need a better understanding of how organizational structures and roles constitute classification devices in their own right and render visible particular features of the world whilst hiding others.

In this chapter we aim to shed light on some of these issues by studying how the restructuring of one company led to a change in the way it represented performance. These changes were introduced with the intent of redefining the company's business and its relation to markets but had a number of unintended consequences, namely raising issues that transcended the scope of the proposed changes. By linking these themes, we propose to examine the interplay between structural roles and modes of calculation at different levels within a complex organization and assess their impact on relationships with suppliers and market demand. The following section is devoted to the design and method employed in our study.

Method

Our empirical study focuses on the case of a fuel-retailing network which, in the course of 2003, shifted from a product to a category management system. This move was accompanied by a radical change in managerial responsibilities, in work processes, as well as in the performance indicators deployed by the company.

As a generic methodological strategy, we made use of Latour's injunction (1987, 2005) to follow actors and artefacts throughout a research site. Our site, a company labelled BEST to preserve anonymity, is amongst the world's leading oil companies with a significant forecourt presence in most European countries. It occupies a strong market position in four of the largest countries in the European Union. It is the retail division of a larger group with sizeable refinery and chemical divisions. The profile of BEST in the sector means that it is an important partner for suppliers, a banner brand with a significant level of awareness amongst consumers, and a player which has the potential to instigate major changes in petrol retail markets.

The first author had previously developed contacts and relationships with key individuals in the focal company as part of a broader longitudinal study over a four-year period, from 2002 to 2006. The study relied on the close and frequent involvement with many managers at BEST, including Joe, Jennifer, and Paul, pseudonyms we have chosen for three managers we name in our subsequent empirical narrative. Joe and Jennifer were heavily involved in the crossover from the product to the category management era, and Paul was in charge of coordinating the key retail activities of petrol stations, namely, car wash, restaurant, and shop (CRS).

Our study tracked the use of key performance indicators before and after the change to a category management structure, in an attempt to understand the logic used by managers when measuring the performance of products and suppliers in a particular category. The research design is best described as a form of ethnography or participant-observation, given the period of involvement of the first author with the focal company as a trainer and consultant prior to the start of this research project (see Atkinson and Hammersley 2007). In management research, this method has been mainly employed in ethnographies of managerial work involving long periods of residence at one site (Kunda 1992; Watson 1994). The orientation of the researcher was deliberately biased towards an outsider or observer-as-participant role, bearing in mind that observation was inevitably affected by the prior involvement with the company (Ackroyd and Hughes 1992: 135). The justification for the use of participant observation methods is that they facilitate a largely unstructured access to insiders' views on their working lives and capture a variety of data (e.g. photos, documents, computer files, field notes, formal, and informal interviews) which more structured and shorter forms of access may struggle to replicate. One obvious challenge in deploying this method is the balancing of the dual roles of researcher, which advises an outsider orientation, and participant, which steers the researcher in the opposite direction. The issue of adopting dual roles (e.g. service worker and shopper) and writing ethnographies based on these roles is discussed by Pettinger (2005).

The construction of ethnographic texts can follow a variety of genres (see Atkinson 1990). The narrative in the following section is framed by our theoretical concerns regarding the effects of the changes prompted by the move from product to category management. In particular, we focus on how changes in calculative spaces, by grouping and displaying a different set of performance indicators, constructed a different version of performance at the level of products and categories of products, with important implications for how suppliers were ranked and consumer demand represented.

From product to category management

ACT 1: MANAGING FUEL VS. NON-FUEL ACTIVITIES

Before 2003, the unit of analysis at BEST was the petrol station. The role of a station was to deliver fuel to motorists. The building attached to the forecourt was designed to facilitate the payment of fuel refills. The objective assigned to store sales was that they should cover the distribution cost of fuel so that the fuel margin was maximized.

To manage the business in this configuration, as Joe explained, a store manager was responsible for forecourt operations and reported to a district manager who looked after the development of forecourts in a region. In addition, the store manager was responsible for the network's security policy. To help the store manager deal with the development of store sales, or 'the diversification businesses' as it was then known, the district manager had an assistant, the shop adviser, whose task was to help store managers pursue sales activities. In practice, the shop adviser ensured that the products listed by the company, according to the recommendations of product managers located at regional headquarters, were properly merchandised.

Product managers were not expected to analyse markets or understand their dynamics. Their narrower remit was to develop the planograms of assortments defined and negotiated by the retail director, who was in charge of both the fuel and store businesses. Once planograms were defined, product managers worked with suppliers to select sales promotions. They were predominantly concerned with identifying the best deals proposed by manufacturers and rolling them out across the network. Product managers interfaced mainly with field managers (district managers, shop advisers, and store managers) and spent the majority of their time on the phone dealing with day-to-day routines such as checking product codes or ensuring that store managers knew how to order through wholesalers, etc.

To assess how the business was performing, product managers used simple dashboards. The term dashboard, more closely associated with car and aircraft cockpits, is a way to describe the consolidation and display of a variety of snapshot data in one convenient location (e.g. instrument dials, a computer screen). At BEST, the performance of the store was assessed with measures taken at the product level, in the first instance. Figures were aggregated at a product family level for a store, cumulated for stores at the regional level, and summarized with a few key performance indicators (KPIs): sales in volume and value, the profit margin calculated as the value of sales minus the purchasing cost of goods, and the number of stock keeping units (SKUs, a unique identifier for each product sold). A series of ratios were calculated using these KPIs: the contribution (the weight of each segment on the total) to volume, to sales, to profit margin, and to assortment. Table 5.1 is an example of such a dashboard.

Two or three times a year and before supplier meetings, product managers would carry out a simple analysis comparing the various ratios in order to decide which segment and supplier was performing best. Joe explained how he analysed the business in October 2003 before meeting beverage manufacturers:

The table shows that some segments are doing well with a major contribution to volume, sales and margin. The colas achieve 30% of the volumes and 31% of the total sales, 30% of the total margin with an average margin rate of 42% and they achieve this result with a number of SKUs representing 22% of the total assortment. The energy drinks achieve a high level of sales (12%) with a limited number of products (6% of the assortment), a high margin rate (45%), above average for the family (43%), and a good contribution to margin (13%).

The performance of the colas and energy drinks were 'good' because the product families were major contributors on all indicators. Joe further commented that they performed well because a reduced number of SKUs generated a higher contribution to volume, sales, and/or margin. Joe also noted the poor performance of other segments such as the juices. With nine SKUs representing 3 per cent of the assortment, this family achieved 4 per cent of the volumes and 3 per cent of the sales only. Its contribution to margin was 3 per cent and its margin rate (33 per cent) was below the average for the segment (43 per cent). The performance of the juices was poor because their weight in the total business was insignificant and the family was thus dilutive of the total margin. In Joe's mind, this product family was not addressing 'customer needs'.

To analyse the evolution of the business, Joe compared the 2003 data with the previous year. At the time of the annual market review, the cumulative sales were based on twelve comparable months including the high season. The conclusion was that the relative performance of the segments did not change from 2002 to 2003. This analysis was based on demand measured by volumes and sales. It was built upon simple accounting numbers, with the profit margin generated by each family as the key measure. The indicator linking the number of SKUs with sales performance suggested that limited resources could be expected to produce a high level of return. It was better to have a high turnover with a limited number of SKUs, rather than the same turnover with a large number of products.

Table 5.1. BEST company—sales performance dashboard

What are store keeping units? (SKUs)

Sub-group	Unit sales	Contribution to volume (%)	Sales excl. VAT	Contribution to sales (%)	Profit margin	% Margin	Contribution to margin (%)	Nb of SKUs	Share of assortment (%)
				Year 2003					
Cola	2,317,778	30	£2,152,202	31	£898,681	42	30	59	22
Sport	967,985	13	£953,084	14	£383,179	40	13	31	12
Still	1,238,956	16	£910,776	13	£498,340	55	17	26	10
Energy	692,930	9	£836,297	12	£374,788	45	13	16	6
RTD	886,807	12	£642,616	9	£257,793	40	9	34	13
Fruit	653,015	9	£569,799	8	£225,967	40	8	33	13
Juice	268,881	4	£229,055	3	£75,081	33	3	9	3
Flavoured	263,241	3	£204,715	3	£98,584	48	3	8	3
Lemonades	145,930	2	£154,999	2	£73,676	48	2	4	2
Pure juice	116,840	2	£107,668	2	£46,440	43	2	19	7
Concentrate	33,937	0	£52,738	1	£20,833	40	1	10	4
Sparkling	29,051	0	£19,644	0	£11,732	60	0	2	1
From concentrate	15,011	0	£11,283	0	£3,571	32	0	5	2
Mixers	7,805	0	£8,630	0	£3,295	38	0	5	2
Iced tea	7,010	0	£5,855	0	£2,826	48	0	2	1
Smoothies	2	0	£3	0	£1	26	0	1	0
Total	£7,644,679	100	£6,859,364	100	£2,974,785	43	100	264	100

The discussion with Joe explored the assumptions behind this mode of reasoning. As Joe assumed that a concentration of the assortment on major segments would lead to higher performance for the family, we enquired if some segments should be discontinued. The same analysis might have led him to reduce significantly the weight of the fruit juices in the assortment, for example. A deeper analysis was required at the SKU level. Joe analysed the performance of each SKU as well as the performance of the product family with tools such as classification and class analysis. In Table 5.2, based on the cola segment, we can see that the ten best-performing SKUs were doing three times better than the next ten.

The detailed analysis of the ten best (Table 5.3) and ten worst items (Table 5.4) showed equally strong concentration effects.

To prepare for his meetings with suppliers, Joe explained, the data would be aggregated to give an overall picture of the supplier's performance. Taking an

Table 5.2. BEST company—best and worst sellers in volume

Cola	Annual sales	Weekly sales
10 First	8915	171
SKU 11–20	2759	53
SKU 21–30	1217	23
SKU 31–40	665	
SKU 41–50	97	
SKU 51–60	0	
Total	13653	263

Table 5.3. BEST company—ten top selling cola products

Ranking	Designation	Sales	In %	Cum. in %
1	Coca Cola 500 ml	1898	14	14
2	Diet Coke 500 ml PET	1478	11	25
5	Coke 2l	1252	9	34
6	P7 Coke 3 for 1.90	918	7	41
3	Coca Cola 330 ml	915	7	47
8	P6 Coke 3 for 1.90	789	6	53
7	P3 Coke deal 2 for 1.25	539	4	57
4	Diet Coke Can 330 ml	485	4	61
9	Dr Pepper 500 ml	324	2	63
10	Diet Coke with Lemon 500 ml	317	2	65
	. . .	. . .		
Total	Total Cola	13653	100	100

Table 5.4. BEST company—lowest ten selling cola products

Ranking	Designation	Sales	In %	Cum. in %
. . .	. . .	. . .	. . .	. . .
41	P8 Irn Bru 2 for 1.30	135	1	
42	Coca Cola 2× 2l	100	1	
43	Pepsi Twist PET 500 ml	50	0	
44	Vanilla Coke PET 2 l	35	0	
45	Diet Coke Vanilla 2 l	30	0	
46	Coca Cola 6× pack Can for 1.99	30	0	
47	Diet Coke 2× 2l for 2.29	28	0	
48	Diet Coke 6× pack Can for 1.99	25	0	
49	Diet Coke 2× 2l	20	0	
50	Coca Cola 2× 2l for 2.19	20	0	
Total	Total Cola	13653	100	100

Table 5.5. BEST company—commercial margin by supplier

	Purchase	Sales	Commercial margin		
	In value	In value	In value	Margin in % of sales	Contribution to margin
Category 1					
Supplier A	120	167	47	28	32
Supplier B	110	167	57	34	39
Supplier C	100	143	43	30	29
Total category	330	477	147	31	100

example from the beverage business, he showed how Table 5.5 could be extracted from the data—the names of the suppliers are disguised for confidentiality reasons.

Joe commented:

[Supplier B] delivers the best margin as a percentage of sales, in absolute value, and therefore in contribution to margin. [B] is the preferred supplier. [Supplier A] delivers the poorest margin on sales. But considering the absolute margin in monetary terms, it is the second best contributor, behind [supplier B]. Because I have limited time to spend on the data, I am focusing on the product families that apparently perform best; I identify the suppliers of the best selling products and I tend to trust their recommendations.

In this case, Joe would be inclined to implement B's sales promotion proposals and push its products more often. It became clear that the perception of a suppliers' performance, defined through the lens of a specific dashboard, had an effect on the acceptance of their marketing proposals and, consequently, a bigger impact on consumer demand.

The case analysed by Joe was a simple one. In reality, many suppliers had a product range covering different segments. What happened to poorly performing products belonging to a globally successful supplier? Joe commented:

It may well be that they are kept in the assortment. This explains why the fruit juices are still very important in the range displayed in the stores whereas their sales performance is poor.

In the existing structure, it was the decision of the retail director rather than the product manager to discontinue products. He added:

There are also specific deals that the retail director may have concluded with the suppliers. I am not aware of them, they are kept secret. The extra margin points given by the suppliers are not included in the product manager's dashboards.

ACT 2: BREAKING DOWN NON-FUEL ACTIVITIES

The vision of the business described above prevailed until a market research project showed that forecourt stores were much more important to customers than the retail directors of BEST imagined. Because BEST aimed to become the European leader in fuel retail, the marketing department had carried out extensive research in all European countries to better understand why motorists stopped at petrol stations. The results came as a surprise to senior management. Customers visited stations for many reasons other than to refill their cars. Customers often stopped to take a break during long journeys or used stations as convenience stores on their way home. In some countries, up to two-thirds of the drivers who stopped at forecourts did not even purchase fuel.

Leading marketing managers of the company felt they had to pursue the business opportunities uncovered by these findings. However, some traditional fuel managers argued against expanding the retail side of the business by invoking the identity of the company as a key player in the energy sector. If diversification was to be pursued, the area of green energies should be targeted, they argued. Long discussions on the subject followed, before the senior marketing managers of the company concluded that, even if the company decided to abandon the fuel retail business, a competitive network was required to attract potential buyers.

A food offering was identified as a good opportunity for the retail network to become a preferred stopping point for motorists. A new structure was proposed by the senior managers of the retail division of BEST. The idea was that management should be specialized by product category. Fuel should be one of those categories, an important one, but still only one offering among others. To supersede the distinction between the fuel and non-fuel businesses, a new classification was proposed. In addition to fuel, three key product categories were set up: car wash, restaurant, and shop (CRS). A new CRS department was created in March 2003, headed by a manager reporting to the retail director. The proposal was to measure the performance of each of these broad activities, which eventually meant measuring the performance of each product category within each of these activities.

To further understand the impact of this reorganization, we interviewed Paul, the senior manager of the retail division in charge of CRS. The shop business is a complex one, he explained. To cover all its aspects, CRS is staffed with a restaurant manager, a car wash manager, and category managers for each class of goods sold in the stores. Each category manager was in turn responsible for the product lines that made up a category, for instance, non-alcoholic beverages (NABs). The task of a category manager was to manage all processes related to this business, as Paul explained:

...he is responsible for all activities from the purchasing of the products, through developing marketing activities, down to their implementation in the stores. While the mission of a product manager was very operational—he was developing and implementing primarily planograms and promotions—the job of a category manager is to be the general manager of his business. He is now responsible for the strategic, horizontal dimensions which were not part of the mission of the product manager, such as purchasing and investment decisions.

To track the performance of their categories, managers needed new tools:

In this new configuration, the category manager has access to some aspects which were so far the business of the retail director. The over-rider deals, for example.

When manufacturers seek to persuade a retailer to list one item in the assortment, they can agree to give extra points of margin, as Paul illustrated:

The commercial margin of a product is calculated by comparing the purchase price of an item with its selling price. Let's say 35%. We can get extra points of margin if we accept to follow one specific aspect of the manufacturer's marketing policy. Let's say, to carry one specific line in our assortment. When manufacturers want to launch a new product, they will give a budget to the retailer to cover the risk of under performance in the first year. They usually have important market research and advertising budgets, and they can assess, in quite precise ways, the chances of a product to perform well. [...] After some time, the business figures tell us the truth and one can see if the innovation did well in reality. If it did not, the purchaser will threaten the manufacturer with delisting the item. And to give the product a further chance, an extra incentive can be given to compensate for the slow up-take of sales. Category managers have now the responsibility to negotiate these budgets.

To demonstrate how this mechanism worked, Paul directed us to Jennifer, the category manager for NABs. The acceptance of over-riders by the retailer could be analysed in two ways: as the means to secure an extra margin at no risk, and as a danger, since they incentivize the retailer to stock products with a low sales rotation. Jennifer commented:

After some time running after over-riders, one ends up with an assortment that is completely wrong. Indeed, a secure margin may not compensate the commercial margin that a high rotation item may have generated.

Over-riders are thus part of the global negotiation with suppliers. A manufacturer would propose to list some of its best-performing products together with a few, less well performing items. Part of the back margin may be paid to the retailer immediately, but usually it is attached to conditions such as the achievement of annual objectives and paid at the end of the year. This was the reason why, before category management was introduced, these monies were not spread across the SKUs. No adjustment of the commercial margin was made. It was kept as a global package attached to a manufacturer and no basis for apportionment was sought. The over-riders were considered a bonus that would come on top of the margin on operations (MO), to improve the operating profit. Paul explained this mechanism, using Table 5.6 as an example. The MO had been calculated for each supplier A, B, and C. The MO was then aggregated into a total margin for each supplier. Finally, the over-riders would be added to reach the operating profit.

With a category management structure in place, each manager wanted to see exactly what part of the over-riders would be integrated in the global margin. Following requests by the category managers, the profit and loss account was changed to the format given in Table 5.7.

Table 5.7 shows how the over-riders were treated: they were added, for each supplier, to the commercial margin to form a total net margin. In this system, a category manager could use the over-riders to lower the price of a product, if he or she thought that it would drive up volume. Jennifer remarked:

Table 5.6. BEST company—margin on operations, supplier breakdown

	Supplier A		Supplier B		Supplier C		Total	
	Val.	%	Val.	%	Val.	%	Val.	%
Volume	10000		30000		15000			
Retail selling price	1.15		1.05		1.1			
Sales incl. VAT	11500	100	31500	100	16500	100	59500	100
Sales excl. VAT	9361		25641		13431		48433	
Cost of goods sold (COGS)	−7475	−80	−21735	−78	−9075	−68	−38285	
Commercial margin	1886	20	3906	12	4356	26	10148	21
Cost of operations	−575		−1970		−1650		−4195	
Margin on operations	1311	14	1936	6	2706	16	5953	12
Over-riders	230	2	1575	6	1320	10	3125	6
Operating profit							9078	19

Table 5.7. BEST company—margin on operations including over-riders, supplier breakdown

	Supplier A		Supplier B		Supplier C		Total	
	Val.	%	Val.	%	Val.	%	Val.	%
Volume	10000	18	30000	55	15000	27	55000	
Retail selling price excl. VAT	1.15		1.05		1.1			
Sales incl. VAT	11500		31500		16500		59500	
Sales excl. VAT	9361	100	25641	100	13431	100	48433	100
Cost of goods sold (COGS)	−7475		−21735	69	−9075	−68	−38285	
Commercial margin	1886	20	3906	15	4356	32	10148	21
Over-riders	230	2	1575	6	1320	10	3125	6
Net margin	2116	23	5481	21	5676	42	13273	27
Cost of operations	−575		−1970		−1650		−4195	
Margin on operations	1541	16	3511	14	4026	30	9078	19
Operating profit							9078	19

What counts is the total margin on operations in value. I can decide that I don't need to have 30% of margin on operations for supplier C since the average is 19%. Thus 25% is enough for me if the total value increases. With this new system, I can use the over-riders as a real tool in the management of my category.

In other words, Jennifer could now turn the over-rider into an instrument to manage demand. Furthermore, the ability to capture over-riders reflected her negotiation skills. Sales promotions were also added to the category manager's armory. Promotions are a common mechanism used to enhance the performance of a product—e.g. amplify seasonality, block competitors' moves. But promotions are also used to boost the sales of flagging products. The special price that the retailer would get during the promotional period is usually passed on to the consumer to generate incremental sales.

Manufacturers had different policies on promotions. Some used promotions sparingly and preferred to advertise heavily on TV. Others thought that spending their budgets on activities closer to the point of sale was a better bet. The impact on sales could vary greatly. Some product families had a high sensitivity to sales promotion and were rather 'promo-dependent'. In some cases, promoted volumes could reach 40 per cent of the sales. But conversely, other product families would only be modestly affected by promotions. In the previous structure, Paul explained, promotions were negotiated at the field level by the district and store managers. With category management, promotions were in the hands of people like Jennifer, who could decide what promotion should be done with which supplier, according to strategic goals rather than merely reacting to suppliers' proposals as was previously the case with product managers.

In this new landscape, Paul observed, the category manager had a pano-ramic view of performance. However, the dashboard used to monitor this performance needed a further adjustment, as Jennifer explained:

If we were to have full control over the margin and use it in the most appropriate way, to set prices right, for example, we had to combine the three dimensions of margin: the upfront commercial margin, the over-riders and the promotional rate.

With the implementation of category management, Jennifer was responsible for purchasing as well as marketing. Because she was accountable for the performance of the category, she naturally tended to combine factors which previously were kept separate and she could spot opportunities and problems that product managers were unable to see. While negotiating with suppliers, she would link this new information with what she knew about the market. With the earlier, coarser-grained perspective on performance, only the com-mercial margin was monitored. Now, Jennifer and her colleagues requested a dashboard which would show the total margin, including the three types of margin described above. Table 5.8 shows the resulting table combining the commercial or upfront margin with the promotional and back margin (or over-riders).

With this new dashboard, suppliers' performance is shown in a different light, Jennifer commented. Table 5.8 shows that Supplier A delivers the highest level of total margin, both in percentage and in absolute value, but it is only the third supplier on upfront margin rates (28 per cent). Supplier B, who was the preferred supplier on the basis of the upfront margin, is now the worst and below average when considering the global deal. Lastly, supplier C delivers an average 40 per cent total margin, since its below-average upfront margin (30 per cent) is compensated by a high back margin. From this perspective, the initiatives of supplier B will be the least interesting since B is now the 'worst-in-class' supplier.

The business objectives given to Jennifer were largely based on the total margin in value. With this tool, she could mix and match her negotiation tactics—she could focus on supplier A, for example. Or she could play with the margin mix in trying to push supplier A to give her the upfront margin she got from supplier B, and push them to reach a better back margin, as offered by supplier C. Jennifer's scope for negotiation increased dramatically with this broader view of her options. This aspect was also interesting for suppliers who could now spot new opportunities, as Jennifer stressed. Since the analysis of product performance was mainly influenced by the segment to which the product belonged, the classification of a new item was crucial.

Jennifer zoomed in on the water segment she was responsible for. Supplier B had developed an innovation which consisted of a mineral water with a touch of fruit flavour. Flavoured water could either be classified as a sub-segment of the mineral water segment, or as a sub-segment of the fruit

Table 5.8. BEST company—total margin, supplier breakdown

	Purchase	Sales	Upfront margin			Promotional margin			Back margin			Total margin			
	In value	In value	In value	Margin in % of sales	Contribution of total margin (%)	In value	Margin in % of sales	Contribution of total margin (%)	In value	Margin in % of sales	Contribution of total margin (%)	In value	Margin in % of sales	Contribution of total margin (%)	Share of margin (%)
Category 1															
Supplier A	120	167	47	28	66	20	12	28	4	2	6	71	42	100	37
Supplier B	110	167	57	34	88	5	3	8	3	2	5	65	39	100	34
Supplier C	100	143	43	30	75	7	5	12	7	5	12	57	40	100	30
Total Category 1	330	476	146	31	76	32	7	17	14	3	7	**192**	40	100	100

Table 5.9. BEST company—sales growth in non-alcoholic beverage (NABs) segments

	Margin rate (%)	Sales growth (%)
Mineral water	58.84	−4.58
Fruit beverages	45.48	−10.46
Flavoured water	56.49	42.58
. . .	. . .	. . .
Total NABs	47.94	6.69

beverages. The performance implications were significant. Let us look at the growth of the segments and their margin rate (Table 5.9).

Placed among the waters, flavoured waters had a marginally lower margin than the average for the segment. But flavoured waters had a high sales growth when compared to the water segment which was in slight decline. Should flavoured waters be classified as carbonated fruit beverages, not only would they deliver a good margin rate, but their sales growth would be seen as a way to boost the entire segment. In addition, supplier B was the leader in the water segment. For them, the development of sales in the carbonated fruit beverages would also generate less cannibalization than if the product was placed in the water segment.

Category management also added a financial dimension to performance measurement and ushered in a 'return on investment' (ROI) logic. On the occasion of a collaborative project with a supplier, Jennifer was involved in the calculation of ROI for the implementation of fast lane chillers. Four types of inputs were now being considered: the cost of land, buildings, merchandising furniture and working capital (essentially stocks in the case of petrol stations). Because Jennifer was keen to develop the category, she naturally sought to increase the number of chilled cabinets:

As my product family was perceived to be very profitable in comparison to other product groups, it was legitimate to ask for an increase in the space allocated to beverages. And to do this, you have to go through our Capital Expenditure Request (CER). If a category manager wants to get engineering hours to get the job done, she has to fill in a CER and use the traditional investments appraisal tools: return on capital employed, payback, discounted cash flow and internal rate of return. This is where I became that one square meter in a store is the addition of a fraction of land, building, furniture and stock. And all this has a cost. You have to measure the gross margin ratio of a product family to the cost of one square meter. And you want to make sure that the product family will pay its fee. This ratio is called Gross Margin Return on Surface (GMROS).

Using the category logic, all beverages were deemed equal because they shared the same chiller:

One brand of beverages is competing against another brand of beverages and one does not need to consider the investment. It is as if the space was given to you and you don't have to pay any rental fee.

However, if the proposal was to expand the space attributed to beverages, a decision has to be made on the allocation of space, on a supra-category basis. Paul, as CRS director, was familiar with these procedures:

The CRS director is the one who decides if ten additional square meters of space should be given to the beverages, to the sandwiches or to automobile spare parts. This decision can be made within the category management department. But as soon as a special construction or a modification to the building is required, and this is the case when you want to install a chiller, the technical department will have to give it a green light.

With the new category management rules, the reason for undertaking any activity started to be discussed in unexpected ways. Smiling, Paul took us through some examples:

The toilets need a lot of space and do not contribute to turnover but, they are the number one reason why drivers stop at petrol stations. The fuel section requires huge investment in security and environmental protection and it delivers a significant amount of margin, particularly if one adds the upstream margin to the retail margin. The grocery items deliver a great margin but they also require specific investments which they need to contribute to. And their contribution to profit, once the investment is included in the calculation, is no longer a dream number.

If a chiller has to be installed, the investment would be charged to the beverage category. The investment would no longer be included in a global investment package attributed to the store. Compared to other businesses, such as the sandwiches, confectionary, or tobacco, the beverages needed more resources to be operated. In contrast, the sale of DVDs and telephone cards took up little space, required no additional investment, and delivered a great margin and return. Referring to Jennifer's NABs, Paul added:

When compared to these new businesses, the beverages deserve fewer resources and their expansion in terms of space allocation is difficult to justify financially. This is the counterpoint to the autonomy awarded to category managers: they have to justify how they use the resources given to them. And this dimension has been totally underestimated by everyone. Category managers should in fact be very senior if they want to stand up to the technical department with regard to financial issues.

In summary, the implementation of category management challenged the way the performance of the activities was perceived as well as their role in the business model of the retailer. It allowed category managers to see phenomena that were invisible under the previous structure. As the different components of the retailer's margin were progressively integrated in one single dashboard, the ranking of suppliers changed which, in turn, impacted upon their ability to influence the retailer's decisions. When launching new products, suppliers now have to consider the grouping of products at the retail level because their performance can be significantly influenced by the category to which they are assigned.

Analysis

Our case sheds light on the dynamics of calculation processes as our focal company changed from a product to a category management structure. This move was prompted by the requirement to see stores attached to forecourts as more than an appendix to the fuel business. By adopting category management, the focal company aligned itself with the practices of retailing and, as a result, took a different perspective on the role of its forecourt network and its relationships with suppliers and consumers.

The analysis of the dashboard used by product managers suggested that there should be a balance between contribution to volume, margin, assortment, and consequently, share of shelf space. By influencing the retailer's market representation, suppliers acted to shape retailers' assortments (e.g. which product should be selected and displayed in stores) and norms (e.g. the share of shelf space should be equivalent to market share). In short, the remit of product managers gave them a partial view of demand and suppliers' performance, and helped focus negotiations with suppliers on a narrow range of performance indicators.

The introduction of category management signalled an important shift in outlook. The reference market became generic retailing rather than just fuel retailing. Retailing activities were now managed and monitored in a more focused and fine-grained manner. The grouping of previously dispersed activities and metrics under category managers led to new ways of aggregating, combining, and interpreting performance indicators. For example, as soon as the upfront margin was displayed side by side with over-riders and promotional margins, the performance of suppliers was cast in a different light. The choice of product assortment was now dependent on the aggregate of different types of margins and category managers could take a much more comprehensive and rounded view of suppliers' performance. The negotiations between the retailer and its suppliers could now contemplate multiple fronts, with concessions on one front, say promotional rates, being able to compensate for deficiencies in others, e.g. low sales rotation.

But, as we have shown, negotiations between the focal retailer and its suppliers did not revolve solely around calculative spaces and tools. What constituted a category and how new products should fit into existing categories was also a source of contention. For example, should flavoured waters be classified as part of the water or the juices category? The answer did not merely affect how products were displayed on the shelves but, as we have shown, had an impact on the performance of the category to which the new product was assigned.

Whilst the new system brought a great deal of autonomy to category managers in their external dealings, the financial dimension of their role introduced novel modes of internal accountability. As category managers sought to expand their business, they were confronted by new modes of calculation as they interacted with other corporate functions, such as the finance and technical departments. A mundane decision, such as the installation of a chilling cabinet in a store, pushed category managers into a world of capital expenditure requests where additional calculating tools (e.g. return on employed capital) came into play. With these metrics in place, corporate functions pursued a vision of petrol stations as spaces of financial flows where every product category should be able to pay its way and justify the investments it required.

This financial logic raised strategic issues about how to use the space of a petrol station and how the returns on that space can be maximized. Why, for example, should the company sell fuel when the costs of securing fuel in retail environments are so high? Why not sell apparel or electronic goods as the operating margins for these categories are high and little shelf space is required? The move to category management thus triggered a shift in interaction patterns within the broad corporate structure and brought into play another range of performance indicators, whilst opening up new strategic vistas for the business.

In short, a 'volume, sales, margin' vision of performance was progressively replaced by a scenario where category managers, combining purchasing and marketing responsibilities, took a rounded view on supplier performance and were made internally accountable for returns to invested inputs. The shift towards category management had considerable impact on how the company viewed its business, its relationships with its suppliers, and its representation of demand.

Conclusions

The use of performance metrics has largely been treated as an intra-organizational phenomenon. Ahrens and Chapman (2007) suggested that the accounting literature has tended to gloss over the work done by management control tools such as performance dashboards (e.g. tables, charts, and figures) and their appropriation as practical resources in managerial work. Our study has broadened this line of enquiry by focusing on the evolution of performance dashboards, as our focal company moved from a product to a category management structure.

In particular, we have tried to flesh out Callon and Muniesa's view (2005) of calculation and situate it in a broader context. At a basic level, our empirical data illustrates how the construction of calculative spaces such as the performance dashboards that informed product and category managers framed actions. Dashboards condense in one convenient location what a manager needs to know about the fine-grained performance of products. Through a series of transformations, results at the SKU and store levels were aggregated to produce one result (a ranking) that informed how the company should relate to proposals of particular suppliers.

But dashboards proved just as important for what they focused on as for what they hid from view. Product managers had a truncated picture of what went on in the relationship between the company and its suppliers. These relationships encompassed many more parameters than product managers could see and involved other roles within BEST's structure.

The move to category management was accompanied by an important shift in modes of calculation at all levels. The sale of fuel was now placed on a par with other retail activities, stores now being aggregates of three major activities (CRS), which were further split into finer categories. Products were classed into categories and these new calculative spaces brought together a broader range of indicators, enabling further calculations and producing different sets of results on supplier rankings and product assortments. As Czarniawska and Mouritsen (2009: 172) remark, inscriptions simplify complex objects such as people, technologies, and organizations, by representing them as sets of simplified traits and making them visible as discrete entities. It is this separation of objects from their contexts that allows control and intervention. But simplification is not without costs. Inscriptions move some things into sight whilst obscuring others. In reintroducing inscriptions into new contexts, managers have to deal with a new set of complexities and linkages.

Category managers were now general managers of their own businesses, combining both purchasing and marketing responsibilities. As the story of Jennifer illustrates, category managers did not simply use the dashboards they were supplied with. The development of their role featured a dynamic iteration between interpretations of how they should relate to suppliers as well as the development of new dashboard formats based on the figures they saw as enhancing their negotiation role.

Although Callon and Muniesa's view (2005) of calculation proved useful to analyse our empirical data, we conclude that it is insufficient to understand how multiple calculative spaces are connected at different levels within the same firm and mobilized for a variety of ends. For example, the product category is mobilized in relation to negotiations with suppliers to help decide how to carve out limited shelf space amongst competing offerings within the same category. The retail store is a calculative space aggregating multiple categories and where each category competes for retail space on the basis of new performance criteria (e.g. internal rate of return). At each stage, entities are placed within calculative spaces associated with particular sets of figures, transformations are then performed on those figures, and results extracted. But these distinct stages are hardly self-contained modules. Changes at one level have the potential to transform relationships between levels (e.g. category managers to corporate functions) as well as affect multiple levels (e.g. factoring in all the resources required to sell a particular product category).

In conclusion, we have shown how changes in calculation are linked with managerial responsibilities and modes of internal and external accountability. Reconfiguring managerial responsibilities often implies changes in the relationship amongst modes of calculation within the firm and often, across firm boundaries (e.g. relationships with suppliers). As we have also highlighted, this process of multi-level reconfigurations can trigger new strategic interrogations and drive them in unexpected directions—for example, should a fuel retailing company set up stores where no fuel is sold?

6 Markets are trading zones

On the material, cultural, and interpretative dimensions of market encounters

JOHN FINCH AND SUSI GEIGER

Purpose

In this chapter, we apply the concept of trading zones to markets. We do so in order to highlight the multiple material, cultural, and interpretative dimensions of actors' organizing, trading, buying, and selling work, which they normally undertake in order to make an exchange. Trading zones also highlight the multiple areas of conflict, miscomprehension, or incommensurability that can arise between buyers and sellers in markets. Drawing on extant descriptions of how firms interact with customers, this chapter aims to show the diversity of buyer–seller interactions that can underlie apparently smooth market exchanges. As a contribution to marketing theory, drawing on the concept of trading zones helps us identify the sometimes long, multiple, and contested channels by which producers present—and anticipate presenting—their offers to buyers, and by which buyers encounter an array of offers. Parties to exchanges may well develop cognitive models of one another (Bagozzi 2009). However, the obdurate material, cultural, and interpretive practices of making exchanges have a strong influence on marketing, which is more or less constitutive of and proximate to those exchanges.

The present volume's aim is to re-focus marketing's attention on markets as socio-technological phenomena, rather than merely an abstract or institutionalized collection of buyers and sellers, explaining market exchanges through analysing actors' practices in connection with the objects involved therein. The stream of research represented in this book considers markets as 'bundles of practices including material arrangements that contribute to perform markets' (Araujo et al. 2008: 8) and has suggested, for instance, that material objects such as shopping carts can have a significant influence on how market actors act in market spaces (Cochoy 2008a, 2009). We develop this agenda by arguing that in emphasizing socio-*material* practices in those market spaces, the material continuity observed may conceal discontinuities and boundary work in associated socio-*cultural* practices, for instance around actors' interpretative activities, that are often pertinent to undertaking exchanges.

We are especially interested in the differences between buyers and sellers in their respective sense-making and negotiation of the meanings of exchange because for Callon (1998*a*) and many other researchers in market practices, questions of incommensurability are not as important as calculative agency. Actors in markets overcome incommensurability in this interplay through material objects and devices that shape and constrain their calculations (Callon et al. 2007). Furthermore, because calculation as a competence or capacity is located in the interplay between human and non-human elements in the actor-world, questions of interpretation can be overlooked. These cultural and interpretative dimensions represent bases of misunderstandings, disputes, and incommensurabilities, which we argue are important characteristics of actors' encounters in markets with the potential of stimulating actors' imagination and creativity (Finch and Geiger 2010).

We develop Peter Galison's use (1997, 1999) of the trading zone concept by inverting it in order to investigate how markets and their exchanges become organized, with varying degrees of collaboration and contest. We are particularly interested in those scenarios in which material continuity—a smooth transition of a firm's product or service through a good in a market to a usable object settled into a buyer's life or world—betrays signs of actors negotiating and contesting the material or calculative arrangements and meanings of exchanges. We are also interested in the processes by which actors in markets represent their activities and interpretations pertinent to such exchanges. We demonstrate that the concept of trading zone allows researchers and market actors to examine how trading is accomplished and how the 'sphere of practice ... continues unbroken' (Galison 1999: 138). While often taken as a given, continuation is remarkable due to the potentially radical differences in market actors' anticipations, imaginings, visualizings, calculations, or estimations of value; differences we refer to as 'incommensurability'. We add to Galison's account by exploring additional dimensions of trading zones beyond the linguistic one and demonstrate how, taking these into account, the stability he sees guaranteed in the trading zone is fragile and often fleeting.

The remainder of the chapter will proceed as follows. After an introduction of the trading zone concept in sections 'What are trading zones?' and 'The negotiation of meaning and levels of incommensurability', we will draw upon published case material for four examples of ideal types of trading zones in business-to-consumer markets in the section 'How buyers and sellers shape exchanges in trading zones'. Section 'Discussion' will then critically discuss the contribution of the trading zone concept to the market studies project in general and to this book's theme of 'Reconnecting marketing to markets' more particularly. Section 'Conclusion' concludes the chapter.

What are trading zones?

Peter Galison (1997, 1999) introduced the concept of trading zones into the field of science and technology studies (STS) in his historical analysis of the development of physics into fragmented subdisciplines. Galison drew on the interactions and relationships of theoretical and experimental physicists in the Rad Labs of MIT in the 1940s, extending to include engineers in making instruments, to argue that physicists had formed subcultures. Members of the subcultures traded, and, of particular relevance to the current chapter, worked out ways of trading that were material and linguistic. In other words, physicists managed to cope with their discipline's growth by means of fragmentation through developing and performing new ways of coordinating their increasingly disparate activities. Borrowing from anthropologies of neighbouring ethnic subcultures, Galison defines trading zones as follows:

Anthropologists are familiar with different cultures encountering one another through trade, even when the significance of the objects traded—and of the trade itself—may be utterly different for the two sides.... when we narrow our gaze to the peasant buying eggs in a landowner's shop we may see two people, perfectly harmoniously exchanging items. In fact, they depend on the exchange for survival. Out of the narrow view, however, are two vastly different symbolic and cultural systems, embedding two perfectly incompatible valuations and understandings of the objects exchanged.... What is crucial is that in the highly local context of the trading zone, *despite* the differences in classification, significance, and standards of demonstration, the two groups can collaborate. (Galison 1999: 146; original emphasis)

Galison argues that physics and other sciences comprise subcultures, which are inter-dependent, quasi-autonomous, and (crucially) a little out of step with one another. He contrasts the 'out of step' character of trading zones with the two totalizing narratives in the 1940s physics, logical positivism and relativism or constructivism, which presume an easy interplay of theory, instrumentation, and experimentation, but with radically different meta-theories.

In the case of the Rad Lab, instead of easing the way to totalizing or unifying meta-theories in physics, physicists' theorizing, experiments, facts, and instrumentation added further chains and qualifications to their arguments and scientific processes, translating the 'locus' of theory, fact, and instrument into locales and subcultures. The new science featured incremental changes in recognition of the awkwardness implied by theory, empiricism and instrumentation being typically a little resistant to one another, so reinforcing the locales. Rather, physics became a culture of subcultures, each with its material arrangements and practices, which its participants negotiate through their interactions.

Gorman (2002, 2005) and Collins et al. (2007) develop Galison's concept by relating interactions between scientists and other professions in trading zones to their levels of expertise and their capacities to acquire power over their counterparts in exchanges and trades. Their overriding question is of how members of two communities or subcultures can interact in a mutually beneficial manner (i.e. trade one thing for something that comes to be valued similarly), given that the relationships between their respective communities are characterized by incommensurability. In answer to this question, Gorman (2002, 2005) describes three types of trading zones: (*a*) elite control, (*b*) approximate parity, and (*c*) shared mental models. While in the elite control type of trading zones, one group controls evolving exchanges through their unilateral expertise, the shared mental models type of trading zones stretches beyond individuals' expertise. Gorman acknowledges that in between these two extremes, the approximate parity type of trading zones covers the broadest ground, encompassing all inter-actions among groups with broadly equal if different areas of expertise and ranging from attempts at dominating the exchange to truly democratic collaboration.

Building from these three categories, Collins et al. (2007: 657) investigate trading zones as 'the locus of incommensurability' where alongside an apparent material continuity (the exchange of a good), difficulties of communication and culture are negotiated and overcome. They amend their typology by taking into account the extent to which power is acquired, formatted, and used by one party to enforce the trade (axis 1), and the extent to which trade leads to the emergence of a new culture (axis 2). Hence, Collins et al. present four types of trading zones, as depicted in Figure 6.1.

'Enforced' trading zones—as a development of 'elite' trading zones—are characterized by little attempt from either party to engage in each other's culture; the powerful party black-boxes its expertise to the trading partner; interchange of meanings is limited to the minimum level where the bargain can be understood by both parties. In 'Subversive' trading zones, the powerful 'expert' party remains largely in control of the exchange, but endeavours, above and beyond the trade, to supplant the other group's culture and vocabulary with its own, leading to a homogeneous (if unilaterally shaped) new culture emerging from the continued exchange. The other party can offer resistance to this process in the subversive trading zone, but commonly this resistance only serves the 'expert' party to further reinforce its own vision of the exchange.

Collins et al.'s two collaborative types of trading zones (2007), representing the top half of Figure 6.1, are more reciprocal in nature. 'Fractionated' trading zones are characterized by approximate parity of expertise and an interaction of both groups' cultures to make the exchange happen, even if cultures do not give rise to an 'intercultural' or inter-language zone. Fractionated trading zones fall into two camps, depending on whether the trade is mediated primarily by a material or a mainly linguistic boundary agent (i.e. the boundary object trading zone and the interactional expertise trading zone).

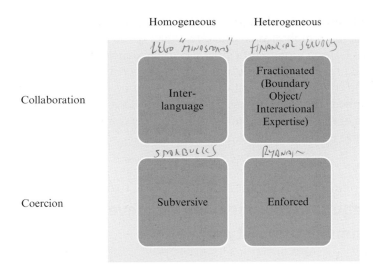

Figure 6.1. Four types of trading zones (adapted from Collins et al. 2007: 659)

Finally, 'Inter-language' trading zones are those that Galison described in his original work, where sustained interaction and a common interest in the trade give rise to an inter-language in the form of a pidgin or a more durable Creole. In these zones, 'all actors in a network have high inclusion within a technological frame, including a shared mental model of what needs to be accomplished' (Gorman and Mehalik 2002: 502). Despite potential material differences (e.g. of being producer and consumer), groups manage to develop jointly a local platform to trade collaboratively.

Gorman and colleagues' work presents an interpretation and development of Galison's concept of the trading zone. Galison's argument explains how physicists made physics incrementally and by overcoming material and linguistic differences, which were themselves consequences of physicists specializing in theorizing, experimenting, and developing instruments. While Gorman and colleagues draw on additional cultural, broadly cognitive, and social factors, some of which seem to be general factors pre-existing the particular locales studied, we highlight the possibility that some actors may seek to acquire the power to dominate others, such as in the few-to-many relationships typical of the market settings of exchanges between businesses and consumers.

Markets are complex places of interaction and organizing. As with all attempts at organizing across diverse subgroups (Kellogg et al. 2006; D'Adderio 2008), apparent material continuity in market trading zones may betray the vulnerability of the interaction that is threatened at all times by a potential breakdown of the local negotiation of the meanings of the exchange.

Indeed, Baird and Cohen (1999) contend that in a commodity economy, trading zones exhibit greater instability than in the 'gift economy' in which they see Galison's physicists operate. A tendency to greater instability makes the trading zone concept even more pertinent to markets—from which the concept was drawn originally—than in sciences to which it has been applied. In the following section, we explore the different bases and elements of this instability, and how actors may work with or around them to organize exchanges nonetheless.

The negotiation of meaning and levels of incommensurability

By utilizing the trading zone metaphor, we aim to examine the processes by which actors in markets interact to create material continuity in an exchange, arrive at a calculative basis for the exchange, and develop languages and means of communication to represent the activities pertinent to the exchange. This section delves deeper into potential sources of ruptures or incommensurability during market processes. We explain how investigating markets as trading zones can enrich the conceptualization of markets as collective calculative devices (Callon and Muniesa 2005), which has featured heavily in the approach represented in this volume. Trading zones also help us reconnect marketing to 'really existing' markets by drawing attention to the interpretative and cultural activities of marketers and their counterparts, a theme which we will return to in our discussion in section 'Discussion'.

To reiterate, to Callon et al. (2007) as well as many other researchers, questions of incommensurability are not as important as those relating to calculative agencies. In recounting Garcia's study of the strawberry market in the Sologne region of France (Garcia 1986, Garcia-Parpet 2007), Callon (1998a) demonstrates just how much effort is exerted in constructing devices which constrain and shape actors' calculations to the extent that, socially and communicatively, their market exchanges become easy 'clean breaks'. The clean breaks also ensure ease of material continuity as objects pass through production, market exchange, and use. Our focus is on those instances where breaks and continuations are not smooth but 'messy' and contested.

The first potential locus of messiness and contest are the languages actors use to engage in the trade. For market actors, languages are immediate and fairly flexible ways of uttering plans, valuations, descriptions, and representations, and can cope with being transformed from informal conversations to being written, recorded, and broadcast. In his exploration of scientists' trading zones,

Galison (1999) refers to localized pidgin languages, which are more or less stable, simplified, and functional contact languages between two groups, extending to symbolic systems. Hence, where markets can be described as trading zones, we are likely to find traces of a contact language or pidgin, which provides the communicative basis for actors' trades especially if the material dimensions are in the making, as with new techniques or instruments of measurement or experiment. The advantage of a restricted contact language over a full translation of one community's language to another is that a pidgin can be limited to the functional requirements of the local exchange, so that the communities are not required to fully engage with their counterpart's symbolic, cultural, and material worlds. Like material devices, the use of a pidgin language establishes a common ground for trading between market actors. At the same time, as Galison has indicated, the use of such languages often hides vast differences in actors' calculative bases that could emerge and disrupt trade at any stage.

Interpretation is the next potential for incommensurability. Like calculation, interpretation in its broad sense is concerned with the question of 'what counts' to a market actor. While Callon (1998a) allows for interpretative differences when describing cultures as accounting for 'differences in equipment' of people's calculative capacity, he claims that they can be overcome by (material) market devices: 'Markets are collective devices that allow compromises to be reached, not only on the nature of the goods to produce and distribute but also on the value to be given to them' (Callon and Muniesa 2005: 1229). In other words, markets sort out the messiness of actors' conflicting meanings, interests, and interpretations.

'Sorting out' requires two things of market actors, which we contend are often not achievable in markets: that all actors are content to step 'into' the market frame and compromise on their (often socially and culturally coloured) interpretations of 'what counts'; and that the material devices, which referee the compromises, are available and undisputed. What happens if actors do not or are not willing to shed their own interpretations when 'stepping' into the market? Chan (2009) offers such an example in examining how companies providing life insurance in China met varying degrees of resistance among potential customers, in connection with a longstanding and shared discomfort in talking about death. Or when social or cultural differences between actors are such that categorizations and therefore valuations are incompatible, such as in the interactions between policy makers and AIDS activists that Gorman and colleagues studied? Or if the material devices themselves are open to interpretation and do not provide the clean break a market exchange needs, as was the case in Baird and Cohen's report (1999) of two major instances of breakdown in the trading zone between Magnetic Resonance Imaging physicians and instrument makers? In the latter case, interpretive differences became so obvious in the trading zone that Baird and Cohen (1999: 250) described trading as a 'community-dividing' rather than 'community-forming' process. Thus, even if an inter-language exists in a trading zone, it may not succeed in hiding underlying differences in culture, interpretations, or power to enforce the exchange.

To summarize, trading zones depict rich and messy episodes of interaction rather than clean boundaries in between parties of an exchange. In the following section, we discuss four previously documented cases of business-to-customer interactions, drawing upon Collins et al's classification (2007) of trading zones in Figure 6.1, to draw out how exchanges happen in the face of incommensurability, understood as some combination of material, social, linguistic, or interpretative processes.

How buyers and sellers shape exchanges in trading zones

We follow Collins et al's assertion (2007: 658) that 'not all trade is conducted in trading zones. . . . We define "trading zones" as locations in which communities with a deep problem of communication manage to communicate. If there is no problem of communication there is simply "trade" not a "trading zone".' In relation to market exchanges between businesses and their customers, we are not considering 'non-contentious' exchanges in this chapter, in which buyers and sellers enter and exit the market as if strangers, and where calculative orders appear as clean-cut, settled, and uncontested (Callon 1998a). Instead, we investigate cases in which trade is dependent on 'zone work' by one, two, or multiple parties, and in which actors either contest local meanings or threaten to expose incommensurability of global ones, and thus potentially impede successful trading.

THE ENFORCED TRADING ZONE: RYANAIR

What part of no refund don't you understand? You are not getting a refund so f*** off. (Michael O'Leary, CEO of Ryanair; quoted in Kerrigan 2006)

Can a market encounter be 'enforced' in a capitalist, non-monopolistic market? Collins et al. (2007) give the ideal-type example of Roman galley slaves to illustrate their 'enforced' category. While our market example of an 'enforced' trading zone may not rely on 'brute physical repression' (Ibid.: 659), it nonetheless represents a case where the constitution of the trading zone and its terms and conditions are governed unilaterally by one party. Furthermore, those on the receiving end of this control 'are obliged to change their practices . . . but are not required to adopt the cultural viewpoint of the dominant group' (Ibid.). This is the case of the airline Ryanair. Amply documented elsewhere (Calder 2003; Creaton 2004, 2007; Brown 2006; BBC 2009), Ryanair has built a successful business model based on a thorough pursuit of its low-cost and no-frills agenda. Yet, it is at the same time one of the most profitable airlines in the world, carrying 58 million passengers in the year 2008 with an average load factor of 81 per cent per plane and a twelve-month profit of €480 million for year-end March 2008 (Ryanair 2008). So trade it does, with a large number of customers every year. However, is there a trading zone, and if there is one, how is it stabilized?

Ryanair pioneered the low-cost aviation business model in Europe in the mid-1990s, shortly after the European Union's deregulation of the industry. Rather than providing an alternative to existing airlines, Ryanair taught air travellers a novel process of market exchange, which was adopted in part from the low fares pioneer Southwest Airlines and included some novel practices. Ryanair proposed low airfares and frequent promotions to a public used to mostly government-owned flagship carriers in exchange for Internet-only booking, baggage that should be carried on board rather than put in the hold, no allocated seating but instead an optional 'priority pass' at extra cost for avoiding queues, no refunds for no-shows or cancellations, and no patience in waiting for late passengers.

Anyone who has flown Ryanair knows how profoundly its innovative processes have changed passengers' exchange practices and their practices and experiences of being passengers. On a Ryanair flight, passengers form queues in the designated areas sometime before boarding is announced; they carry cabin-sized trolley-bags into the plane, minimize Ryanair's offloading and turnaround time by sprinting in and out of the plane, and clean up their rubbish. Ryanair has done away with back-of-seat storage facilities, so there is little alternative to handing over one's rubbish to the flight attendants. As with the removal of back-of-seat storage facilities, Ryanair has put a wide range of material and communicative devices in place to facilitate and enforce these practices. For instance, default options on the website lead customers to accept many of the additional charges that form part of Ryanair's business model (BBC 2009). Airport check-in has been abolished so that passengers have no option but to check in online and print out their own boarding pass, an activity for which they are charged £5 by Ryanair. On board, seats cannot be reclined, increasing the aeroplane's load capacity.

Ryanair has continually justified these often uncomfortable changes to exchange practices by pointing out their necessity in order for the airline to fulfil its low-cost promise and to 'give passengers what they really need' (Ryanair Passenger Charter). In the market space, Ryanair considers any service attribute outside its 'low cost promise' as a spillover and therefore part of other clearly distinct market exchanges conducted in other zones.

Choice for passengers in this trading zone is minimized and essentially restricted to trading or not trading with the airline. Ryanair's version of market calculation has been challenged by a plethora of journalistic investigations (e.g. BBC 2009), anecdotes, and litigation cases by disgruntled passengers attempting negotiations and expressing to Ryanair their versions of 'what counts' in their market exchanges, thereby disputing the meanings of 'low cost' or 'what they really need' imposed by Ryanair. The challengers have not yet caused the airline to either change its market approach or its rhetoric nor to be apologetic about its practices (Calder 2003). Ryanair has continually pointed to the fact that the passengers—maybe begrudgingly—continue to trade. A recent exchange, as reported by the *Daily Telegraph*, indicates the level of incommensurability of interpretations in this trading zone:

A Dutch company [EUclaim] which specializes in launching actions against airlines has instructed lawyers in Dublin to start proceedings against the Irish-based no-frills carrier. EUclaim is offering to handle compensation claims from passengers. When individual passengers approached the airline for compensation they were informed that the delays or cancellations were due to 'weather conditions' or 'technical problems', a spokesman for the company said. "In most cases airlines will reject claims made by individual passengers, stating 'extraordinary circumstances' as the cause of the delay or cancellation. But more often than not this is not the case." It is virtually impossible for passengers to object to airline statements about technical circumstances. As a result airlines have been able to effectively hide behind the claim of extraordinary circumstances. "... A spokesman for the Air Transport Users Council, said that carriers were loath to pay out even when passengers were entitled to compensation." There are very few examples of airlines paying out for cancellations, they have routinely avoided it.... "They are using all sorts of excuses to avoid paying. They will claim there has been weather disruption, three days after there were real problems." Airlines will also cite crew shortages, when really it is their job to roster their staff properly. "There have been complaints of cancellations being classified as delays—in at least one case of 24 hours. EUclaim's intervention was dismissed by a Ryanair spokesman." Ryanair customer service only deals with passenger complaints made directly by passengers in writing. We will never deal with greedy, ambulance chasing organisations who promote a compensation culture where people claim for anything and everything. Ryanair will carry over 58 million passengers this year, have the best on time performance of any European airline with 88% of flights on time, lose just 0.5 bags per 1,000 passengers and cancel fewer flights than any other major European airline. From time to time a small number of passengers may feel disgruntled. These passengers should contact Ryanair customer services in writing as set out on our website www.ryanair.com and can expect to have a reply within seven working days. (Milward 2008, © Telegraph Media Group Limited 2008)

Ryanair's categorization of a 'delay' may differ from that of a passenger or indeed lawyer who would classify the same incident as a 'cancellation'. However, Ryanair has refused many times to be drawn into any negotiation of its categorizations and uses of language. Its terms of exchange are by now well understood by all concerned—low airfares for a minimal level of service—but in practice these are unilaterally formulated and enforced terms. Ryanair has devised a powerful material and communicative strategy that determines 'what counts' in this market exchange. Beyond citing passenger numbers it has chosen not to heed passengers' interpretations of their needs, even if these passengers try and invoke other actors such as courtrooms and regulators, so trying to make these other actors proximate to the market. Negotiations of meanings are overtly refuted. The trading zone's presence is signified by contest and stability because one party's stance of categorical 'no negotiations' leaves the other party with the choice of not trading at all or accepting the calculative frame imposed by Ryanair.

THE SUBVERSIVE TRADING ZONE

We changed the way people live their lives, what they do when they get up in the morning, how they reward themselves, and where they meet. (Orin Smith, Starbucks CEO; quoted in Clark 2007)

But why would anyone think having 14,000 stores around the world all being exactly the same be a good thing? (Blogger, Willamette Week Website, http://wweek.com/popup/comment.php?story=9911#comments_add)

Collins et al. (2007: 660) argue that 'in a subversive trading zone . . . [authority] gradually supplants the alternatives until it becomes the socially appropriate response'. They speak of colonizing by one party of both the language and the subculture of the (less powerful) other party, to a point where cultural hegemony is established and where the exchange offered is taken for granted as the default option. While alternatives may still exist, actors gradually write these out of their calculations and rarely put them into practice. Collins et al.'s account of the subversive trading zone has many parallels in critical marketing and consumer research where researchers have analysed some firms' interactions with their customers in terms of their hegemonic influence on local subcultures (Firat and Venkatesh 1995; Klein 2001; Holt 2002; Thompson and Arsel 2004; Cromie and Ewing 2009). Starbucks—alongside other global corporations including Microsoft, Coca Cola, or McDonalds—is an oft-quoted example of a firm whose claim to 'cultural authority' (Holt 2002) over a market has shaped consumers' buying practices in many parts of the world (Ponte 2002). As of February 2008, after a decade of worldwide expansion, Starbucks had a presence in forty-three countries outside the United States through close to 2,000 company-operated and almost 3,000 licensed stores while owning over 7,000 and licensing another 4,000 stores in the United States (Company Fact Sheet 2008).

While aiming for a similar 'total domination' (Clark 2007) of its industry, Starbucks (unlike Ryanair) has always been at pains to present itself as a benevolent trading partner to consumers and supply-chain partners alike.[1] Its guiding principles include to 'develop enthusiastically satisfied customers at all times' and to 'embrace diversity' in its trade dealings (Company Fact Sheet 2008). Yet, as websites such as www.ihatestarbucks.com, www.starbucked.com, and www.delocator.net stand to witness, the brand is a prime target for antibrand movements, protesting against the infiltration of local cultural meanings by the Starbucks business model. As Thompson and Arsel (2004: 632) put it, 'a hegemonic brandscape provides a constellation of objectified meanings (i.e., discourses, material goods, and servicescape atmospherics) that consumers can incorporate into their worldviews and put to a wide variety of interpretive and identity-constructive uses'.

One sign of the subversive change of meanings is evident in the uses of language as customers engage in exchange at and with Starbucks. Starbucks has introduced a new coffee vocabulary such that ordering a coffee becomes an adventure in creative Italian. Consumers are required to use the new language to trade with Starbucks at its coffee shops. Corroborating the notion of a subversive trading zone, Starbucks mixes consumers' normal linguistic coffee conventions with its own argot into a 'coffee Creole'; the trading language in this market exchange. Starbucks offers a type of translation service where, for instance, the new words for sizes that it would like customers to learn (*tall*, *grande*, and *venti*) are illustrated by a sample of coffee cups on the cash desk or where the often highly creative names of their coffee beverages are back-translated into colloquial English on the menu. Moreover, when repeating back the order to consumers, baristas usually change whatever 'old' coffee-speak was used into Starbucks' coffee Creole, as the following outburst by a poster on the website www.ineedcoffee.com witnesses:

'Will that be a Tall, Grande or a Venti?' Starbucks' menu language is just stupid—especially for espresso drinks. All I have to say is 'tall' is small. The barista or cashier will not speak to you in normal cafe speak either... If you order a double cappuccino, you get the most dreaded question of all—'Will that be a Tall, Grande or a Venti?'

The standardized material arrangements in Starbucks are another sign for its assembly of a trading zone that becomes the default manner of trading and therefore has subversive qualities. Starbucks has created an instantly identifiable version of the 'third place' (Oldenburg 1989) as a combination of material aspects of the public and the private space, which Thompson and Arsel (2004: 634) claim combine to form 'Starbuckified structures of common difference', which include sofas, distressed-looking and carefully arranged helter-skelter tables and chairs, light jazz or world music, tasteful 'young' art, and bohemian-looking staff. By setting standards for what a coffee shop should look and feel like, Starbucks has engaged in extensive cultural engineering, shaping customers' cultural expectations, and calculated comparisons for this type of market encounter: 'In American metropolitan settings, a coffee shop is more or less like Starbucks in much the same way that a fast-food restaurant is more or less like McDonalds' or a theme park is more or less like Disney World' (Ibid.: 633).

Even though Starbucks invokes allies in other market actors such as coffee growers through their fair trade policies, Starbucks' cultural authority gives rise to fierce resistance by some against being subverted (McGinnis and Gentry 2009). Recently, however, according to the following newspaper clip, Starbucks has started to 'subvert' the anti-subversion front by embracing rather than rejecting their interpretations:

In a move that will seriously confuse anti-chain consumers who live and breathe for morning pick-me-ups that are authentically artisan, the cafe franchise Starbucks is ditching the unfashionably common Starbucks brand from a number of its US stores. Each of the 'Starbucks by stealth' stores will be given a 'local' name, such as Seattle's 13th Avenue Coffee and Tea, with the new names designed to give caffeine-dependent commuters a dollop of faux-community feeling along with their appreciably more bohemian Americanos. But all revenues from these undercover franchises will go straight to that alleged evil destroyer of independent coffee houses, Starbucks. (Slattery 2009)

So, through much work to address meanings, language, and culture, Starbucks' 'third place' has come to represent the easily accessible, safe, and predictable 'default option' for the majority of its customers, having successfully shaped our expectations of what visiting a coffee shop entails and the way market actors calculate (and how much they spend) when approaching this trading zone. For those it has yet to convince of this cultural recipe, Starbucks continues to try and appropriate their meanings in order to secure an exchange.

FRACTIONATED TRADING ZONES

Thankfully, the FSA has not danced around this: it has banned the payment of commission. The result is that consumers will be able to seek financial advice in the knowledge that the cost will be agreed at the outset and that the advice will be geared towards the investor's interests and not the adviser's commission account. (Andrew Fisher, CEO Towry Law, 2009*a*)

In Collins et al.'s classification (2007), enforced trading zones are characterized by very minimal cultural interchange and subversive trading zones operate by imposing one culture on another. By contrast, in fractionated trading zones, occupying the top right hand corner of Figure 6.1, participants within different cultures interact selectively and often through the mediation of material and cultural elements. Collins et al. draw on a rich literature in organizational studies on boundary objects and boundary spanners. In the settings of markets, boundary agents' mediation allows the fractionated trading zone to approximate material and cultural continuity. Hence, a market's actors may develop confidence in the fairness and reliability of that trade even though their knowledge of and direct interaction with their trading counterpart (producer or buyer) is minimal.

We take as an instance of fractionated trading zones the market for financial services and products in the United Kingdom (Devlin 2003). This is a contested terrain as the market has been beset with cases in which tied and independent financial advisers have mis-sold products and services, including endowment mortgages and personal pensions. Financial advisers are regulated in the United Kingdom by the Financial Services Authority (FSA). Cases of mis-selling continue to arise. Most recently, Swinton Group, a UK insurance company, was fined £770,000 for bundling payment protection insurance, with premiums of £15 to £20, with car and home insurance policies without making it sufficiently clear to customers that the additional payment protection was optional (Cumbo 2009). The FSA described Swinton Group's approach as an 'assumptive selling technique'.

The financial products and services considered individually and as an array are complex. The regulator, the FSA, is intensifying its efforts to act in the market and be a powerful market actor. Financial advisers have, with the encouragement of the producers of the financial products and services, established themselves to mediate between producers and buyers in the market. Financial advisers are tied to the producer, such as a bank or insurance company, and can only advise on their employer's products, while independent financial advisers can offer advice across the market's array of offers. Ross (2009*a*) reports that 'there are 35,000 independent financial advisers in the United Kingdom, 25,000 in banks and life insurance companies and a further 25,000 who are registered to give advice but are not currently giving it'. After a review lasting three years, the FSA is overseeing a change in the design of the retail market by outlawing from 2013 the practice of independent financial advisers being paid a commission by the producers of financial services when advising customers to buy these products. Instead, advisers are to agree a fee for their services with their consumer clients. Further, financial advisers are to become more highly qualified and their companies are to have much larger capital requirements, increasing from £10,000 to £350,000. The FSA and the advisers' industry association in the United Kingdom, the Association of Independent Financial Advisers, see the benefits of changing the mediation in retail markets to promote a smaller and more professional group of advisers (Ross 2009*b*).

The relationship between the FSA and the financial advisers (tied and independent) could be considered highly complementary. The FSA has a specific website directed at customers in the retail market (Money Made Clear, TM, http://www.moneymadeclear.fsa.gov.uk/). Crucially, the site makes a virtue out of its use of 'clear English', under its strap line of 'no selling, no jargon, just the facts'. However, the FSA's review of retailing in financial services seeks to reorient independent advisers by breaking their material connection of commission with producers and establish a new material connection between advisers and customers through ensuring that advisers charge fees. Andrew Fisher, CEO of Towry Law, begins a provocative discussion article with: 'The public it ostensibly services has been exploited for 20 years. Regulatory authorities have finally decided to force a change on a series of archaic practices, where poorly qualified "experts" administer inappropriate advice to the unwitting and are paid billions in commission to sell potentially harmful products' (Fisher 2009*b*).

Gorman (2002) and Ribeiro (2007) draw attention to the interactional expertise required of the boundary spanner whose job it is to 'buffer' between two 'forms of life'. As Ribeiro (2007: 577) notes: 'Its goal is to allow interaction between participants of two social worlds that present linguistic-cultural or conceptual discontinuities'. Selling financial services is complex and contentious. The discussion above shows that the intermediary can easily become a centre of activity, culture, business, much as the instrument makers became a subculture alongside experimenters and theorists in Galison's discussion of the development of physics. The actions of the UK's FSA in its retail review demonstrate the considerable additional effort it can take to stabilize relationships where commercial interests are significant and a shared culture, as physics, is missing.

INTER-LANGUAGE ZONES

When the first MINDSTORMS set came out (1.0), I picked it up immediately. I had waited for something like this for years and have been building robots ever since. When word got out that LEGO was seeking input from fans, I felt that this would be my chance to help shape the product and its future. I wanted to bring my ideas to the table and help test the new features like Bluetooth and the new functionality such as the built-in rotation sensors on the motors. (Lead User, Lego Mindstorms Community website)

Often seen as the 'original' type of trading zone, matching that described by Galison (1997), inter-language zones are characterized by two independent groups moving toward a homogeneous platform through the development of an inter-language that borrows and combines elements of both cultures. It is important to note that even in these groups, there is still *trade*. Groups remain as largely autonomous entities, and while boundaries will blur, the groups will not be *in toto* subsumed into a larger social entity. This is the difference between the gift economy and a commodity economy, in which social ties move the exchange outside of the market, as is the case in open source software development (Zeitlyn 2003), or in the academic reviewing community mentioned by Baird and Cohen (1999). The explicit element of trade also distinguishes inter-language zones from other kinds of communities such as communities of practice, which are similarly characterized by shared mental models, parity of power, and a common language between otherwise autonomous actors (Lave and Wenger 1991; Roberts 2006).

Within the broader umbrella of brand or user communities there are an increasing number of examples of inter-language trading zones, such as customer co-design communities (Piller et al. 2005), communities of creation (Sawhney and Prandelli 2000; Von Hippel 2001), or the value co-creation cases presented by Cova and Salle (2008) in the business-to-business realm. In these zones, customers' expertise is utilized by firms in the design or marketing process of a product or service, facilitated by a 'configurator' or 'configuration system' which familiarizes the customer with the socio-technical frame in place, such as a software platform. The trade conducted in these communities is mutually beneficial; firms gain valuable insights into customer needs and get customer expertise and input for free; customers gain social and psychological rewards from the co-design process as well as higher utility from commercial products that truly fit their needs (Jeppesen and Frederiksen 2006).

This is the case, for instance, in the robotics world of Lego Mindstorms, launched in 1998. From a corporate perspective, the Mindstorms project represented a huge departure for a company that had been thus far known for 'going it alone' and maintaining complete control over partners and suppliers (Oliver and Roos 2003). Originally set up as an educational satellite project to the corporate Lego universe and given little strategic attention, the mission of the Lego Mindstorms project included the guiding principle of 'be[ing] a real partner' (Ibid.). This attitude allowed the Lego Mindstorms team to open up their firmware to their early adult fans, rather than to answer those fans' attempts to hack into the software with the legal challenges that had been the expected response by some of these hobbyist 'meddlers' (Wallich 2001). While the Mindstorms project had not initially included a communication strategy for adult fans, soon firmware codes were jointly developed; gatherings of fan communities were sponsored and encouraged; lead users were 'hired' to the Mindstorms Developers Programme and their profiles and ideas featured on the Lego Mindstorms website; and creations by customers were used for trade shows and marketing tours and often commercialized. During its ten-year existence, Lego Mindstorms has owed its high user and producer value (retailing at an average price point of over £150) to both parties adopting what Sawhney and Prandelli (2000: 31) call a 'new open and democratic regime of knowledge creation and idea sharing'. In this case, the trading zone is based on shared interpretations of what the product came to represent (a relatively simple, modular, and customizable entry point into robotics for children and adults alike); jointly developed (programming) pidgins; hardware and other material products such as books; and Web-based platforms for exchange that are encouraged but uncontrolled by Lego.[2] Indeed, the Internet universe of Mindstorms, consisting of an endless number of programming websites, blogs, and user forums, seems to be an almost seamless material blend between corporate Lego and its fans.

The question of how market goods come to count in this type of market exchange is moulded by a high level of negotiation between the market actors. While in this particular inter-language zone there has not been any open contestation of the exchange or threat of power imbalances, market exchanges are made 'messy' because of the high level of sharing and joint investment. As Callon (1999) observes, where parties cannot leave 'as if strangers', markets do not function as intended. The other three trading zones that we explore are contested because of *in*commensurability; in this instance it is the growing level of *commensurability* of corporate and non-corporate 'Mindstormers' with associated feelings of investment and co-ownership that may impede the trade. We witnessed commensurability in the near-endless discussions on some of the Lego Mindstorms user blogs about the most minute details of potential future Mindstorms developments, one of which culminates in the emotionally exasperated outcry of an involved fan: 'Why then does LEGO ignore our dreams?'

Discussion

In the previous section, we investigated through empirical vignettes four zones where trade between actors is contested (see Table 6.1). The trading zone concept's origin in science studies and its adoption in organizational studies (Kellogg et al. 2006) have demonstrated its potential for explaining 'trade' in many different intra- and inter-organizational contexts. We contend that by (re-)introducing trading zones as heuristic zones in a market context, the analysis of the cultural and linguistic elements of market exchanges as potential points of disruption, contention, and creativity forms a useful complement to extant market studies research focusing on the work invested in guaranteeing material continuity in exchanges. In our vignettes, to use Callon and Muniesa's (2005) words, the process of momentary detachment or objectification of the exchange object has failed and the work undertaken by market actors to organize the market exchange remains visible. By drawing our attention to these often still-visible material, cultural, and interpretative traces of exchange work, the trading zone concept allows us, in the spirit of this volume, to 'reconnect marketing to markets'. In other words, we explore the multi-dimensional and often fragile negotiations that form the basis of a market exchange. Table 6.1 provides a summary of such work in our four case illustrations.

Table 6.1. Four examples of trading zones in markets

Trading zone type	Enforced	Subversive	Fractionated	Inter-language
Example	Ryanair	Starbucks	Financial Services Authority	Lego
Cultural interaction	Minimal	High, one-way	Minimal	High, two-way
Language use	Restricted to terms of trade	Hegemonic	Interpreter	Creole
Control of interaction	Unilateral	Unilateral	Mediation qualified by socio-material practice of commission	Bilateral
Socio-technical apparatus mobilized	Rigidly structured website, airplane design, pricing structure	Retail space designed as mock 'third place'	Translation aids such as websites and brochures and forecasts using calculation and criteria approved by regulator	Interactive websites, user forums, customized hardware, network of users
'What counts'	Price emphasized as the only basis for calculation	Imposed or 'taught'—not quality or service, but 'experience'	Mediated/translated and regulated	Jointly constructed
How is incommensurability overcome?	'We're not negotiating'—not overcome, but accepted as part of the trade	'We'll show you that our way it better'—cultural muscle/submissiveness (but also resistance by fringe groups)	'I understand you both'—third party showing intimate knowledge of both worlds	'Let's do it together'—joint effort at creating shared interpretations and value

We liken the case of Ryanair to the category of enforced trading zone. Ryanair does not attempt to prepare the good for re-attachment to the buyer's world; instead, it lays out the conditions for trade and otherwise adopts a stance of 'take it or leave it'. Marketing work here concentrates on ring-fencing the terms of exchange from any attempt at negotiation or re-interpretation and on organizing the exchange in such a manner, materially and linguistically, that others encounter the least possible amount of freedom to reconfigure market practices. Starbucks approximates the category of subversive trading zone, with its marketing working by 'luring' buyers into exchanges. Then Starbucks uses its cultural resources (a carefully integrated unity of discourse, design, and practice) to replace buyers' normal practices and ways of calculating the value of the exchange with its own (Starbucks has managed to increase the price paid for a cup of coffee by 300 per cent in relation to 'comparable' goods). Starbucks' marketing practices also entail a certain amount of heavy-handed organizing with little space for counter-practices, but because marketing acts more at the level of cultural persuasion than material constraint, as in the first example, Starbucks expects reactions and anticipates some specifically.

Retail financial services in the United Kingdom proved to be a loose approximation of a fractionated trading zone. The recent review and interventions of the regulator, the FSA, indicate that once independent advisers are compelled to charge fees to their customers and undertake more extensive training and qualification, rather than earn commission from producers of financial goods and services, the fractionated model may be approximated more closely. In particular, the regulators' actions are designed to convince customers that independent advisers are free to develop and deploy their expertise, so becoming intermediaries.

Finally, in the inter-language zone of Lego Mindstorms, the object combines joint investments of buyers and sellers and becomes incapable of acting as a 'pure' market good. Marketing work here focuses simultaneously on uniting and distancing, that is, making exchanges happen *despite* the high levels of attachment to the buyer's world that the product possesses from the word go.

If the trading zone concept allows for a multi-dimensional analysis of marketing work, it has two additional qualities that may allow researchers to trace how market exchanges are organized. Collins et al. (2007) highlighted both the fractal and the vectorial qualities of the trading zone concept. Fractally, the trading zone concept allows researchers to investigate the same marketing work at different levels of 'granularity', that is, to describe practices contributing to the exchange at different loci and levels of interaction. To use Starbucks as an example, the trading zone concept can be used to describe the marketing work at headquarters in which marketers imprint materials with meaning, aiming overall to make the Starbucks style of exchange general as a cultural default for coffee houses. Similarly, anti-Starbucks activists undertake the counter-interpretative work against the corporation on websites with the aim of re-appropriating what 'coffee culture' stands for. By the same token, the trading zone concept can be used to examine if and how such marketing and anti-marketing practices are mirrored at the more fine-grained level whenever a cup of coffee is ordered in 'non-Starbuckified' language.

From a vectorial perspective, we can use the trading zone concept to trace processes in market exchanges. For instance, in countries where Starbucks has been established for some time and has proved successful in its 'subversive' work, trade may have 'settled down' into a less contested market exchange that no longer contains any visible trace of negotiation or dispute. Other versions of coffee houses may have been marginalized in a neighbourhood, which is another important process to trace and explain in socio-material, cultural, and interpretive ways. In Collins, Evans, and Gorman's words (2007), our Starbucks example may have 'fallen off' Figure 6.1 in a Westerly direction. Thus, the trading zone concept not only allows researchers to zoom in and out of local and more aggregate market exchanges but it also allows for evolution to be traced during repeated or prolonged market interactions.

Conclusion

Researchers have translated the concept of trading zone from science and technology studies and the sociology of translation to organizational studies. We argue that trading zones can usefully be applied to our growing understanding of markets in the making; of market forms and marketing practices. We see three advantages in adapting 'trading zones' into the vocabulary of market studies: (*a*) the concept helps us sort out different ways in which actors engage in and organize markets exchanges; (*b*) it draws our attention to the material, cultural, and interpretative activities of market actors as they try to understand each other's calculations and channel them into desired directions; and (*c*) the trading zone can be noisy, or at least leave audible or readable trails that can allow researchers to track some developments, such as on websites devoted to questioning a marketer's way of calculating (hence, anticipating and typifying) an exchange, and can allow others to gain some clues as to how to join the market in the making.[3]

While this chapter is intended as an introductory piece laying out the different configurations and practices in trading zones, we think that future research could investigate instances of contested market interactions empirically, at a more granular level. Research should be mindful both of the practices market actors engage in and also of how these practices betray and alter material, cultural, and interpretive configurations in the actor-world. Marketing research generally, and consumer research in particular, has explored the interpretive and emotional factors influencing individual actors in market exchanges (e.g. Bagozzi 2009). By contrast, market studies research has made impressive inroads in investigating the material dimensions of such exchanges. In this chapter, we provide a framework that allows researchers simultaneously to explore several of the relevant facets of exchange practices as well as their mobilization in acquiring power over trade counterparts.

■ NOTES

1. For an analysis on how global chains such as Starbucks have changed the coffee supply chain markets, see Ponte (2002).

2. The Mindstorms experience seems to have contributed to a sea-change in corporate culture at Lego. It has since developed the Lego Factory, where customers can order their own or other customers' home-made models and vote for those models that

should be adopted into the product line; has an extensive two-way communication process with its customer base through corporate magazines, email newsletters, blogs, forums, and design galleries; and even publishes the coveted blueprints for some of its own Legoland models.

3. A recent example of such 'noise' in the financial services industry was Ann Minch's YouTube video 'Debtor Revolt Begins Now' on how Bank of America increased her credit card interest rate to 30 per cent without any warning and calling for others to join her in the 'debtors revolt' (http://www.huffingtonpost.com/2009/09/14/debtors-revolt-woman-refu_n_285394.html).

7 Tinkering with market actors

How a business association's practices contribute to dual agency

LIV FRIES

Introduction

Business associations are interest associations for firms that operate in between markets and politics, connecting these to each other through representation, rulemaking, and information. As representatives they are part of the political system which they are often trying to influence. As an association for their members they provide an arena for collaboration and the creation of common standards. Research into business associations tacitly assumes that the business association acquires its agency by demonstrating that it represents and speaks for its members, often in political or regulatory spheres at arm's length from those firms' 'normal' industrial and marketing activities (Doner and Schneider 2000a, 2000b; Greenwood 2002; Streeck et al. 2006). Similarly, this stream of research identifies business associations with agency in the political sphere, leaving under-researched their roles in shaping the member-firm's industrial and market settings. This chapter examines the question of how business associations and their employees go about acquiring dual agency, of firms acquiring political agency alongside their industrial and marketing agency, and of business associations acquiring agency to shape their members' markets and industries alongside their activities in a political and regulatory sphere.

Callon (2007b: 139) urges us to 'give up the idea of substantive definitions of the economy and politics that can serve to distinguish between that which is economic and that which is political'. In broad terms, Callon is encouraging us to see how company managers, politicians, and regulators encounter problems and opportunities for action, which seem to be broadly to do with economics, or markets, or politics, but probably some combination. Law and Akrich (1996) investigate how people change swiftly from being market actors to being academic actors, examining how they can acquire market and academic agency in close succession; so the chapter's second question is how actors switch between forms of agency and what they can carry over between spheres.

This chapter presents and analyses the case of Almega, an industry association for the service sector in Sweden that includes in its normal activities negotiating wages, lobbying politicians, and promoting and communicating with a multitude of non-members about its members' industry and markets. Almega is a federation of seven business associations, which are co-located. Almega pools resources between its associations and organizes some common functions, including lobbying, providing information, and administrative services. Almega employs 135 people, many of whom work for more than one of its associations, or work part-time for Almega itself and part-time for one of its associations. Almega's seven associations have a combined membership of 9,200 firms, covering sixty industry or market sectors. The member firms can be grouped into three: firms offering services in relation to manufacturing, such as IT and engineering consultants; firms offering auxiliary services that companies had outsourced, including cleaning companies and employment agencies; and a large group of firms active in the recently transformed public sector in Sweden, particularly in health care, education, pharmacy, and postal services.

Almega is governed by its members, but can be understood as a distinct entity with goals of its own. It is not really part of its members' markets and industries, but its employees have considerable expertise and experience of its members' normal activities. Hence, through this case study, I begin to form an argument that industry associations, such as Almega, have or can acquire agency in their members' markets and industry, and so shape markets.

In the next section, I review theories of multiple agency and relate this to empirical research published on business associations. I then describe the research design, upon which this chapter's case study is based. In section 'Analysis', I describe the case of Almega, beginning with how it has acquired political agency and then considering its agency with respect to shaping its members' markets.

Multiple agency

Callon and Muniesa (2005) and Callon (2007a) have, in the emerging research area of market studies, developed a version of the long-standing question in science and technology studies of how actors acquire agency by being equipped with tools for calculating. Hence, agency as the capacity to act is an outcome, continually acquired and re-acquired, of joint action among humans and non-human devices (Law and Akrich 1996; Callon et al. 2002). The stream of research in market studies is in part methodological as it directs our attention to practices (Law 2005).

In later years the term *agencement* has increasingly been used in situations where 'actor network' was previously used (Miller and O'Leary 1994; Kurunmäki 2004; Callon 2007*a*, 2007*b*, 2008). *Agencement* refers to how the actor is surrounded by material as well as social actors, practices, and devices, which together create agency and uncover restrictions to actions, which in fact is quite similar to an actor network. Hence, it draws attention to agency as a collective achievement. Sets of framings can include some combination of models, theories, tools, and regulations that propose what counts. Framings also exclude other actors and factors, labelling them, provisionally, as entities which do not count or as overflows (Callon 2007*b*: 140).

In developing an economic sociology of markets, researchers have focused particularly on the performative qualities of markets (MacKenzie and Millo 2003; MacKenzie et al. 2007). Specifically in the marketing discipline, Kjellberg and Helgesson (2006) argue that many different theories, concepts, and ideas come to be performed in markets. Hence, we can expect a rich agential diversity among actors' market practices (Andersson et al. 2008). Others have shown how actors can acquire multiple agency, in which actors acquire overlapping forms of agency, which can emerge as a stabilizing effect across its entities, but can feature entities destabilizing one another (Sjögren and Helgesson 2007; Simakova and Neyland 2008).

By beginning with the performativity of agency, researchers encounter methodological consequences, such as the considerable difficulties of not knowing for sure who and what are interacting. Callon (1998*b*) argues that markets should be framed, for instance, through regulations, standards, models, and means of calculation. A part of agency involves actors in framing what is and is not relevant to their actions at a particular moment, extending to non-human devices, which both imply frames and can contribute to others' framing. For example, Goffman (1959) refers to people taking on different faces, performances, and notions of self, in anticipating others' expectations in their normal interactions. March and Olsen (2004) argue that an actor's roles imply others' expectations of those roles. Similarly, Ahrne and Brunsson (2008) argue that firms draw upon industry associations as ways of providing them with an additional identity, a collective identity like a family name.

In the literature on business associations, researchers have a strong tendency to analyse business associations as part of either the political (Doner and Schneider 2000*a*; Greenwood 2002; Streeck et al. 2006) or the market system (Fligstein 2001; Hall and Soskice 2001), underestimating the specific quality of being a part of both the political and the market sphere. Business associations develop standards, represent the industry to politicians, and provide a common arena for firms within the same industry. They have many different roles (Lenox and Nash 2003; Berk and Schneiberg 2005; Ronit 2006; Bartle and Vass 2007; Bennett and Ramsden 2007). The economics literature has concentrated on finding out whether business associations assist or impede the efficient functioning of markets (Doner and Schneider 2000*a*), while researchers in the neo-corporatist tradition started out with an assumption that trade associations are effective in contributing to the governing of the economy (Schmitter and Streeck 1981). This chapter departs from the established literature on trade associations by addressing how they influence firms' possibilities for being both political and market actors and how firms and the association itself achieve agency as actors.

Method

I conducted the case study inductively, drawing on grounded theory (Glaser and Strauss 1967). I focused on Almega for the case study because it carries out the usual actions that business associations undertake, but is particularly active in relation to its political sphere and in its members' markets and industries. This pronounced pattern of activity allows for the consideration of how, as a trade association, it goes about acquiring agency and a capacity to act in these two spheres. Given the attention paid to practices in the emerging market studies literature and to research into how actors acquire agency, I adopted an ethnographic approach. Others working in this area have also approached their field work ethnographically (Hess 2001; Knorr-Cetina 2001; Hine 2007). 'Ethnographic' is of course a broad term, and I focused in particular on how actors enacted practices, rather than examining culture or social structure (Mol 2002; Latour 2005).

At Almega, I observed the work of its lobbying department. I spent two or three days a week in the department or at Almega over a period of eight months. Almega is a federation of business associations and only some departments, including lobbying, are common to all member-associations. Furthermore, the lobbying department was also involved with two other vital departments at Almega, namely the departments of information and negotiation. Therefore, the lobbying department offered a possibility to gain an overview of the activities of Almega in respect to lobbying and shaping its members' markets and industries.

My main strategy of gathering data involved shadowing personnel (Czarniawska 2007). I followed seven lobbying specialists in their daily activities, also accompanying them to external conferences and seminars, while taking the opportunities to ask questions and have their activities briefly explained to me in addition to interviewing them. Additionally, I took part in the department's weekly meetings. My shadowing work at Almega's lobbying department allowed me to gain access to other actors and to gain insights into the different business associations within the federation. The work within the associations was mostly organized as working groups, which were led by an Almega employee and in which member firms cooperated. I followed a number of working groups for several weeks, covering lobbying, environmental policy, and groups for collaboration with authorities. I also followed project groups and meetings concerning the upcoming wage negotiations and planning groups for various events. Occasionally I was invited to attend board meetings of different associations within Almega. The shadowing, especially as it occurred in the working groups and in the weekly departmental meetings, provided some structure to my data gathering, allowing me to consider the particular activities and committees as sources of variety and comparison across my data. In effect, the different groups formed multiple sites and cases within the case (Czarniawska 2004). I also attended a board meeting, which occurred within my eight months of working within Almega. Not all the meetings included personnel from the lobbying department.

I undertook semi-structured interviews with personnel at Almega, to include: the CEOs and board members of two of Almega's members, Almega's CEO, and members of the information department. I had lunch with Almega's employees, talked with them over coffee, and hung around listening, observing, and asking questions. I was able to use any free desk in the lobbying department's office and could listen to and observe the everyday activities. I took detailed notes during the meetings and interviews and also made notes of the informal small talk in the department. I recorded some of the interviews. I analysed and coded my notes and transcripts, developing a wide range of themes. In this chapter, I consider especially instances where Almega's employees expressed opinions regarding how member firms should behave or how specific markets ought to be organized.

Analysis

ASSEMBLING THE POLITICAL ACTOR

In this section, I show that Almega has acquired political agency by encouraging its employees and members to become experts and advisers, and by using and regrouping the identities of its member associations. Almega operated at larger scale and broader scope than its member associations and the member firms. It could support the activities of secondees from its member associations and firms and also share part-time employees with the associations, developing experience and expertise especially in its lobbying and information activities.

I present an excerpt from a conversation which occurred in a lobbying meeting. The participants are representatives of large education companies that provide primary and secondary education. Their schools are privately owned and the students' fees are paid by the municipality. An executive of Almega's lobbying department organized the meeting, which was also attended by two employees of the Confederation of Swedish Enterprise, the main umbrella association for Swedish business associations of which all seven Almega federations are members. This is one of several meetings in which the companies were discussing unfavourable press generally, and how they should manage their encounters with those politicians who were critical of private schools. In the excerpt, those present are discussing what to do, who should do it, and in the name of which organization.

[Representative of Firm 1, F1]: I think we should participate in the party congresses... [Almega employee]: We should be a part of the programme in that case [not just have people handing out brochures]. It should probably be an Almega-hat on that, or maybe [the national umbrella association: CSE]. And we should have something at Almedalen [major national political event] too this summer. [F2]: Then it should perhaps be the association for private schools that is inviting? [F1]: Yes, but we [the group of companies] should provide the content. [Almega employee]: You are important actors that drive and personify the issues. [F1]: The forum is different, then it should not be the private schools nor [a company] that invites, then it will only signal that now it's time for publicity... [Almega employee]: It is important to talk about economies of scale instead of hiding behind cooperatives [who are smaller, and also preferred by some political parties]. [Employee of CSE (CSE 1)]: We are talking about it [at the CSE]. I believe that we should take on that task. [Almega employee]: It is fun with large actors—they do the work themselves. [CSE 2]: I have been talking to [the chairman of the association of private schools]. He can put their logo on [a brochure that is supposed to explain the difference between profit and dividends and why profit is necessary and good for the customer]. But he insisted that it should be this group that produces the text. [Almega employee]: We in the organization will take a look at Almedalen and at the congresses. We can stage seminars. The message will then be that economies of scale are beautiful and create quality. (Working group meeting at Almega, 4 February 2009)

In the meeting from which the verbatim account above is drawn, those present are discussing rather mundane matters. Each participant represents an organization or company and has at least one other role. During the opening round of introductions, participants mentioned that they were also a journalist, an owner, a CEO, a member of a think-tank, and a member of a political party. During the meeting, participants realized that their collective 'other' roles could be put to use later on when taking action. Those in the meeting referred to their set of other identities as entities that they could draw upon later so that they could become part of another setting.

Likewise, the organizational identities are referred to by the participants as identities or framings that can be drawn upon and used to become part of one another's setting. They are discussing using the identities of firms (large firms preferably), but they also want to draw on the legitimacy of the associations available, choosing among Almega, the national business association, and an association for Private Schools (not formally part of Almega). The meeting was organized by Almega, but it is noteworthy that the formal organization of the relationships between the firms and the different associations is subordinate to the message that the firms want to communicate. The meeting's participants used the associations as framings, which convey a message, as an additional identity.

ASSEMBLING AN ORGANIZATION TO ACHIEVE POLITICAL AGENCY

On other occasions those involved in Almega's lobbying department sought to assemble new organizations, with varying degrees of temporariness and formality, for the purpose of making communications in part by making identities. The head of lobbying at Almega described these new organizations as 'forceful devices' for communicating with politicians. An instance of creating an organization occurred among cleaning companies that at the time were part of a larger national organization, which was also a member of Almega. The cleaning companies faced a particularly significant problem in that their customers preferred to buy cleaning services illegally and so tax-free. Cleaning services had become a matter of political controversy. Some politicians argued that cleaning services should be tax-deductible, but others—notably on the left—argued that it was inappropriate to pay someone else to clean one's home and were also worried about the possibilities of exploiting a workforce that was predominantly female. After a few years of lobbying by Almega, politicians decided to make cleaning services tax deductible.

I discussed the case of cleaning services with the head of lobbying at Almega. He identified Almega's commissioning of an economic report, which showed the positive economic effects of the change in policy to making cleaning services tax deductible. He also saw the decision of Almega's executive committee to create a separate business association for the cleaning companies as being vital in making the breakthrough in political lobbying: 'It was very effective. I could bring the same person as before to a politician, but when this person was the president of the business association it was a completely different thing. Then they could listen'. Politicians were literally unable to listen until Almega and the companies formed the new organization. Previously, listening could be interpreted by any 'other' as unfair competition, so becoming unproductive or incompetent lobbying. The cleaning services industry comprised six companies, all of which seconded a board member and from the politicians' perspective this was sufficient for the group to acquire a collective identity of representing an industry.

The industry association served to demarcate those six companies, which could now present themselves as legitimate tax-paying companies, from those myriad of anonymous providers of services that were acting illegally by not including taxes in their charges. In other words, the new organization shaped the market too by introducing a framing device such that the market actors could distinguish between companies which paid taxes and those that did not. Furthermore, the new association allowed the cleaning companies to draw upon Almega's resources. Since the cleaning companies were identified as a particular group rather than being part of a larger group of companies and federations, the other federations could now act as (relatively) independent supporters instead of fellow members of the same association. They might all be part of Almega, but sometimes it was more useful to underline their separate identities. The other members had a variety of reasons for supporting the lobbying effort, but the cleaning companies could draw upon this support as a new resource in the context of Almega's lobbying activities. More generally, Almega used the experience of the cleaning services companies as a method for acquiring political agency for other companies and business associations.

THE ART OF BEING AN EXAMPLE

Lobbying required that some firms, or representatives of firms, took on the new role of being a representative. When members first encountered the question of lobbying, they typically sought to persuade members of Almega's lobbying department that they should write and collectively sign an article about the issue and try to get it published as a 'comment' article in an important national newspaper, or that Almega should undertake its lobbying activities by seeking to 'educate' journalists. If only the public and politicians could learn about their particular industry, problems could be solved quite easily, their argument went. An employee of Almega commented:

I don't believe in 'comment' articles, they are more for the members themselves, they want to see some action and then they think the question is solved .... What really counts is when other people, outside of the organization, start saying things I have been talking about in seminars and reports, and in meetings with politicians.

Another employee of Almega supported this: 'It is closer at hand for many— especially smaller—companies to think like business people and apply a marketing idea; that it is only about saying what is good about the product and how much better it is than others'.

For some members, Almega's work was in coordinating companies' strategies. For other companies, Almega's lobbying work was a completely new experience. Larger companies had plenty of experience in interacting with politicians, but smaller and newer companies tended not to have this accumulated experience. Some members were unaware that Almega could influence rules and laws, but acting politically requires know-how and Almega offers such know-how to its members. Almega employees were aware that they often had to teach members new ways of acting, and especially talking. Often, Almega's employees met with politicians and brought representatives of firms with them. Almega's employees then worked in the background as advisers, arranging further meetings and working with the members to prepare content for discussion. Almega employees advised their members that when meeting politicians they should try and represent their industry, to underscore a role of being a representative and also draw on experiences from their own company as examples. This way of acting was a contrast to a 'marketing' way of thinking and acting. It involved representatives of firms suppressing their market identity and acquiring the new one of being a representative of the industry. Representatives of firms could acquire greater legitimacy in the eyes of politicians than the employees of an industry association, but only by very clearly playing down their market identity as firms, putting this aside in favour of an industry identity.

An Almega employee recalled a member who was particularly good at bringing out different versions of himself when representing. He had said: 'So who do you want me to be today; the owner, the burdened small enterprise, or the expert in public procurement?' This was a CEO of a small company who had been working with the business association for several years. He had acquired experience of handling public purchases and was often invited to make presentations. He presented various aspects of himself and adapted his story to the role that he was taking on at that moment, to the audience. His skill was unusual and he appreciated that transforming oneself into an example was an art. Most members of Almega required more guidance.

KNOW-HOW OF PROCESSES AND NORMS

In addition to providing its members with a model for acting politically by demonstrating a capacity for representing, or being represented by, others, Almega also provided advice in taking the political system into account, for instance, when a group of companies wanted to approach a minister. Whereas the firms' representatives wanted to write a letter to the minister, the Almega employee advised them to wait. He knew that a letter would become public due to the Swedish law on access to public records. The episode occurred towards the end of a period of negotiation, which parties regarded as being sensitive. Letters that would be available publicly would have the effect of making compromises difficult, of hindering the flexibility of parties to nego-tiate and make concessions. Instead, the Almega employee sent an email to the minister, suggesting a meeting and indicating that the companies might have some views that they could perhaps share. The Almega employee timed the email well and the minister agreed to a meeting.

The Almega employee had familiarity with the formal routines and proce-dures. In addition, the employee displayed an understanding of politicians' agendas, placed in the context of the norms of the different political parties. Returning to our discussion of the meeting involving Almega employees and representatives of the private schools (at the start of this section of the chapter, above), a recurrent theme was understanding the strategies of poli-ticians and the routines and norms of political parties. Sometimes, the group invited consultants working for 'friendly' politicians to talk about current policies and alliances concerning education policy. Those in the group who represented schools found it amusing that members of the Green Party would seek to meet Almega in pairs, one male and one female, and travel by train or bus. Additionally, a particular member of the Social Democratic party was often very influential in policies that the schools were interested in, even though this person had now moved to a different area of policy. Despite the person's continued influence, all committee members agreed that they could not approach this politician formally due to a convention whereby a former office holder would leave the ground clear for his or her successor. Hence, the politician was unlikely to make public comments in an area of former responsibility.

ACQUIRING POLITICAL AGENCY

In summary, I have shown four ways in which Almega employees work with their member associations and with the companies that are members of these associations by: assembling political actors, creating entirely new actors, affording members the ability to shift identities, and acquiring and offering members know-how of processes and norms in the political sphere. The immediate focus of these collaborations, and I have concentrated on Almega's lobbying department in this section, has been to allow companies to re-frame their corporate, market, and industry identities in ways that are consistent with the political sphere. Almega has equipped its member-firms with ways of shaping their markets and industries. In particular, the member-firms seemed initially to require clear representations of their markets and industries, and then some guidance about ways of acting on these by political means.

Taking on the role of being a market actor

While acting politically, Almega also prepares and performs many descriptions and representation of its members' markets, as good as any statistics or diagrams. Kjellberg and Helgesson (2006) argue that markets are continuously recreated through the interaction of exchange, normative, and representational practices. Almega's representations of its members' markets required some practical theory of how the members liked to see their own settings given their identities as market actors, but in ways compatible with politicians' understandings.

AN ASSOCIATION IS NOT A FIRM, SO CAN IT BE A MARKET?

Almega's employees occasionally acted as spokespersons for markets, voicing claims about what actions and policies would be good for a market considered as a whole. Members rarely agree on a representation of the market; after all they are market actors with subjective positions in and perspectives on 'their' market. In one instance of health care, Almega's head of lobbying tried to convince the members that one kind of solution in a market was preferable: 'I told them to think of future members.' Our discussion continued:

[LF] But it wasn't for you to make that choice, was it? It must have been the politicians and the members?

[AHL] No, it was really hard. But finally the board made the choice of actually pursuing the [voucher solution]. And the firms are not doing that from a citizen's perspective, but because it will be more like an ordinary market. In a voucher market, those with happy customers survive. In a [market based on contracts] political preferences and other things play a huge part and not necessarily those who perform best.

While the members made the decision, Almega's head of lobbying argued in great detail for the system of a market based on vouchers to be used by those seeking health care directly, with the providers being remunerated by the state. The alternative was a tendering process in which some providers were awarded contracts over certain durations by the state. Almega's head of lobbying thought that his argument was persuasive as he could represent a system of vouchers as being more market-like. He could also draw on the experiences of comparable systems that were operating in neighbouring countries. His projection of a future was important too. A tendering and contracting system put the market as a form of social and economic organizing at risk, meaning that many firms could be 'locked-out' and would then leave. A voucher system would be more competitive, in terms of giving more firms more opportunities to join in the market at any time. Competition in the market was also aligned with politicians' perspectives. Generally, vouchers were consistent with a 'better' market.

Almega's employees are not obviously acting on behalf of their members when depicting a version of a market. Rather, they are persuading their members of a course of action and directing the development of a market towards having a particular form in the future. Almega has the capacity of making a market 'visible' and can also show how a market comprises the interdependent decisions and interactions of those actors that participate in the market. By interpreting and representing the market to its members, Almega also acquires agency for itself in relation to its members.

MEMBERS DEVELOP NEW MODELS OF BEING MARKET ACTORS

Many of Almega's members were active in businesses that historically had been publically operated, such as health care and education. We have seen above that politicians were uncertain as to what kinds of markets they wanted and were still involved in shaping the markets at arm's length, for instance, in considering whether firms in the market should compete through tendering or through vouchers. But, perhaps surprisingly, some of Almega's members, which are of course companies, were also unclear as to what it meant to be a market actor. A board member of the association for health care, part of the Almega federation, explained that she, like many of her colleagues, began her career in the public sector. She valued the ideals of professional nursing highly and she wanted to learn from her association what being a market actor meant and entailed. I observed a meeting in which she was a participant along with representatives of the association for Swedish municipalities, Almega, municipalities' procurement activities, and member companies. She sometimes said things that were not typical of business associations, such as claiming that collective bargaining over employment contracts and wages was the most important issue. The Almega employee discreetly shook his head at this point as this was not the association's official view.

From the perspective of the association of health care, those members for whom she spoke were not trained in economics and finance. Indeed, she felt a little alienated by the idea of business and, politically, its right wing connotations. At the same time, she thought it important that the members of the association of health care (companies), and the association itself, should develop identities as market actors. She suggested that her association hired an economist or accountant to provide practical advice to members, a suggestion that the other board members rejected. Another board member agreed with her description of the member companies and the association for health care: 'most care-givers see themselves as care-givers primarily and not businessmen. But growth demands a business mind set.'

TELLING OTHERS ABOUT MARKETS, CREATING STORIES

The market making and shaping activities of Almega and its member associations and firms took place against the backdrop of a broadly encompassing story and Almega's lobbying department was involved in creating a coherent storyline for all Almega's activities. I became aware of the storyline when I participated in a weekly meeting of the lobbying department in autumn 2008, at which the financial crisis was on the agenda. The director spoke about how members and employees should talk publicly about the crisis and its consequences for Sweden's service sector, indicating that they could depict the crisis as a structural transition from manufacturing to services. Such an account should, however, be qualified to take into account the gravity of the crisis. The meetings' participants were familiar with the line of argument, as an Almega employee later explained:

One has to find a framing story that can work. In this case, the Social Democrats have historically been good at managing structural transitions, they are good at embracing change. One has to be flexible in relation to politicians and this should work for them. ... We are contrasting the service society to the industrial society, saying that old solutions won't do anymore, they are structures from another time. Old cogs won't go with new gears. We have tried the story and it works. It is good too for other areas [Almega's member associations, negotiations with trade unions]. Rhetorically, it works well. There is contrast, hope and analysis behind it.

In another discussion, the head of lobbying said that he had started working on the storyline a few years ago. He wanted to create a common image that everyone could use. When he presented the story for the first time to politicians he showed them a classic picture of a factory with smoke coming out of chimneys. He followed this with another picture of a small cottage on an island to represent the new service society. The storyline was elaborated and refined regularly thereafter. In summer 2008, Almega deployed a slogan: 'We don't want to change the model—we just want to sharpen it'. 'The model' refers to 'the Swedish model'; the long-established way of organizing labour markets. During 2008 and 2009, Almega's lobbying and information departments and a consultant worked on how they should represent the service sector but could not develop a suitable image or picture. In one meeting, the consultant said that they considered dropping the term 'service' as it seemed to evoke fairly simple tasks such as laundry and juxtaposition to manufacturing. The working group developed an image of 'competitiveness' in markets for services during my period of study. Almega's information department often received calls from journalists, seeking a person or firm that could illustrate an item of news, and the employees were often looking out for people and stories that could be used in contact with media and politicians to broaden the view of what the service sector was, or what it needed. In autumn 2008, I accompanied one of the employees to a presentation concerning an academic book on markets. She hoped to hear some good stories, but ended up trying to enforce Almega's view. During the seminar she asked the authors why they had not written about companies within the service sector? Why was the service sector so invisible in their account of markets? She complained later that politicians and researchers alike often did not associate innovations with services: 'It is always about some Japanese robot. They need better examples.'

MAKING OTHERS FIND OUT WHAT THE MARKET ACTORS IN SERVICES ARE FOR

Almega attempted to convince politicians and others outside the markets that their stories were compelling. Almega employees tried to undertake this activity subtly by concentrating on the societal benefits of their members' markets. One means of persuasion was in writing pamphlets for publication to include the analysis and presentation of economic data. In the discussions about the negative public opinions concerning private schools, participants recognized as a vital question that of how the firms could convincingly argue that profits and market solutions went hand in hand with an effective education system, which benefited society. Politicians of the left wanted to prevent private schools from making profits but did not want to abolish the market entirely. The politicians of the left were interested in a the market's capacities in engendering competition that would remove companies' profits. At the same time those working with and in companies were actors in markets because they envisaged the prospect of profits. The following exchange brings into close relief different understandings of profits among the private schools:

[Manager, Firm 1]: We have to make a distinction between the notions of dividends and profit. We do not have to distribute dividends but we must make profits.

[Almega employee]: To restrict dividends would also be detrimental; just think of the investors.

[Manager, Firm 2]: Parents want the school to have a sound finances, but they don't like the idea of profits.

[Manager, Firm 1]: Today there is a fine imposed on schools with poor financial positions. Would it be better if schools were bad and unprofitable?

In addition to developing representations of what markets are like for politicians and for consumers, Almega also became involved in presenting versions of markets to other companies that were in business-to-business relationships with Almega's members. One might expect that this would be unnecessary because the buyers are themselves companies and so are also market actors. But Almega's question involved making space for a new market. Sweden's law on public procurement regulated how the majority of members' services were purchased. Many members did all their work with public agencies or directly with the state and others included the public sector as a significant client. Almega employed an expert in public procurement law and, while companies called for advice, so did the municipalities, public agencies, politicians, and agencies for purchasing companies. During 2009, Almega's expert in procurement travelled widely as the law on procurement had changed and he was invited to advise on these changes:

I usually tell them [public agencies] what the law [on the voucher system] means. I provide them with knowledge and information. Then it is the arguments: Why should one buy services rather than produce them? I give a few arguments for that, some-times tell them about the [national economic] growth argument, other audiences do not need that... When I talk to firms I usually don't have to sell the idea of public markets [markets in former public sectors]. But in certain groups I meet traditional companies, small sub-suppliers, middle-aged lads. They don't get this, they are not part of it. They don't sell to the public sector, still they are an important target group. They are strong business representatives locally. They are not against private service companies but they need to learn. They can be strong spokespersons since they are all members of important local organizations. They need to be able to explain why we need other kinds of companies in our municipality, not only middle-aged gentlemen.

The verbatim account above illustrates a trick with roles and identities. Almega's employee wanted members of the established industry to argue in favour of the emerging new industry, focusing on the new 'public markets'.

Almega's expert in public procurement was in demand to such an extent because buyers and sellers active in the new public markets were uncertain as to how to interpret Sweden's procurement legislation, itself within the context of the EU's law on procurement. A contentious part of the legislation was the strict clause of 'no contact', which led to situations in which public buyers and the companies had very little interaction and so could not really get to know one another. Buyers and sellers can, however, make contact with one another before and after tendering and contracting processes. An Almega employee tried to address how companies worked with the clause of 'no contact' by arranging meetings between firms and their public purchasers at local and national levels. He wanted both parties to discuss questions such as the requirements to be included in tender documents and to promote an under-standing of the terms of business relationships generally. Some municipalities had little understanding of how their potential supplier companies worked and particularly of why some of their conditions and requirements made it impossible for smaller companies to participate in tendering processes.

SUMMARY: ENHANCING REFLEXIVITY IN MARKETS

The examples set out in this section illustrate how Almega's employees helped enhance the reflexive capacity of their members' markets. Almega enhanced the capacities of its members to reflect about what it meant for them to be market actors and to acquire agency by being market actors. New members had opportunities to learn from other members about what it meant to be an entrepreneur rather than, for instance, a professional nurse. Firms were reminded that they had to make sure that the market remained competitive— because it was good for the market as a whole, and for preventing politicians from interfering. Further, Almega employees could use their identities as outsiders and as non-market actors to speak on behalf of their members' markets, using the role as spokesperson in part to make members aware of how their actions and interactions shaped their markets. Finally, Almega employees devoted considerable energies into creating a story in order to contrast what was currently in a market with what could be.

Discussion: Almega's capacity to shift between agencies

In the previous two sections, I have presented illustrations of how Almega acquired political agency, promoting some of this capacity among its members, and then of how it acquired market agency, again promoting some of this among its members. Analytically, this chapter set out to examine how an actor can acquire multiple agencies, with the multiplicity implying that an actor could and should be able to shift between its forms of agency.

Callon's uses of *agencement* (2007*a*, 2007*b*, 2008) in place of agency draws on Deleuze and Guattari (2004) and refers to a network or arrangement of actors, practices, and devices, which are stabilized temporarily (Miller and O'Leary 1994; Kurunmäki 2004). Hence, if actors have agency, they have acquired it through a combination of framings and also exclusions of entities. The spheres of markets and politics, as depicted in this chapter, exhibit the characteristics of *agencement*, of interlinked networks. Actors, as an association or a representative carrying an appropriate label of association together with appropriate behaviour, create temporary *agencements* that provide enough stability to be perceived as an actor and enough coherence to have agency. *Agencement* is the act of organizing different elements into an order. The actions within the business association put frames, individuals, and organizations to work and make them become actors with agency.

In order for firms to become political actors, their personnel need to know how to act within the political sphere. Almega, as an organization with an identity that is distinct from its member firms and member associations, is capable of articulating representations of its members' markets. The representations help create agency because politicians can recognize the member firms and Almega's association as a political actor in a political network or *agencement*. Furthermore, it is able to use its representation of the market to assist in its members' attempts to acquire market agency, by helping them consider new ways of negotiated actions and activities that can change the shape of their market.

This chapter presents a new view of business associations, thereby contributing to that stream of empirical research. Almega makes markets, industries, and political norms visible and does so by means of its employees' practices and the different resources such as roles, people, stories, associations, and different ways of combining them. Almega's employees made use of Almega's 'decided order', by which I mean the formal rules that distinguish between the different associations, and make the different associations formally different from each other, even though they might have different members (March 1988; Seidl 2005; Ahrne and Brunsson 2008). Still, it seems as if the formal boundaries are far from impermeable. In fact, it is the messiness of who belongs to which association or who works for whom that is often put to use, and the ability of the different organizational forms of Almega and its associations that makes it useful for its members, in particular, in the contacts with politicians and media. Almega employees or the logos of the various associations could be present or be absent from a particular scene or brochure, either leading meetings or leaving meetings to the member associations and companies. And this careful staging of being present or not draws attention to the dependencies and connections between the various *agencements* that were crucial to Almega's activities in representing and shaping markets: the Almega federation in all its parts, different representations of markets developed specifically for lobbying questions, and the material arrangements and normal practices of the member companies' markets.

Barry and Slater (2002) and Callon et al. (2007) encourage researchers to examine how technologies can create calculative agency. Almega, as an *agencement*, created multiple representations of market actors, thereby making them visible and calculable to politicians, providing some view of processes, of likely outcomes. Almega's members could also draw upon the representations in order to calculate their activities as market actors and to understand how other actors—firms and politicians—can influence them. In all these instances, actors are drawing upon representations as part of their activities, making the representations performative.

Almega, through its connections and scope, performs a critical role in acquiring agency for itself and those it works with. Almega is the space within which the ordering of things—the combination of actor, label, organization, and formulation of the issue at hand—takes place, which results in different framings of possible actors. Andersson et al. (2008) show how a physical technology, an online purchasing system, comprised in part some predetermined binary actions. Almega's actions were not predetermined so precisely, with there being a myriad of possible actions. But the relations between actors, including the association, the firms, the employees, bring out the possibilities for making representations of markets. Almega devoted considerable efforts to configuring not only those organizations close at hand but non-member firms, firms of the future, politicians, and its members' buyers. Like Simakova and Neyland's (2008) study of a marketing department, Almega developed a number of compelling stories by which it sought to arrange and represent its constituents in an *agencement*. In the case of Almega the compelling stories had to do with framings of the questions it was engaged in with its members, such as why a municipality should buy rather than produce services, or why private schools should be allowed to be profitable. What is interesting though is that Almega not only engaged in the framing of a question through language but also constructed macro actors. Furthermore, Almega's employees identified different actors to convince, as with the industry members that were not part of the service sector, but none the less good spokespersons for it. These 'other actors' or potential allies became part of a new *agencement* that consisted of stories, actors, and organizations.

Conclusion

In this chapter, I have shown how a business association can conceive of itself as a locus of *agencements* that helps its member-firms, politicians, and itself shift agency, especially between the interdependent spheres of the political and the market. The interactions between the firms, the association's employees, and the association assist in enhancing the reflexive capacities of actors as well as in pulling together appropriate representations of markets and market actors so that it can be visible in the market and political spheres. What does the case study say about markets and marketing?

For one, politics and markets are intertwined (Callon 2007*b*). The way actors seek to design or format markets has political consequences, and firms act both as profit-making organizations and as part of a community. The case indicates how the political sphere differs from the market sphere, which is made clearer as firms learn to recreate the differences between the two spheres and re-enact their differences. To adapt to the political sphere, they have to play down certain aspects, like making profits, and bring out others, like competing. The market as a political actor is a framing of a market, one of many aspects of it. Callon (Ibid.) argues that markets can be singled out and objectified in ways comparable to the singularizing of products, and business associations can be of use in this process.

Second, the framing activities of the actors considered in this chapter's case study are part of what can be understood as marketing. Marketing is usually focused on, or in some way 'about' customers. Lobbying could be perceived of as another attempt at marketing, but in relation to politicians rather than customers. In order for this to work we saw that firms needed to stop 'applying a marketing idea', identifying themselves with being actors in their market, and adopt a way of presenting themselves that politicians and regulators found to be acceptable. Within marketing research it is common knowledge that successful marketing is carried out differently in different situations. Marketers pursue different programmes and the internal balance between these programmes might vary. The need for business associations to develop and adopt particular business models and marketing techniques may be more or less important in different industries and especially at different stages in the development of a market. Within Almega, the firms that were active within the former public sector were particularly engaged in lobbying activities, while firms within the construction industry tended to engage in discussions with other associations of firms within their industry, rather than with politicians. That the intensity of activities varies according to the current time can also be seen in other countries and cases (Granovetter and McGuire 1998; Fligstein 2001; Berk and Schneiberg 2005).

Third, this chapter shows how the business association's activities especially contribute to the creation of reflexivity in the market among other market actors (Andersson et al. 2008). Representation allows actors to ascribe properties to situations, themselves, and others. In business associations like Almega, actors are both constructed and represented given their identities relative to their markets. As a result, firms become more competent in discussing the ways in which their markets are regulated, and the ways in which their markets result from their combined actions. Callon (2009: 541) asks for more interaction between those who provide models for the organizing of markets, including academics and regulators, and those who meet the problems and overflows that certain framings entail. This seems to be exactly what the employees of Almega strived for, while addressing legislators and sellers rather than the theorists behind the markets' laws and rules. Politicians and buyers were reluctantative of to discuss the shaping of markets with firms, but agreed to discussions with the association, which seemed less threatening, and unambiguously representative of a collective interest.

In this chapter's Introduction I quoted Callon's claim that there are no substantial differences between that which is economic and that which is political (Callon 2007*b*). This chapter has shown the amount and the character of work that goes into uniting political demands and values, societal demands and market ideals, framings of actors, and their possibilities for action. There might not be any substantial differences, but actors do create differences between the political and the economic, and re-enact differences in behaviours.

It has also shown the need for firms to frame themselves as actors of different kinds in order to be able to achieve agency in the political world, but also how the association works to make a particular market possible, through ensuring collaboration with firms in other industries, politicians, public officers, and so on. The role of the association seems to be to link together and create new *agencements*, which make both political and market agency possible for member firms.

8 The unexpected effects of gas market liberalization

Inherited devices and new practices

THOMAS REVERDY

Introduction

The liberalization of the gas market in Europe was intended to establish competition between suppliers and create a European wholesale gas market with large numbers of transparent transactions taking place between producers and suppliers. It was also expected that the spot market would fix a price for gas and that this price would become a reference for all transactions, as is the case for other commodities like crude oil. Finally, the gas market was intended to support the development of hedging against price fluctuations.

The actual gas market is still very different from these expectations. First, regulatory tariffs have been maintained and many industrial customers have not opted for the free market. Secondly, the prevalence of long-term contracts between major producers (from Russia, Norway, or Algeria) and existing suppliers hinders the development of a large and transparent gas marketplace. Competition is limited to incumbent suppliers. The gas spot market and the gas price index are not recognized as a reference for all transactions. Because of the long-term contracts, the price of gas is indexed to the oil price. Inherited practices and devices like regulated tariffs, long-term contracts, and the oil index coexist with new practices and devices encouraged by liberalization, like calls for tender and indexed gas contracts, creating a confusing context for industrial customers.

The ongoing transition of the gas market offers a good opportunity for studying change dynamics in market practices. For instance: how do market actors make sense of this changing context, anticipate how it will evolve, evaluate its risks, define new offers, calculate, and choose between offers, etc.? Because of the liberalization, industrial customers have to manage new issues like forecasting consumption and gas prices variations, while suppliers have to adjust marketing and sales practices and define new offers and contracts combining the physical supply with financial services. New types of actors have also entered the market: consultants promote new purchasing practices such as calls for tender; bank analysts offer financial services and provide information about anticipated prices and market structure. Through their various practices, all these actors contribute to shaping the gas market.

This chapter investigates how market actors develop new practices on the basis of inherited and novel 'market devices' (Callon et al. 2007). My starting point is to regard market transitions, like the one following the deregulation of the gas market, as processes of socio-technical change. I argue that an important part of this process is the development of new practices employing 'market devices', which work as cognitive prostheses for market activities. Effectively, in this case, purchasers, marketers, salespeople, and consultants shape the market by combining inherited devices, such as long-term contracts and the oil index, and new practices such as benchmarking, price anticipation, hedging, etc. In this process, market devices, such as the 'price index' (Caliskan 2007), reduce uncertainty and support suppliers' offers and purchasers' calculations (Callon and Muniesa 2005).

More specifically, I investigate the ambivalent status of market devices in calculation and transaction practices when their relevance is questioned. In most markets, and most of the time, established market devices work as 'black boxes' (Latour 1991); they are taken for granted and employed by the actors without questioning. This 'black boxing' occurs when actors accept that the devices simplify the complicated and confusing context in which they must act. However, in a transition situation, 'black boxes' may be 'reopened'; their relevance and reliability may be questioned if they no longer seem to fulfil their initial promise. Major regulatory change, such as liberalization, can weaken inherited market devices and promote the adoption of better-adapted devices. Thus, in the gas market, both new and inherited market devices are being questioned: are new contracts more restrictive than regulated tariffs? Is the oil index a relevant reference for purchasing gas? And so on.

As a consequence, the envisaged effects of regulatory change do not occur immediately: there is a transition. During this transition, some inherited market devices remain in use although their fundamentals may become more and more precarious. As these market devices support established practices, it is difficult to abandon them. At the same time, new market devices are not immediately employed because they have yet to prove their relevance. During transition, the relevance of market devices, that is, their capacity to reduce uncertainty and support calculation without disregarding market fundamentals, becomes a major issue for market actors.

On the basis of my empirical study, three important observations can be made concerning the role of market devices in selling and purchasing practices, and by extension, in market transitions. First, the relative stability of inherited market devices can prolong such transitions, or produce other results than those expected at the outset. Secondly, market transitions imply learning processes for market actors, who evaluate the relevance of inherited and new market devices for the practices they engage in. Thirdly, the weakening of certain market devices during market transitions may introduce asymmetries in calculative capacities which affect power relations in the market; for example, customers may become more dependent on suppliers or consultants who have been better equipped to deal with uncertainties linked to the new market situation.

The next section presents my analytic frame for studying market transitions as socio-technical changes. The following two sections provide an introduction to gas market practices and describe how the empirical material was collected. I then present my results concerning five issues: how liberalization introduced new forecasting and monitoring practices; how new devices affected the formation of prices; how suppliers and consultants compete to organize market competition; how calculation practices developed around price uncertainty; and how use of the oil index became controversial. I end the chapter with a discussion of the stability of inherited market devices during market transitions.

The development of transaction practices in a context of liberalization

This section establishes an analytic frame for studying market transitions as socio-technical changes in which actors' attitudes towards and uses of market devices is central. 'Liberalization' (or, more accurately, 'reregulation') is an ongoing process where new regulations are tested, implemented, evaluated, negotiated, etc. (Crew and Kleindorfer 2002). In this context, transmission and distribution networks for gas can be conceived as 'natural monopolies'. In other words, it is not justifiable for each competitor to have its own network; all competitors should share the same infrastructure. The aim of regulation is then to organize competition within this infrastructure. Furthermore, incumbent suppliers possess equipment, networks, long-term contracts, and so on which disadvantage newcomers. The regulation should thus balance the market power of incumbent suppliers and new entrants so that competition is enabled. Indeed, a 'liberalized' market can be far more complex and tightly regulated than a public monopoly.

Market transition is not the result of regulatory change alone; it also stems from endogenous market processes involving marketing and purchasing practices (Kjellberg and Helgesson 2007a). As argued by Araujo et al. (2008: 8):

'markets are in constant evolution both in terms of the practices that shape them as well as the forms they assume as a result.' Historic analyses of gas market reorganization suggest that it relies not only on regulatory change but also on strategic appropriations by producers and purchasers, maintaining inherited arrangements and abandoning them when important structural changes occur (Stern 1997; Wilson 1997; Kjärstad and Johnsson 2007). The market transition triggered by liberalization would thus seem to offer a suitable context for studying multiple and often conflicting efforts to shape markets, to which buyers, sellers, regulators, consultants, and others contribute by producing new devices and defining new practices. This process is further likely to include 'efforts to shape markets as well as efforts to operate in markets qua structures and the intended and unintended interactions between these practices' (Araujo et al. 2008: 8). As liberalization is a multi-actor process, studying it requires overcoming the 'distinction between market-making practices—defined as activities that shape the overall market structure—and marketing practices—defined as firm-based activities aimed at developing an actor's position within a structure' (ibid.).

The perspective adopted here strives to be symmetrical, that is, it looks at activities undertaken by both buyers and sellers. When analysing a transition towards a 'liberalized market', characterized by complexity and continuous experimentation, the purchasing side must be considered in its own right (Kotler and Levy 1973; Caldwell et al. 2005). Demand is far from being constructed, restricted, and marked out by supply or prescription alone. In particular, the way in which purchasers are able to understand different supply and pricing solutions, how they evaluate these (Juliusson et al. 2007), and how they anticipate market developments, are of central import to the transition.

In this respect, one of the most interesting aspects of the socio-technical approach to markets (Callon 1998) is the possibility it offers to study the distribution of calculative capacities in markets. According to this approach, market practices are intimately linked to market devices, that is to material and discursive assemblages (Callon and Muniesa 2005). These devices become intertwined with human actors in economic *agencements* that have certain capacities to act, for example to produce prices. Depending on the constitution of these *agencements*, their calculative capacities will differ. Thus, market devices play an important role in producing calculative capacity. If a market device is detached from a specific economic *agencement*, its calculative capacity is likely to be affected. This suggests that actors' adoption or rejection of specific market devices is a key issue in market shaping. This becomes particularly relevant in the context of liberalization, which is often legitimized in the name of the customer who is supposed to benefit from more offers and lower prices produced by competition amongst suppliers. But the level of supplier competition also depends on the ability of these customers to influence competition through their purchasing practices (Caldwell et al.

2005). This ability, in turn, depends on their calculative capacities, which are intimately linked to the market devices they employ.

Economic theory suggests that a market can be more efficient than a public monopoly. In terms of economic sociology, this implies that distributed cognition (Hutchins 1995) between market agencies, including purchasers, suppliers, regulators, and the market devices they employ is more efficient than a more bureaucratic and centralized organization. Given the complexity of a reregulated market, purchasers have to be equipped with calculative capacities to match the level of market complexity. The question is whether purchasers have enough autonomy and are sufficiently independent of suppliers to be able to play their role and shape competition between suppliers. Their independence, their skills, and their access to market devices and information will determine their ability to calculate, that is, to interpret physical and financial gas markets and to act in these markets.

An introduction to gas market practices

The supply of gas to an industrial customer is based on the following principles: the industrial customer purchases an anticipated volume of gas for the following year (sometimes for the following two years). The suppliers need a defined volume in order to check that the overall volume of gas they sell matches the volume contracted with gas producers. Suppliers also have to book transmission capacities. This means that contracts between suppliers and industrial customers are always defined on an annual basis. To avoid penalties, industrial customers have to abide by the consumption volumes defined in the contract. A second difficulty concerns the definition of price in the contract: the price of gas varies over time, which means that the industrial customer is confronted with a price risk. This price risk can be managed through fixed or indexed prices or by using financial instruments such as oil price hedging (Levy 1994).

Taking an in-depth look at purchasers' calculative practices (Callon and Muniesa 2005) helps us to understand how they build their sourcing and price control strategies and how they assess what is on offer. A distinction can be made between two levels of action: first, there is the type of transaction adopted (e.g. regulated tariff or eligibility, fixed or indexed price, prices indexed to the gas or oil markets), and secondly, within the chosen type of transaction, there is the way in which the different offers put forward by the various suppliers are ranked.

The first action involves technical and financial uncertainties that are difficult to evaluate and quantify. It therefore requires understanding and interpreting the way the gas market works and evolves (e.g. marketplace, long-term contracts) and the implications of this for a business (e.g. supply risks, price fluctuations). Purchasing strategies can be divided into several types: regular consultation, call for tender, or membership of a purchasing consortium. Several types of contracts are possible; e.g. fixed-price contracts (one or two years), contracts indexed to the gas market price, to the oil market, or even based on regulated tariffs, and contracts where it is possible to 'fix' part of the indexed price in order to seize upon a market opportunity.

The second level of action operates in a more structured way and has more to do with optimization of purchasing parameters: comparing similar offers, choosing the date when fixing the price, etc. The two types of action do not necessarily occur sequentially: purchasers will drift from one level to the other to compare product offerings. Many actors test each form of transaction before opting for one or a mix of them.

A note on method: collecting market practices and market devices

The empirical study behind this chapter is based primarily on interviews with salespeople, energy purchasers, and energy managers (sixty interviews in all). In-depth semi-structured interviews were carried out. In the first part of the enquiry, interviews with salespeople helped to establish an overall picture of purchasers' practices. The salespeople described the background of the purchasing practices employed by their industrial customers. They proved to be very familiar with many purchasers' practices, such as calls for tender, information seeking, financial decisions, etc., because they are directly affected by these activities. However, due to the nature of their business relationship, some purchasing activities remained hidden to them; for example, the exchange of information with alternative suppliers, or the purchasers' real motivations.

This is why I conducted in-depth semi-structured interviews with industrial purchasers and technical managers about their activities, what is at stake for them, how they develop their role, and perceive services and salespeople's attitudes. The energy purchasers interviewed had two to six years' experience of the gas market. The interviews, which lasted between 1½ and 3 hours, were recorded and transcribed verbatim to keep a complete record of the arguments put forward by the interviewees.

Interviews are an excellent means of establishing how purchasers justify the practices they engage in. However, this method is not usually considered the best way to investigate the practices themselves. To this end, the interviews with the salespeople proved to be helpful. With the salespeople, I was able to draw up a list of events, decisions, and problems facing their customers, which revealed many practices that purchasers engaged in. Subsequently, the customers were asked to evaluate their business relationship, to express views about service and product supplies, and also to justify these views. They described concrete situations where, for example, they found a salesperson helpful or unhelpful. The interviews also revealed their doubts about particular practices and the difficulties they have explaining their choices to their managers. These interviews did not allow me to understand all the practices in detail: direct observation, for instance, might have helped in developing a more comprehensive picture of practices. However, the in-depth discussions about specific events, including crisis situations, did reveal the conditions and resources of their day-to-day activities.

The purchasing practice background of each industrial customer was reconstructed with the salesperson by considering events, outside influences but also their own learning. An attempt was made to trace the skills of those involved in these new activities and their training in energy purchasing; changes in their purchasing practices; the reasons behind these changes: significant events, influential messages, experience, etc. Apart from carrying out interviews, the research also involved studying marketing and institutional documents, publications from the French Energy Regulation Commission, and communications by industrial associations.

The following sections present different examples of competition between alternative transaction frameworks. The first relates to the transition from regulated tariffs to free market transactions. The focus here will be on new requirements in terms of forecasting and monitoring. The following sections look into price definition, competition, and risk management, which have become vital issues for industrial purchasers.

New forecasting and monitoring practices

In France, the gas market was opened up in several phases between 2000 and 2004. Since July 2004, all non-residential customers have become eligible, that is, legally empowered, to purchase their gas and electricity on a competitive market. The liberalization process has created a transitory situation where customers are encouraged to abandon existing, regulated contracts and adopt new, free market contracts.

COEXISTENCE OF REGULATED TARIFFS AND NEW OFFERS

Rules governing market operation and network access have been defined allowing competition to develop despite the existence of a monopoly on transmission. At the request of industrial customers, however, the state has maintained regulated tariffs, delivered only by the incumbent suppliers. The state's regulatory action has therefore led to the coexistence of two different forms of transaction: the regulated tariff and competitive offers (made by both incumbents and other suppliers). The question to be explored is how the transition from the former to the latter has been made.

The incumbents have developed their sales operations so as to facilitate their customers' transition. They have tried to develop their supply in other countries, either by buying out existing suppliers or by investing in their sales activities. In the early years (2000–4), the market supply was (with a few exceptions) cheaper than the regulated tariff. The state, professional bodies, and alternative suppliers strongly encouraged the 'exercise of eligibility' through extensive communications. A large number of customers switched from the regulated price to the market offer, in many cases staying with the incumbent supplier because its price was the most attractive. Still, a certain amount of competition appears to have been created since alternative suppliers have gained a significant market share. Most major European energy suppliers have substantially increased the volumes sold abroad, whilst their domestic sales have dropped.

However, these general observations do not explain how the transition was made. What is the calculative capacity (Callon and Muniesa 2005) of an industrial purchaser faced with a choice between regulated tariff and market offer? How do they identify alternatives and prioritize them? Before answering these questions, we must look in detail at the economic and technical context in which a purchaser operates.

THE LEARNING OF NEW PRACTICES: CONSUMPTION FORECASTING AND MONITORING

In the gas and electricity markets, the regulated price proposal (the tariff) and the eligible contract (market price) do not follow the same rules in terms of physical supply: with a regulated tariff, the industrial customer is not affected by peaks and troughs in consumption. Prices are primarily based on quantities actually consumed, without a requirement for forecasting or follow-up. This is not the case with eligible contracts. The contractual separation between transmission infrastructures (which have remained a monopoly) and trading in energy has led to additional constraints for industrial customers in terms of consumption forecasting and monitoring. These constraints are explained by a new distribution of roles in the market: suppliers are responsible for the balance between what they deliver into the distribution network and what their customers consume. The pressures on the network to maintain the balance are transferred from the network manager to the supplier. For the supplier, the only way of guaranteeing this balance is to impose strict consumption forecasting and monitoring rules on their customers, or have them pay for the privilege of flexibility that their own users need.

ADJUSTMENTS TO FORECASTING AND MONITORING RULES

Looking more closely at how industrial customers compare the two supply contracts on offer (regulated tariff vs. market price), the assessment of consumption, including its fluctuation and future development, stands out as a major issue in their calculation. Our survey showed that many buyers experienced problems in assessing and managing these issues due to a lack of human resources, skills, and measuring devices on each industrial site. Some large customers thus preferred not to take the risk of turning to the free market. Furthermore, energy purchasers who did opt for eligible contracts for gas did not always fully understand the subscription rules, e.g. in terms of power requirements for their equipment. Not all these rules were fixed at the outset. As the rules firmed up, the owners of the distribution networks sought to help their customers access the market by maintaining a relatively lenient position towards them: many penalties for subscription overruns were thus not enforced.

Another issue concerned the relationship between suppliers and their customers regarding consumption commitments (e.g. over a year, over a quarter, over a month, etc.). The salespeople of some suppliers sought to teach their customers how to incorporate these needs for flexibility into their calculations. Their aim is to identify their customers' flexibility needs. Salespeople use their knowledge of industrial sites, their consumption and procedures, to inform energy purchasers (who are often not aware of these problems) of the risks they are taking with overly rigid contracts.

Paradoxically, the new contracts are more restrictive due to the regulated access to the gas supply network. Transition difficulties are explained by the important investment in socio-technical reorganization of gas consumption of industrial sites. In the transition period, not all industrial customers were organized to meet this requirement and thus risked ending up paying more than the regulated tariff if they accepted market offers. As a result, not all industrial customers exercised their option to use the deregulated market and instead, continued to purchase gas according to the regulated tariff. Thus, from the physical side of supply, we witnessed the incomplete stabilization of practices and devices; the coexistence of regulated contracts and market contracts; and the partial implementation of new rules by the gas supply network in order to facilitate the development of the deregulated market.

Inherited market devices and their effects on price construction

The liberalization of the gas market introduced some uncertainty concerning gas prices for industrial purchasers. When the market was opened up, the choice of a price reference was the major issue for industrial purchasers. The oil index competed with the gas index to act as the reference in price negotiations with suppliers. Industrial purchasers tried to understand market structure in order to evaluate the relevance of the gas and oil indexes. Most of the time, the selling price defined by the supplier (downstream market) depended on the supplier's price negotiation with gas producers (upstream market).

There are two types of upstream gas markets in Europe, depending on whether the country in question is an importer or exporter of gas. The United Kingdom and Denmark are both importers and exporters and have an active upstream wholesale market. Many transactions between producers and suppliers are conducted transparently on a marketplace. Prices on these markets are publicly available. On the downstream markets, suppliers offer their industrial customers prices that reflect supply: the formula is indexed on the wholesale market plus a distribution margin. The other European countries do not have their own production and depend on imports from producing countries like Russia, Algeria, and Norway (upstream market). Before deregulation, these imports were organized through long-term 'take-or-pay' contracts based on the oil price index (e.g. the Platts Brent Index). Both producers and suppliers considered these long-term contracts (10–30 years) as the best means of financing the heavy investments needed for operation and transmission. In these contracts, the supplier committed to buying a fixed annual volume of gas from the producers, at a price that was not fixed ahead of time. The prices negotiated were based on a 'net-back' principle: this calculation takes into account the price of the fuel oil sold to the consumer and removes the estimated transmission and distribution costs and margins—see box below. The objective of this indexing was to ensure the competitiveness of gas in relation to fuel oil and to guarantee that certain volumes of gas were sold.

The liberalization of the gas market has not fundamentally changed this practice. In 2006, around 95 per cent of the gas imported into France was

---

Type of price formula
  $P = Po + Ax(G - Go) + Bx(F - Fo)$
  P(Po) = purchasing price from the producer/index o: initial date of contract
  G/F = average price over 3, 6, or 9 months for light fuel oil G, or heavy fuel oil F
  A/B: coefficients

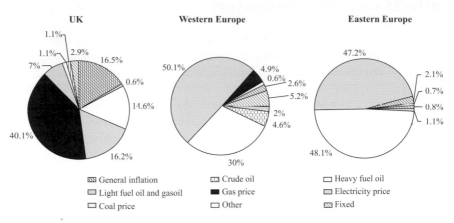

Figure 8.1. Indexation in supply contracts

purchased via 'take-or-pay' long-term contracts from gas producers. More recent events show that this transaction type is still favoured by suppliers. The difference between the volumes purchased via long-term contracts and actual gas sales is covered by purchases on the wholesale markets. In continental Europe, gas wholesale markets only account for a small proportion of total sales: the Zeebrugge market in Belgium and the TTF market in Holland are the most developed, but are not yet liquid enough to provide sufficiently representative indicators of market prices. Since they only account for a small part of total sales, they are very sensitive to gas availability. As can be seen in Figure 8.1, transactions in the wholesale market only account for around 5 per cent of the indexation in Western Europe. In the United Kingdom, the gas price is defined at the National Balancing Point (NBP), a virtual trading location for the sale and purchase of UK natural gas.

On the downstream continental market, suppliers offer their industrial customers a varied price formula. The price formula defined by suppliers combines supply portfolio with financial instruments: suppliers join forces with investment banks to offer their customer a different price structure based on a combination of their sourcing arrangements and financial instruments (Figure 8.2).

PRICE REFERENCES AND RISK MANAGEMENT IN THE CONSTRUCTION OF SUPPLIERS' OFFERS

As noted above, the price defined by gas suppliers in the United Kingdom reflects their purchasing portfolio: their price is indexed to the wholesale gas market. Customers are advised to seek support from specialized banks to

British gas market

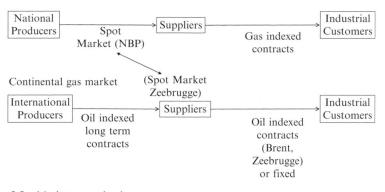

Figure 8.2. Market organization

manage the risks attached to these fluctuating formulae. So, the risk management for prices developed in a disjointed manner: services are offered directly by banks and target the customers' finance departments rather than their energy purchasers. In continental Europe, suppliers had developed partnerships with investment banks, using derivatives to spread the financial risk arising from the difference between the price formula at which they purchased gas (mostly long-term contracts) and the formula offered to their customers. When offering customers a fixed price, suppliers buy a 'swap' on the financial market to cover the risk of price increases on the upstream market.

The key role of long-term contracts in gas purchasing in continental Europe and the limited influence of wholesale markets make it impossible to establish a specific gas market reference for suppliers and industrial customers. And suppliers do not want to reveal their supply price structure and thus offer their customers diverse price structures, with fixed and indexed prices. The indexing formulae employ the oil price index (such as Platts Brent) or the spot gas market index (such as Zeebrugge). The choice of reference index was far from straightforward and the two indexes competed to act as the reference in price negotiations.

TRANSFER OF OIL PRICE ANTICIPATION SKILLS TO THE GAS MARKET THROUGH OIL INDEXATION

From a practical point of view, the oil index offers many advantages. Oil price anticipation skills are traditionally the domain of oil producers and investment banks. However, today gas suppliers have developed partnerships with investment banks in order to be able to accecss these skills and provide their customers with price anticipation services.

Investment banks have developed calculation capacities based on a spread between market price and the so-called 'fundamentals', such as infrastructure, speculation, weather forecasting, disasters, geopolitical conflicts, political decisions, etc. Trade desk analysts always try to evaluate the effects of events and macro shifts on supply and demand trends. They build scenarios that integrate changes of fundamentals. For example, just after the 2005 Tsunami disaster in Thailand, the market anticipated a substantial drop in the oil price and banked on a decline in the South Asian economy. The market settled on a low price for a few days, until a correction kicked in. Market actors underestimated the real impact of the disaster, but some trade desk analysts were able to evaluate the gap between market price and fundamentals.

In continental Europe, gas prices are set by processes similar to those found on other commodity markets. However, these prices have a sophisticated structure that attempts to offset the absence of a shared gas price reference by reusing a price reference that already exists, that is the oil price index. This 'prosthetic construction' (Caliskan 2007), based on an inherited device, makes it possible to use financial hedging derivatives from the oil market and compensate for the incipient financial hedging on the continental gas market. Market actors have developed price guarantees for gas contracts (e.g. fixed prices, indexed prices, contracts with different price references, hedging) as if gas were an oil by-product. This reveals the strength of inherited market devices, such as the price index, and also the flexibility of their use. Market offers overlap devices and practices inherited from the old gas market (i.e. before liberalization) and from the crude oil market. This has resulted in innovative solutions to meet the needs of market actors.

Competition to organize competition

Purchasing activities rely on organizing competition. Indeed, it might be said that this is the 'raison d'être' of purchasing. In the context of liberalization, organizing competition between suppliers may be seen as straightforward. However, it is interesting to look in greater detail at how competition is being organized in the gas market.

Industrial customers have been strongly encouraged by consultants (in fact, agencies depending on UK and Norwegian suppliers or producers) to adopt UK practices: putting out a call for tenders at a given date, which is planned in advance on the basis of an indexed formula. With the help of a consultant, the purchaser compares the formulae proposed by suppliers using a simulation based on the probable index changes. The objective of the call for tenders is to reduce supplier margins as far as possible, and also to identify the most favourable price formula and the one that suits the company's needs best.

Having purchased their gas according to an indexed formula, customers can also use financial services (provided by the supplier or a bank) to 'switch to a fixed price' thanks to market derivatives when they feel they have obtained a good price or need to set their energy spendings as part of a budgeting process.

Consultants advise their customers to initiate calls for tenders with indexed formulae primarily on the Zeebrugge wholesale gas market, hence relying on the development of a short-term gas market. They argue that these wholesale markets are becoming the price reference for the continental market. During the first years of deregulation, a number of industrial customers accepted the idea that the reference price for gas was the Zeebrugge price or the NBP price. They saw it as a limited risk since it was a common price reference and only the wholesale market offered real reductions in relation to the regulated tariff.

Furthermore, salespeople representing the main continental suppliers (who have no production activity and depend on long-term contracts) also play a decisive role in shaping purchasing practices. These actors criticize the use of fixed-date calls for tenders and wholesale gas market indexes. Instead, they try to convince their customers that wholesale markets are not representative of the supplier portfolio or their purchasing practices. They argue that it is preferable to build a formula using the oil index on which long-term gas contracts between producers and major continental suppliers are based. These salespeople have been able to win over industrial customers who have experienced spectacular price variations on the British, NBP, or Zeebrugge markets.

The suppliers' salespeople also explain the shortcomings of using calls for tenders to their customers: the formulae proposed in response to these calls depend on the date of the call (suppliers already use financial markets to construct these formulae). And a call for tender put out at the wrong moment runs the risk of being unfavourable to both customer and supplier, who will have no room for manoeuvre in constructing the formula.

Instead, salespeople encourage their customers to adopt a third purchasing strategy, the so-called 'at the right moment' strategy. This involves defining one (or several) supplier(s), specifying needs and the type of formula to use. The customer then leaves it to the supplier(s) to inform them about prices, in particular when they are attractive. Purchasers set up a contract when they think they have reached a good deal. Thus, the customer benefits fully from their supplier's (and their bank partner's) abilities to anticipate and act on market opportunities.

There is thus competition between two practices linked to different representations of the market. Consultants focus their discourse and practices on promoting competition: they portray themselves as encouraging practices designed to foster the development of a competitive market. Incumbent suppliers, on the other hand, focus their discourse on the value generated by the synergy between the sale of gas and price engineering, in particular by making market opportunities more accessible. Thus, the purchasing practices of industrial customers are partly shaped by a variety of market actors. The way they think about how the market works and how they represent its structure is crucial to the adoption of one type of offer or another.

Calculation practices developed around price uncertainty

Purchasers try to make sense of the market context and formulate a supply strategy. How should they interpret oil indexation? How should they help competition? How receptive should they be to the arguments proposed by consultants and suppliers?

USE OF THE OIL INDEX

Most purchasers suggest that a cautious price strategy fits their organizational context better. In other words, it would be more prudent to use a fixed price, an oil-indexed price rather than be exposed to a speculative gas price.

Oil indexation in long-term gas contracts sets up equivalence between gas and oil products. The oil market is considered as 'liquid' when a considerable amount of arbitrage activity stabilizes the prices and makes this information widely available. Under these circumstances, customers should be able to access a variety of financial products and rich information from numerous investment banks specializing in the oil market. They should further be well equipped with a range of calculation tools.

However, what we observed was very different from this ideal situation. Only a few industrial customers appear to be equipped with information systems and calculation tools, namely, those customers experienced in oil production and trade. These companies also have a team of analysts at their disposal. Other customers rely on their consultants, their gas suppliers, and their associated investment banks. Although the oil index allows the physical contract to be separated from the hedging operation, the supplier's strategy is to reintegrate both dimensions into one business relation in order to foster customer loyalty.

ORGANIZATION OF COMPETITION VERSUS ANTICIPATION OF PRICE

Energy purchasers focus their attention on price variation. Most purchasers see an opportunity to develop a specialized and high profile purchasing function through forward planning and by playing the market. As one purchaser put it:

The added value of the energy purchaser is his understanding of the market and the timing of his purchase. What makes the price is the market. Timing is much more important than negotiating the supplier's margin.

Purchasers try to follow the market to detect the best opportunities to fix the price. Their understanding of the market is essential. They make a systematic effort to understand the context and attempt to forge an opinion about market prices. In the process, they raise many questions: what is the explanation behind this oil price increase? Why have the prices of futures contracts increased more than the spot prices? Does the price reflect market fundamentals? Are there a lot of speculators in the market? How can new events affect prices? What is the state of gas and oil stocks?

Salespeople support these efforts by informing customers about market changes: they present scenarios and attach probabilities to scenarios; they help to build a representation of the market, analyse, and aggregate data to create the most comprehensive picture possible. It is clear that industrial customers construct their representation of the market, thanks to a particular contact, for example a bank seller, especially when they do not have the requisite skills or time to search for more information. These relationships can take on several forms and vary in their intensity. Inexperienced purchasers employ the strategy of 'buying at the right moment', meaning that the customer accepts the supplier's help when deciding on the contracting date. By including both the supply and the financial engineering, this makes the customer doubly dependent on the supplier. It also requires the customer to react quickly, that is, within a few hours, making it difficult to compare rival proposals, since suppliers do not calculate their prices at the same time. This is an increasingly popular approach for purchasers, because it is aligned with what they regard as their main objective: price anticipation. For more experienced purchasers, cooperation with a supplier results in the joint definition of a purchasing strategy based, for example, on fixed intervention thresholds. When these thresholds (i.e. prices) are reached, the customer asks their supplier to switch to fixed prices or to return to variable prices.

SOPHISTICATED PRACTICES UNDERMINED BY AMBIGUITY

In order to manage these conflicting pressures, suppliers propose more sophisticated practices to manage risks. Salespeople defend a price-fixing strategy designed to spread the risk. According to them, fixing the price progressively, that is quarter by quarter, and distributing the amount to be fixed, is the best way of avoiding risky positions. For example, before the end of the first quarter of the year, the purchaser fixes 100 per cent of the price for the second quarter, 75 per cent of the price for the third quarter, 50 per cent of the price for the fourth quarter, and 25 per cent of the price for the first quarter of the following year. During the second quarter, the purchaser must then fix 25 per cent of the price for the next four quarters, and so forth.

Sophisticated purchasers organize three or four calls for tender before deciding on one offer. They compare the formulae proposed by suppliers in simulations based on probable index changes. They also evaluate how these formulae evolve. However, this strategy takes time and reduces the possibility for exploiting opportunities and being flexible. The organization of calls for tender can lead to decision-making situations that are far from ideal.

The practical consequences can be illustrated with an example. Some interviews took place at the end of the budgetary year when the tension between budgeting rules and the need to be reactive was exacerbated. Oil prices had been constantly rising, which meant that fixing the price at this point entailed the risk of purchasing gas at too high a price. Most analysts predicted that the market would adjust itself sooner or later, leading to a substantial drop in prices. However, no one knew whether this adjustment would take place before the end of the financial year. In this context, fixing the price meant that the purchasers would have to take a major risk. These complexities of gas purchasing and price risk management create a situation in which most industrial customers feel uncomfortable. In this context the devices inherited from the era of monopolistic supply are considered a source of stability by providing a satisfactory response to the main challenges, that is price stability and control. In short, these devices still help to structure market practices.

The fragility of market devices: controversies over the oil index

As explained above, oil-indexed, long-term contracts set up equivalence between gas and oil products. For experienced purchasers, this allows a separation between the physical contract, based on the oil index, and the financial activities, developed with independent banks. For less experienced purchasers, it reduces price risks. But the oil index reference is not as stable as incumbent suppliers suggest. The question of which index to use is regularly raised. Underlying this choice is the role of the long-term contract.

CONTRACTING PRACTICES CALLED INTO QUESTION BY THE SPREAD BETWEEN GAS- AND OIL-INDEXED PRICES

Industrial customers using the gas index in their formula have been surprised by its high level of volatility. The UK gas market in particular is characterized by increasing volatility, both in terms of spot and future prices. Having become an importer of gas, the UK is increasingly dependent on other European wholesale markets, which adds further volatility. The NBP has become extremely sensitive to weather conditions, climbing sharply at the end of 2005 and the beginning of 2006 (with prices approaching 40/MWh), due to the very harsh winter, and then plummeting at the end of 2006 (under 10/MWh) during a more temperate winter. These variations applied to both monthly average spot prices and one-year contract prices. At the same time, long-term contract gas prices (based on the oil index) stabilized at around 20/MWh. The low gas price on the the NBP caused industrial customers to question their use of the oil index. However, the contracts signed in advance for one- to two-year periods meant that it was nearly impossible for them to exploit this opportunity. On the other hand, salespeople who promoted the oil index were exposed to the risk of purchasers developing a different representation of the market.

Investment banks argued that it was unclear what the main price reference should be—wholesale market or long-term contracts—and which would deliver the lowest price. But they also displayed an understanding of market fundamentals, focusing their communication on a new type of risk coverage, based on an option, a 'best-of' formula designed to deliver the best price between the two markets. So, complex financial products, such as options, were progressively introduced. For salespeople, persuading customers to adopt their market representations is strategic as it influences purchasers' acceptance of their proposals.

OIL PRICE EQUIVALENCE IS UNDERMINED BY THE LIMITS OF THE LONG-TERM CONTRACT

During my interviews, French industrial customers sharply criticized the short-term spot price market. To them, the development of a wholesale gas market in Europe is unlikely to have positive consequences for industrial customers. They saw the market as likely to be dominated by producers benefiting from their oligopolistic position. One reason for this is that substituting gas with fuel oil is becoming less feasible: fuel oil is mainly used in transportation and dual firing capacity in industry and electricity generation is on the decline. This is likely to foster rising gas prices. Today, long-term contracts indexed to oil products help to limit the market power of producers. Finally, according to the French industrial customers, a wholesale gas market would allow gas producers to redefine their prices and boost profits. The long-term contract is considered as a reliable means of accessing gas resources.

The problem is that long-term contracts do not fully meet demand. Suppliers need to buy the difference on the wholesale market, at spot prices, in order to keep enough reserves for domestic consumption. The relative scarcity of long-term gas contracts introduces a new issue to be resolved between suppliers and industrial customers. This became evident to several major industrial customers in France in 2007. To be able to negotiate better prices, these customers carried over their physical gas purchases for 2007 until the end of 2006, threatening to buy gas from alternative suppliers. The incumbent supplier announced that there was a risk they might face a shortage of gas bought on long-term contracts. The industrial customers refused to believe this. However, this proved to be the case: the incumbent supplier had to buy gas on the wholesale market through futures contracts. Their offers to the industrial customers thus became based on the futures price and not on the long-term price indexed to oil. Throughout the autumn of 2006, the futures prices for 2007 remained higher than the oil-indexed price. To the industrial customers these events revealed the consequences of the development of the wholesale market: the progressive abandonment of oil indexation by suppliers. As a result, industrial customers were forced to enter what they considered to be a highly speculative situation. They felt trapped.

The oil indexation, a taken-for-granted market device, on which complex and sophisticated practices have been built, appears to be an increasingly fragile device. This fragility is due to a significant change in market structure linked to the decreasing role of the long-term contract. However, purchasers are not prepared to immediately abandon this device. The continued use of long-term contracts and oil indexation also affects how purchasers view the market: it focuses their attention on the oil price and leads them to ignore other facets of the gas market.

Discussion

Liberalized markets are particularly complex because they combine remnants of a previous economic order (e.g. a monopoly) and complex technical regulations. I have investigated the effects of this complexity by studying the role of market devices and market practices, and primarily the link between these devices and calculative practices. Among other things, the findings highlighted the stabilizing role of inherited devices during market transitions. In this section, I discuss four specific observations from the gas market: first, the case suggests that the use of market devices relies on their perceived reliability. Secondly, it suggests that market devices allow new practices to develop. Thirdly, it suggests that the stability of inherited devices is due to their integration in ongoing practices, which may persist even when the devices are perceived as increasingly less reliable. Finally, it suggests that liberalization may produce new asymmetries in calculating capacities by weakening inherited market devices that supported purchasing practices.

HOW ACTORS EVALUATE THE RELEVANCE OF MARKET DEVICES

The literature on market devices (Callon et al. 2007) has been primarily concerned with their history (how social organization and materiality are integrated into the device) and has described how such devices support or constrain cognition and action. How actors evaluate the relevance of inherited and new market devices (such as long-term contracts, regulated tariffs, and oil index) during market transitions has not been explicitly investigated. Still, this issue is implicit in many historical accounts of the spread of market devices. For example, MacKenzie and Millo (2003) demonstrate how the spread of one market device (the Black-Scholes-Merton formula) was supported by shared rationality and collective action. The case study presented in this chapter suggests that the adoption of market devices in concrete exchange practices is not a trivial matter. The relevance of a market device is not only related to its calculative ability or technical robustness; it is also a matter of how it is deployed in economic calculations. For this to happen, the credibility of a market device among market actors is important.

From the point of view of industrial customers in the gas market, the relevance of market devices depends on how consistent they are with their assumptions about the market's structure. If prevailing assumptions hold, inherited devices are still relevant. If new assumptions are made about the market's structure, new devices become more relevant. But market actors do not have direct access to market representations. In order to defend the relevance of devices and practices, consultants, banks, incumbents, and alternative suppliers peddle alternative market representations. Each actor defends its own preferred practices and devices, as well as a preferred market representation, through what they communicate in their day-to-day business dealings. So, marketing is largely a matter of communicating market representations, structured around existing or novel market devices, so that the offers put together make sense to the purchasers. Marketing is thus, indirectly a matter of fostering confidence in particular market devices.

INHERITED MARKET DEVICES SUPPORT INNOVATION

My account of the gas market transition suggests that inherited market devices may foster innovation. Even though the gas market is neither liquid nor transparent, gas suppliers and industrial customers have developed practices very similar to those existing on commodity markets. A market device like the oil index stabilizes the equivalence between gas and oil prices and promotes the diffusion of financial practices used in the oil market. Sophisticated purchasing and financial practices for gas purchasing are built on this analogy. The oil index thus reduces uncertainty and allows for the import of sophisticated practices into the gas market. Calculations in the gas market result from the overlapping of market devices and practices. The calculative capacities of gas market actors are thus hybrid and distributed. In this context, marketing involves manipulating, integrating, and/or associating a variety of market devices, both inherited and novel, with new offers.

INHERITED MARKET DEVICES REMAIN DESPITE TRANSITION

The deregulation of the gas market has created a space in which new modes of transaction can compete with one another. However, the inherited upstream economic structure and the practices employed there (the long-term contracts) continue to constrain the downstream market. Incumbent suppliers benefit from inherited resources, that is the long-term contracts and the use of oil indexation. However, the transition renders the basis for these devices fragile and uncertain. The development of a gas wholesale market weakens the equivalence relation between oil and gas. Gas now has its own demand and supply.

Confidence in market devices can be maintained even though the market is changing. Market devices can act as 'black boxes' that simplify a complicated and confusing context, and whose functioning is taken for granted. The fact that all transactions and financial activities pertaining to a gas contract are defined according to the oil price is not necessarily questioned. By employing the oil index in gas market transactions, gas is effectively transformed into an oil product. The oil index remains a reference for gas transactions even though it does not represent supply and demand for gas. This suggests that market devices can live a life of their own, independent of 'market fundamentals'; they can survive even when they have been cut off from their roots. During transitions, 'black boxed' devices may remain in use because they offer security. But they may also be 'reopened' when they no longer seem to fulfil their initial promises. Actors then revisit their hypotheses about the market for which these devices were originally constructed. This is one reason why market liberalization is not an immediate or univocal process. Some market devices remain in use because they remain associated with particular practices and competencies, associated with an old order.

THE WEAKENING OF INHERITED MARKET DEVICES REINFORCES ASYMMETRY IN CALCULATIVE CAPACITIES

Industrial purchasers of gas combine different forms of reasoning and juggle with different transaction forms. Their skills, equipment, and access to information determine their capacity to calculate, that is interpret physical and financial gas markets and operate within those markets (or request others to do so for them). The ability to calculate is a crucial strategic resource that contributes to the position of market actors (Callon and Muniesa 2005).

Surprisingly, French industrial customers prefer inherited devices, such as the oil index, to the gas index. More market actors are able to offer services on the oil market than on the gas market. Many financial actors are involved in the oil market, whereas relatively few actors are able to manage gas price risks. Hence, French industrial customers view oil indexation as a way of reducing dependence on suppliers and traders. Indeed, they seem convinced that long-term contracts and oil indexation make transactions more calculable than the wholesale gas market, even if long-term contracts hinder competition.

By contributing to the calculative capacities of market actors (Callon and Muniesa 2005), the use of market devices also has power consequences. New market devices are mastered only by a limited number of actors, whereas inherited devices reduce calculation asymmetries because most market actors have learned how to make use of them. A purchaser, who accepts that certain inherited market devices have become less relevant, also accepts greater uncertainty and increased dependence on traders and suppliers. Owing to the complexity and price volatility of the gas market, purchasers need help from salespeople to make sense of the market context. Purchasers thus become dependent on traders (e.g. suppliers, financial institutions) with whom they exchange information and advice. The interactions between purchasers and salespeople reflect an asymmetrical relationship where the customer's calculative capacity depends on informal relations with suppliers and bank traders. Market liberalization should have transferred market power to customers but, in some respects, it has increased their dependence on suppliers and banks.

The attachment of industrial customers to the long-term contract and oil index is paradoxical. Long-term contracts foreclose the market, and also constitute a source of power for incumbent suppliers. Furthermore, in a transition context, maintaining inherited devices increases the risk of deviating from market fundamentals, like gas supply and demand. Despite this, and despite the European Commission advocating the creation of a substantial, 'transparent and liquid' wholesale market, French suppliers and customers are converging towards the continued use of long-term contracts (with a common reference index). These devices are considered more effective in regulating the power struggle between producers and suppliers, and between suppliers and industrial customers, than the development of a transparent and liquid wholesale market.

Conclusion

My analysis suggests that marketing and purchasing activities on the European gas market consist in developing, promoting, evaluating, combining, and deploying market devices that support and constrain particular forms of transactions. In particular, my account of the transition of the continental gas market highlights the role of market devices in establishing common references for market exchanges. Although market transition may weaken inherited market devices, such devices may remain in use because they simplify calculations, reduce uncertainties, and limit the asymmetries in the calculative capacities of actors. But the weakening of inherited market devices—e.g. their dissociation from market fundamentals—provides market actors with a choice between abandoning inherited devices and becoming more dependent on others, and continuing to employ them but risk losing touch with the new market dynamics.

9 Marketing on trial

The SAS EuroBonus case

HANS KJELLBERG

A struggle between two market versions

Economic orders are seldom pure. The 'really existing markets' that consumers and marketers encounter typically bear little resemblance with the idealized and abstract characterization of the price mechanism found in economics textbooks (cf. Boyer 1997). And rightly so, one could argue, since the portrayal of markets as the intersection of supply and demand has analytical purposes and is not primarily intended to be descriptively accurate. Yet, considerable efforts are being spent on projects that employ this analytical model as a normative template for really existing markets, not least various regulatory efforts. The observed impurity is not always for the lack of trying (Bauman 1992; Law 1994).

A familiar response to observations of impurity, besides the zeal of true believers, is to denounce the template; if ideal markets are so rare despite the massive efforts, then perhaps the model is not so good (e.g. Miller 2002; Håkansson et al. 2004). This response disregards that any effort to put in place a specific set of circumstances in a market is likely to be just one among many such efforts. Apart from government authorities and NGOs (Sjögren and Helgesson 2007; Ählström and Egels-Zandén 2008), manufacturers of consumer goods (Azimont and Araujo 2007), wholesalers (Kjellberg 2001), retail merchandisers (Barrey 2007), and professional purchasers (Lindberg and Nordin 2008) are all examples of actors that at times devote considerable resources to the more or less explicit reshaping of markets. As Stidsen (1979: 78) noted: 'a marketing strategy is not just a plan for entering or exploiting a market—it is also a plan for altering a market.' The templates on which these various actors model their efforts may differ dramatically. Two likely sources are economics (for market deregulations, auction designs, etc.) and marketing (for loyalty programmes, relationship management, etc.), but in general social science at large is implicated (Law and Urry 2004). This means that any given market typically is being shaped by multiple parallel efforts to realize specific, but different, economic orders (Kjellberg and Helgesson 2006); the market is the continuous, joint outcome of all these efforts, rather than a blueprint of any one effort.

This chapter explores practices contributing to the ongoing realization of one market and how parallel, competing efforts to organize this market came to interfere with each other. As a resource for this, the chapter follows a controversy between the Scandinavian airline operator SAS and the Swedish Competition Authority (SCA) regarding EuroBonus, SAS's frequent flyer programme (FFP).[1] While questioned both from legal and ethical standpoints for offsetting price competition, FFPs became standard marketing practice in the airline industry in the 1990s (Arnesen et al. 1997). The controversy in focus is traced from SAS's efforts to gain acceptance for FFPs in Sweden, via their successful introduction of EuroBonus, to a decision by the SCA that SAS's use of EuroBonus constituted abuse of their dominant position on the Swedish market. A ruling by the Swedish Market Court temporarily resolved the controversy in 2001, imposing a conditional fine on SAS's continued use of EuroBonus. Then, in 2009, SAS reintroduced EuroBonus on domestic routes following a decision by the SCA that the court ruling no longer applied.

The choice of case resonates with previous efforts to theorize about the relation between 'states' and 'firms' in the production of 'market institutions' (e.g. Fligstein 1996, 2001). Rather than focusing on the correlation between social structures and the production of institutional arrangements, however, this chapter explores practices through which control over the development of a market is attempted and at times exercised. In particular, the case details a struggle between two visions of what the market for passenger travel should be. Based on the Swedish Competition Act, the SCA promotes a market inspired by Industrial Organization (IO) theory (applied micro-economics). SAS, on the other hand, seeks to realize a market rooted in contemporary marketing theory, specifically in ideas about the importance of fostering customer loyalty.

The case underscores the importance of producing the requisite circumstances for a market version to hold in the situations it encounters. This becomes especially demanding if rival efforts to produce alternative market versions are underway in parallel. Moreover, the dependence on others, whose repertoire of responses goes beyond support or rejection, casts doubts over the possibility of stabilizing a particular version of a market.

EuroBonus—a successful and questioned market practice

In April 1992, SAS introduced its EuroBonus programme. As we have come to expect from such programmes, it awarded travellers bonus points relative to flight length and ticket type. The points could then be traded for free trips.

Table 9.1. EuroBonus: membership levels, conditions, and benefits (SAS 1999)

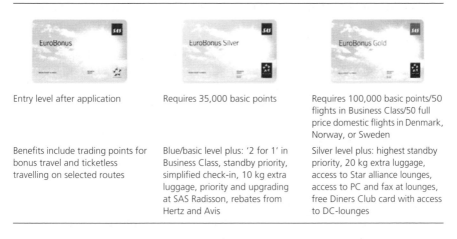

Entry level after application	Requires 35,000 basic points	Requires 100,000 basic points/50 flights in Business Class/50 full price domestic flights in Denmark, Norway, or Sweden
Benefits include trading points for bonus travel and ticketless travelling on selected routes	Blue/basic level plus: '2 for 1' in Business Class, standby priority, simplified check-in, 10 kg extra luggage, priority and upgrading at SAS Radisson, rebates from Hertz and Avis	Silver level plus: highest standby priority, 20 kg extra luggage, access to Star alliance lounges, access to PC and fax at lounges, free Diners Club card with access to DC-lounges

In the words of SAS's EuroBonus manager: 'The core of the programme is increased loyalty and thereby increased repurchase frequency.' The programme included three membership levels, with further benefits reserved for the more frequent travellers (Table 9.1). Within a year, more than 230,000 travellers had joined the programme.

BACKGROUND: AIRLINE DEREGULATION AND FREQUENT FLYER PROGRAMMES

Students of the US airline industry suggest that the introduction and spread of FFPs was triggered by regulatory change (Vietor 1990). The airline industry 'grew up' with heavy regulations, both nationally and internationally. From 1938 to 1978, when the US Airline Deregulation Act was passed, all major economic parameters of airline operations were regulated: entry, routes, frequencies, and prices. As one of several responses to the deregulation and the subsequent difficulties experienced by many airlines, American Airlines introduced its AAdvantage programme in 1981 offering passengers mileage credits (Vietor 1990). Although American is justly credited for having invented the FFP, its marketing director at the time emphasized that AAdvantage was simply a redesign of the highly successful Green Stamp coupon programme (Hoffman 1984; Toh et al. 1993).[2]

In parallel to deregulatory efforts in Europe in the late 1980s, European airlines found their US competitors gaining increased business on transatlantic routes.[3] For SAS, this became evident in the early 1990s when the company was forced to close down several intercontinental flights, including their once so successful Stockholm–Chicago route. SAS identified American Airlines' new direct flights to and from Chicago as a major reason for their lost business. Moreover, they found that American's success largely depended on their AAdvantage programme, to which they had silently recruited 10,000 Swedish travellers. Unfortunately for SAS, their ability to start a similar programme was restricted since flight bonuses were subject to benefit taxation in Sweden.

Based on this analysis, SAS sought to convince the Swedish government of their need to compete on similar terms, and hence the need to exempt flight bonuses from taxation. In a 1991 parliamentary proposal largely based on material supplied by SAS, it was suggested that rebates awarded on the basis of fidelity should be exempt from taxation (Clarkson 1991). Critical voices on the committee on taxation argued that an exemption would sanction activities that bordered on bribery, that were unlawful from both a marketing and competition law perspective, and that would reduce the competitiveness of smaller airlines. Still, in December 1991, benefits earned in connection to international travels became exempt from taxation. With this obstacle removed, SAS soon announced the launch of its own bonus programme for international travels.

SAS developed the EuroBonus programme in collaboration with the American marketing consultancy Carlson Marketing Group (CMG), with which SAS already had ties through their cooperation with Carlson-owned Radisson hotels. CMG had considerable experience both from the travel business (via their sister company Carlson Travel) and from coupon marketing (via the Gold Bond Stamp programme which Curtis Carlson launched in 1938). Also important in designing EuroBonus was the construction of a database enabling SAS to collect, process, and store traveller-specific information, using the IBM AS/400 platform.

THINGS HEAT UP: CRITIQUE, SUCCESS, EXPANSION, AND . . . ?

Even before its launch in April 1992 several groups criticized EuroBonus, including travel agents, competitors, large company customers, trade organizations, and the Swedish Anti-Corruption Institute. One important critique was that the programme would reward passengers also when companies were paying for their tickets. Under such circumstances, the critics argued, rewards should rightfully accrue to the companies. SAS defended EuroBonus arguing that all competitors had similar programmes and that SAS needed EuroBonus to compete successfully.

Travellers were very interested in EuroBonus. In a month, 40,000 members registered and by the end of 1992 EuroBonus had 200,000 members. To increase its attractiveness further, SAS tried to expand the tax exemption to domestic flights, but these efforts failed. Still, EuroBonus continued to attract new members. SAS expanded the programme considerably by awarding bonus also for flights and services supplied by their alliance partners. By the end of 1997, when EuroBonus was named Best International Frequent Flyer Program of the Year, there were nearly 1.5 million members, including 280,000 Swedes. That year SAS also experienced a major setback as the new political majority decided to revert Swedish tax legislation back to the pre-1992 situation. Once again, all private benefits accruing from employment would be subject to taxation. The obligation to report benefits earned and used for private consumption, however, fell on individual employees and their employers rather than on the awarding companies. In anticipation of this change, SAS decided to expand the programme to include also domestic flights from 1 May 1997.

Starting as a strategic response to deregulation by American Airlines in 1981, FFPs had become a global industry practice by the late 1990s.[4] This change had mainly been driven by intra-industry competition, initially in the United States but increasingly in an international context as air travel was gradually liberalized. EuroBonus is one example of this expansion. By 1997, virtually every major airline had an FFP; air travel markets with frequent flyer rewards had been transformed from an idea to a dominant version.

SEE YOU IN COURT!

When preparing their expansion of EuroBonus to domestic flights, SAS asked the Swedish Competitive Authorities (SCA) for a non-intervention notification. The SCA declined: 'FFPs are loyalty creating and can be regarded as fidelity rebates. If fidelity rebates are applied by a dominant company, this can constitute an abuse of a dominant position.' This response should be seen in the light of the deregulation of pricing and entry on the Swedish market for air travel in 1992, which explicitly sought to create conditions for low prices and a consumer-oriented supply of air travel services. This deregulation made the SCA responsible for monitoring the market, and for promoting competition in accordance with the Competition Act.[5] In a 1996 evaluation commissioned by the SCA, the expert economist concluded that the positive effects of the deregulation had not come up to expectations (Bergman 1996). Drawing on IO theory, he also identified FFPs as one reason for this: 'Bonus programs [. . .] hinder competition. In principle, competition would improve if they were banned' (ibid.: 88, trans.). Given this background, the decision against non-intervention was not surprising.

In 1998, SAS's domestic competitor Braathens and the Swedish Federation of Travel Agents filed complaints with the SCA concerning 'the use of loyalty-creating conditions in company-specific contacts, travel agent contracts, and

EuroBonus'. The SCA tried these complaints and found SAS's use of EuroBonus on domestic flights to constitute abuse of their dominant position. In their decision, dated 12 November 1999, the SCA required SAS to cease applying EuroBonus on domestic flights under the threated a SEK 100 million (approximately €10 million) fine. Within a few weeks, SAS appealed to the Swedish Market Court asking that the decision be invalidated on the grounds that the SCA had defined the relevant market incorrectly and against current legal practice within the European Union (EU). Since the SCA disputed this, the Market Court decided to try the case. After an exchange of statements between the two parties and the main proceedings in October 2000, the Market Court reached a ruling in January 2001.

These events shifted the struggle from the competitive arena to an altogether different setting: from a world of travel agents, businessmen, and airline advertising and promotion activities to situations involving legal codes, competitive authorities, market experts, and legal advisers. When the case entered the court system, it was no longer a struggle between an increasingly obsolete 'market *without* FFPs' and an increasingly dominant 'market *with* FFPs'. Here, the global success of FFPs would not automatically favour SAS. In this sense, the playing field was levelled. The next two sections will spell out the arguments put forward by SAS and the SCA in their attempts to persuade the court to rule in favour of their respective positions.

EuroBonus as abuse of a dominant position[6]

The original decision by the SCA drew on the Swedish Competition Act (SFS 1993: 20), according to which it is prohibited for a dominant company to abuse its position in the market. In assessing the legality of EuroBonus the SCA established: (*a*) what the relevant market was; (*b*) whether SAS was dominant in this market; and (*c*) if SAS's use of EuroBonus constituted abuse of their dominant position.

WHAT IS THE RELEVANT MARKET?

According to the SCA, the relevant market must be delimited by determining both the *product market* and the *geographical market*. European legal praxis suggested that relevant product markets depend on the substitutability of different products for those who demand them, whereas relevant geographical markets are areas where the concerned companies offer their products and within which competitive conditions are distinguishable from those in adjacent areas.

The SCA asserted that there were considerable differences between alternative means for commercial passenger travel, for example taxi, bus, train, and air transport, in terms of price, duration, and comfort. Their substitutability also depended on the purpose of the transport: 'Business travellers can stereotypically be said to choose a mode of transport according to the timetable, private persons according to the pricelist.' According to the SCA, this made for a variable substitutability between different means of transportation. Using figures supplied by the Swedish Civil Aviation Administration, the SCA showed that business travellers increasingly chose to fly when the length of the journey increased. Despite a 100 per cent price premium compared to train travel, 59 per cent of the business travellers chose air transport for journeys between 400 and 600 km. For journeys longer than 800 km, the figure was 89 per cent. For private persons, the figures were dramatically different, implying much higher price sensitivity. This led the SCA to conclude that air and ground travel were substitutable only under certain conditions and for certain passengers. For business travellers, who accounted for 76 per cent of SAS's total revenues from domestic flights, air travel could not be regarded as generally substitutable with other means of transportation. In line with this reasoning, the SCA defined the relevant product market as the market for regular passenger travel *by air.*

In determining the relevant geographical market, the SCA argued that special circumstances applied to Swedish domestic air travel. First, SAS had a well-developed network of lines revolving around its hub, Arlanda. Second, passengers were dependent on the network of lines in a hub-and-spoke system when travelling within Sweden. And there was only one such system: that of SAS. This meant that flights between northern and southern Sweden as well as to international destinations went via Arlanda. Since passengers often utilized the benefits of travelling within the same network of lines and since business customers often had bonus agreements comprising the whole or parts of the network of lines, the SCA found that the market could not be delimited to a specific line between two destinations. Consequently, the SCA delimited the geographical market to Sweden, noting that SAS also treated Swedish domestic flights as a separate line of operations.

IS SAS DOMINANT IN THIS MARKET?

With the relevant market defined as the market for regular passenger travel by air in Sweden, the SCA sought to determine whether SAS was dominant in this market. The SCA claimed that a company has a dominant position if it can act independently of its competitors and customers to a considerable extent. A company's market share on the relevant market was said to be an important indicator of this. Additional circumstances also affected the assessment, including financial strength, barriers to entry, access to supplies, patents, technology, and other knowledge-based advantages. However, the SCA noted that there were no absolute criteria for assessing dominance; each case should be judged separately. Still, according to EU-praxis, market shares below 40 per cent did not generally imply a dominant position. Shares above 40 per cent, however, were considered clear signs of dominance. A 50 per cent market share led to a presumption of dominance. Market shares above 65 per cent, finally, made such a presumption almost impossible to vindicate.

According to the annual passenger statistics for domestic flights, the market share of SAS was 67 per cent in 1998. In addition, SAS had extensive cooperation and ownership ties to Skyways, with a 9 per cent market share. All in all SAS and its partners had a market share of approximately 76 per cent based on the number of passengers. Within the business segment, the SCA claimed that SAS's market share was even higher, exceeding 80 per cent. Already at this point, then, the dominance of SAS was clear to the SCA. Additional circumstances, such as economies of scale, benefits of having a well-developed hub-and-spoke system allowing effective and smooth travel, advantageous slots for departures and arrivals, and an attractive loyalty-programme further strengthened this image. Unsurprisingly, the SCA found SAS to have a dominant position on the relevant market.

DOES EUROBONUS CONSTITUTE AN ABUSE?

Having defined the relevant market and established SAS's dominance in it, the SCA turned to the real issue: whether or not SAS's use of EuroBonus constituted an abuse of their dominant position. Since the Swedish Competition Act was modelled on and materially equal to the EU-legislation, the definition of abuse established in EU praxis applied:

The concept of abuse is an objective concept relating to the behaviour of an undertaking in a dominant position which is such as to influence the structure of a market where, as a result of the very presence of the undertaking in question, the degree of competition is weakened and which, through recourse to methods different from those which condition normal competition in products or services [...], has the effect of hindering the maintenance of the degree of competition still existing in the market or the growth of that competition. (ECR 461, 1979)

The SCA concluded: 'a dominant firm thus has a special responsibility not to further weaken the competition in the markets where it acts.' The SCA observed that loyalty rebates in several cases had been found to constitute abuse. In the cited case, a progressive bonus-scale was found to be abusive since it consolidated a dominant position by tying customers to the company.

Once again, however, the distinction between abusive and non-abusive behaviour was said to depend on the circumstances of the individual case.

The two complaints filed against SAS claimed that EuroBonus was very effective at creating loyalty, giving business travellers incentives to disregard both timetables and prices and continue using SAS. The SCA argued that unless a discount system that creates loyalty had an objective justification, such as when volume discounts were offered on the basis of cost reductions, it could be considered abusive. FFPs tied customers to an airline, 'rendering it more difficult or even preventing competitors from entering the market profitably'. This effect was further strengthened by the fact that the programmes targeted the profitable business passengers. Under these conditions, FFPs impeded market access. The SCA concluded:

The loyalty to SAS created by the EuroBonus program strongly implies that the application of EuroBonus for domestic flights [. . .] constitutes an abuse of SAS's dominant position in breach of the Competition Act. . . . The existence of loyalty programs in international aviation cannot entail that a dominant airline on a domestic market can be allowed to apply the program on the latter market if the effects strongly inhibit competition. There is thus no objectively admissible defence for SAS to apply EuroBonus in Sweden in the current way. This application thus constitutes an abuse of the company's dominant position.

EuroBonus as standard marketing practice[7]

In their appeal to the Swedish Market Court, SAS suggested that the SCA had defined the market incorrectly. According to SAS, each combination of origin and destination is a separate market, since this is what customers look for when they travel. SAS also argued that the markets for air passenger travel were undergoing drastic changes and that the SCA had been too narrowly focused on the Swedish case in their decision. Increasing international competition made such a narrow scope impossible for SAS. Most airlines had met this new situation by using FFPs and by forming worldwide alliances, leading to competition between alliances rather than individual airlines. The programmes and their crossover effects within alliances (the ability to switch points between programmes) were thus part of established marketing practice for international airlines.

[M]ost major international airlines apply some kind of FFP. These systems constitute a well-established and generally accepted means of competition in both domestic and international air traffic. The structure of the individual markets play no role in this regard [. . .] For SAS this means that the application of EuroBonus cannot be seen as connected to the particular position that SAS enjoys in the Swedish domestic air traffic market.

Since competitors like Air France and Lufthansa were also dominant in their home markets, yet free to use loyalty programmes, SAS argued that it was wrong to consider domestic flights separately. Further, SAS underscored that since the programme was not exclusive, but open to everyone to join, it could not be considered abusive. In fact, many individuals were members of several programmes. This counteracted any entry barrier effect and made EuroBonus satisfy the conditions set up by the European Commission.

Concerning the definition of abuse cited by the SCA, SAS pointed out that it clearly stated that abuse must involve 'recourse to methods different from those which condition normal competition in products or services'. In fact, in a previous case, the Swedish Market Court had stated that even 'very domi-nant companies may [...] take reasonable measures in order to meet com-petition from other companies'. According to SAS, this clearly indicated that EuroBonus did not constitute abuse.

SAS also supplied an argument against the decision, even if the SCA's market definition was accepted. Malmoe Aviation, a domestic competitor, had grown considerably in recent years, despite SAS's application of Euro-Bonus. In fact, this company was able to charge higher prices than SAS due to its use of an airport located closer to the Stockholm city-centre. According to SAS, this showed that the alleged loyalty-creating and competition-inhibiting effects of EuroBonus were negligible.

EuroBonus on trial

Obviously, the parties' views differed considerably. During the spring and summer of 2000, both sides developed their positions by informing the Market Court of circumstances relevant to the case. Below, provide condensed versions of these extended arguments, before the court proceedings and the subsequent ruling of the Market Court are summarized.

THE DEVELOPED POSITION OF THE SCA[8]

First, the SCA developed their argument concerning the loyalty-creating effect of EuroBonus. In their view, this effect was an established fact. The attempts by SAS to create loyalty constituted deviant conduct, since it made customers choose a supplier on other grounds than price and quality of service. In support of this, the SCA quoted the marketing director of SAS arguing that the SCA's decision would constitute 'a deathblow to the airport in Malmö, since the international route to Copenhagen will continue to produce the beneficial bonus points'. This clearly indicated that the traveller's

Table 9.2. Survey among Swedish companies concerning the effects of EuroBonus on purchases of business travel, no. of responses (Marknadsdomstolen 2000)

Share of occasions	0–25%	26–50%	51–75%	76–100%
How often a traveller chooses SAS despite another airline having been recommended	18 (43%)	11 (26%)	6 (14%)	7 (17%)
How often this choice is made due to EuroBonus	16 (40%)	6 (15%)	8 (20%)	10 (25%)

main selection criteria were not price and quality when EuroBonus applied. With reference to a survey by the Swedish Business Travel Association (Table 9.2), the SCA claimed: 'A cautious analysis indicates that roughly every other time, the choice is made due to EuroBonus.' Further, travellers would benefit the most by earning points with the supplier offering the largest selection of uses for these points. Indeed, the SCA suggested that the programme had a bribery-like character, clearly benefiting the dominant supplier in relation to newcomers.

Second, the SCA addressed SAS's attempt to bring an international dimension into the case. The SCA emphasized that the case concerned the domestic situation and that national law applied. Under such circumstances, European legal practice could provide general insights, but could not be drawn upon exclusively. Each case must be tried locally. Further, the SCA argued that one could not justify measures that weakened domestic competition with reference to harsh international competition. Since SAS was unable to present any other justification for its use of EuroBonus, the practice constituted abuse.

THE DEVELOPED POSITION OF SAS[9]

SAS developed their argument that the SCA had assumed a position at odds with established legal praxis within the EU. Referring to the same sources as the SCA, SAS argued that FFPs normally did not constitute abuse. Only under certain conditions did such programmes run the risk of being illegal, for example if the bonus scale was progressive or if the programme was closed. The diverging position of the SCA meant that SAS would compete on other terms than their major European competitors, who were allowed to apply their bonus programmes domestically.

SAS also addressed the alleged loyalty-creating effect of EuroBonus, arguing that the SCA's conclusion was based on theoretical reasoning rather than empirical investigations. Available figures did not suggest that the introduction of EuroBonus on domestic routes had had any negative effects on SAS's competitors. Not even SAS had noted any major effect. Further, existing empirical investigations showed that FFPs were not very important in determining a traveller's choice of airline (see Figure 9.1).

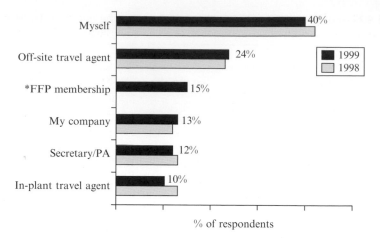

Figure 9.1. Most influential factors when selecting an airline (HI Europe 1999)*—item added in 1999 survey

THE MAIN PROCEEDINGS

During the main proceedings in October 2000, the parties called on selected witnesses to support their respective positions (summarized in Table 9.3). SAS argued their right to protect commercial interests by competing in accordance with normal market conduct. First, the European Commission had a uniform praxis on FFPs, which did not rule out their existence. Secondly, these programmes were a normal means of competition in the air travel market and therefore not abusive. Thirdly, the alleged loyalty-creating

Table 9.3. Summary of the positions during the court proceedings

	The SCA	SAS
Relevant market?	Regular air passenger travel in Sweden	All substitutable means of transport on an individual route
Dominant position?	With a 75–80% market share and advantages from its hub-and-spoke network, SAS is dominant	Generally, no
Abuse?	Yes! (1) Dominant firms like SAS have special responsibilities to uphold competition. (2) The competition on the relevant market is very weak. (3) Comparisons with other markets are irrelevant. (4) FFPs may be abusive and can be assumed so until otherwise proven. (5) The loyalty-creating effect of EuroBonus is strong and offsets competition by means of price and quality.	No! (1) Legal practice within the EU does not consider FFPs abusive. (2) To be abusive, a practice must deviate from established behaviour—FFPs do not. (3) Abusive practices must have negative effects on customers or competitors—there is no evidence that EuroBonus does. (4) By being open to all, EuroBonus does not foreclose the market. (5) Competitors are allowed to apply FFPs on their domestic markets.

effect of EuroBonus must be very small since it had no tangible effects on the market. Finally, EuroBonus was a customer database allowing SAS to better serve its customers.

The SCA challenged SAS's interpretation of EU-praxis, arguing that it had never been developed for a case concerning abuse of a dominant position. Further, in all antitrust cases the conduct under scrutiny should be evaluated in the light of the market conditions prevailing in that case. Any measure that ties customers to a dominant company on a highly concentrated market must be considered unacceptable. And this was precisely the purpose of FFPs: to tie customers to a company in a less costly way than by means of price reductions or quality improvements, and not via normal means of competition. This effect arose primarily from the bonus accruing to the traveller rather than the payer. The customer lock-in that SAS achieved could not be accepted given the conditions on the relevant market; their conduct was an abnormal means of competition. The SCA concluded:

From the Swedish consumers' perspective it is not acceptable to create a *de facto* monopoly in Sweden to allow a certain company to operate internationally.

THE RULING OF THE MARKET COURT[10]

Since the Swedish Market Court has no interrogating role, it must reach its decisions based on what the parties bring before it. After considerable deliberation, the market experts and jurists of the court noted the following in their ruling:

A dominant company is allowed to undertake reasonable measures to meet competition from other companies. The conditions on the Swedish domestic air travel market are such that competition is not easily promoted. It is beyond doubt that bonus programmes have loyalty-creating effects. Since travellers obtain the most advantageous pay-offs from EuroBonus by concentrating their travels on SAS, a considerable loyalty effect arises. This could affect price formation via a reduced price-sensitivity among travellers. Taking into account the limited competition in the Swedish air travel market, SAS's use of EuroBonus constitutes yet another obstacle to its development. SAS's international position and its maintenance of a customer database are not reasons enough to accept the programme. Given this, the Market Court finds SAS's use of EuroBonus to constitute an abuse of their dominant position.

The Market Court only changes the decision reached by the SCA so that SAS, fined SEK 50 million, starting October 27, 2001 is required to cease applying the EuroBonus program [...] on domestic flights and destinations where SAS, or airlines co-operating with SAS, which are connected to the program, face competition through existing or newly created regular air transport of passengers. (Marknadsdomstolen 2001)

In summary, the Market Court ruled largely in favour of the SCA. However, it revised the or its decision in two important ways. First, it lowered the fine from SEK 100 million to SEK 50 million. Secondly, it modified the ruling by requiring SAS to cease its abusive practice only on lines where it faced competition.

A temporary stabilization

SAS COMPLAINS BUT COMPLIES

The SCA is trying to realize this peculiar market modelled on the manufacturing industries. They seem to argue that the market for air travel should be able to sustain 3–4 suppliers since this is the case in other markets. The problem is that this is a theoretical argument. [...] they forget that we have entirely different costs, for security, staff, etc. They emphasise competition for its own sake and lose the consumer perspective. [...] It is obvious that the case is incorrectly judged! (Erik Hellners, legal adviser, SAS, interview 2003-01-31)

SAS was not pleased with the ruling. However, with no possibilities of further appeals and a fine of SEK 50 million, SAS complied. The cost of disagreeing had gone up; the playing field had been reshuffled. When the case left the court, the market with EuroBonus came at a significant cost to SAS. As a consequence, the version promoted by the SCA gained verisimilitude, at least in Sweden. In fact, it gained further ground in November 2001 as the Norwegian competitive authorities reached a similar decision. EuroBonus points earned on Swedish routes where SAS faced competition would no longer produce bonus trips:

The Swedish Market Court has ruled that effective October 27, 2001, SAS must revise the SAS EuroBonus program with regard to points earned on Swedish domestic routes where other airlines compete with SAS and Skyways. The ruling stipulates that points earned on such routes may not be exchanged for bonus flights, or other bonus offers. However, they are still valid for upgrades to higher membership status in SAS EuroBonus. The ruling affects the following routes and is subject to changes [list of routes]. (SAS 2005)

But the ruling was not entirely straightforward:

Are there any exceptions? Yes, there are exceptions and we will explain to you how it works. If you travel with SAS or Skyways on the routes above, and have a connecting flight the same day within Sweden or with an international flight or a non-competitive route with our partners [...] then you will earn redeemable points on the competitive routes. (SAS 2005)

These exceptions complicated the required adjustments and made SAS experience some difficulties. The bonus programmes of SAS's alliance part-ners were connected to EuroBonus, allowing customers to switch points across programmes. The ruling of the Market Court meant that a member of Quantas' bonus programme flying with Thai from Singapore to Arlanda and later to Luleå with SAS in Sweden, was no longer entitled to receive bonus points for the domestic flight in Sweden. Since bonus points could be registered after the flight, for instance upon a passenger's return home, a complicated system of controls had to be set up to ensure compliance with the ruling SAS's problem was that if one of their partners were to register bonus points on a 'forbidden' flight, SAS and not the other airline faced the risk of being fined.

The decision to allow EuroBonus on routes without competition also led to complications: SAS now had to determine what counted as competition. Since several domestic airlines proved to be very short-lived, this created problems. In one case, Goodjet opened a route that forced SAS to change its bonus routines, only to close it again after three weeks. To make matters worse, there were still cases where SAS *could* award bonus points on routes with competition. If the traveller arrived on an international flight (or a domestic flight with no competition) and had a connecting domestic flight (with competition), then that connection did not count as a domestic flight in its own right, but as a continuation of the previous flight.

NEVER SETTLED ONCE AND FOR ALL

Given the court ruling and SAS's decision to comply, the controversy seemed resolved in favour of the market version championed by the SCA. But the success of this market version was still limited. Indeed, the ruling safeguarded that EuroBonus would still be applied on domestic air travels too. The number of EuroBonus members also continued to grow, both in Sweden and Norway (SAS, Annual Reports).

In 2008, SAS made a renewed attempt to gain acceptance for EuroBonus in Sweden, thus indirectly promoting 'its' version of the market. In a reconsid-eration request, SAS asked the SCA to invalidate the ruling of the Market Court, arguing that: (*a*) the market conditions had changed radically since the initial decision in 1999; (*b*) the application of EuroBonus on domestic air travel did not constitute abuse of a dominant position; and (*c*) the SCA and the Market Court had defined both the product market and the geographical market incorrectly.

In their decision, the SCA concluded that the Market Court ruling concerned abuse that was underway at the time, that is, it concerned SAS's application of EuroBonus on the Swedish market for air passenger travel up until the Market Court reached its decision. It did *not* concern a potential reintroduction of EuroBonus in 2009. This is not to say that the SCA agreed to a reintroduction of EuroBonus. The SCA explicitly noted that it might come to try whether an application of EuroBonus constitutes abuse, should SAS decide on a reintroduction. Within days, SAS announced that they would reintroduce EuroBonus on domestic flights. Close to a decade after the initial decision by the SCA, the controversy changed character again. Without the cost added by the Market Court, a full-fledged pursuit of EuroBonus once more seemed possible for SAS.

EuroBonus as part of a performation struggle

Frequent flyer programmes are a prime example of what Cochoy (2007*a*) has called *captation devices*. They purport to transform one predictable customer trajectory (choosing airline and flight based on prices, flight schedules, in-flight services, etc.) into another (choosing airline and flight based on the reception of a redeemable bonus). As such, these devices carry a statement about markets: based on the idea of rewarding loyal customers they propose to make future market exchanges dependent on previous ones.

As argued by Callon (2007*a*), such statements about markets can prosper only if they are accompanied by their own worlds; their diffusion is possible only if the environment they require is made available in the places where they are brought to bear. What this 'required environment' consists in cannot be fully known in advance, varies across situations, and is thus gradually revealed as a statement is brought to bear in specific situations. In this concluding section, I employ a model of markets as constituted by practice (Kjellberg and Helgesson 2007*a*) to identify situations where statements about markets were brought to bear in the case. Specifically the model attends to three interlinked types of market practices: *exchange practices*, which contribute to the con-summation of individual economic exchanges; *normalizing practices*, which contribute to the establishment of normative objectives for actors engaging in such exchanges; and *representational practices*, which contribute to produce images of markets.

The making available of required environments for specific practices is, of course, complicated by the presence of competing efforts drawing on other ideas about markets, a state of affairs that characterized the EuroBonus controversy. In this sense, the case outlines what Callon (2007*a*: 330–2) calls a *performation struggle*—the interference between two processes of adjust-ment of statements and their associated worlds. One of these processes comprised the efforts of SAS and others to realize international passenger travel markets with FFPs; the other comprised the efforts of the SCA and others to realize a domestic Swedish market for air travel with competition

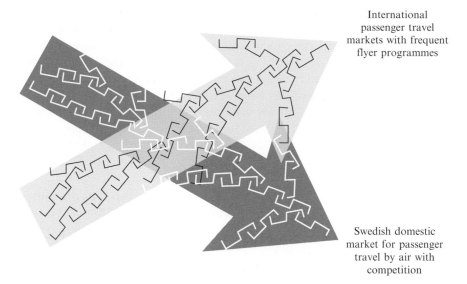

International
passenger travel
markets with frequent
flyer programmes

Swedish domestic
market for passenger
travel by air with
competition

Figure 9.2. The EuroBonus controversy as interference between two chains of translations

(see Figure 9.2). These processes of adjustment can be conceived as chains of translations through which ideas about markets are concretized (adjusting the world to the map), and/or through which abstractions are made from working markets (adjusting the map to the world) (Kjellberg and Helgesson 2006). Below, I present some observations concerning the introduction of FFPs before discussing the interferences between the two processes of adjustment.

ADJUSTMENTS TOWARDS MARKETS WITH FREQUENT FLYER PROGRAMMES

Ongoing exchange practices in the markets for air travel constituted one set of situations in which the statement about markets carried by FFPs were brought to bear. The introduction of programmes like EuroBonus into these settings revealed an important requirement for the proliferation of the statement: the participation of customers. The new device had to become part of the exchange situation. This meant that customers needed to recognize the programme as a relevant entity to take into account when buying airline travel, either by becoming convinced of its benefits or in some other way being induced to use it. Here, the distributed character of the customer is important. The programmes were directed at individual travellers. Arguably, the collective that constitutes a customer of air travel always includes one or more travellers. But travellers need not correspond exactly to customers.

Most importantly for the FFPs, companies, their travel policies, and possible external travel agents also participate in constituting business travel customers. By directing the rewards to individual travellers, the success of the programmes required no specific actions on behalf of these others. In fact, given the views expressed by many companies regarding whom to reward for loyalty, their actions constituted a threat to the success of FFPs.

The airlines' efforts to attract customers through loyalty programmes under certain competitive conditions were of course preceded by the inscription of a set of ideas into specific programmes with explicit rules for membership and loyalty rewards. The normalizing practices of adjusting (if necessary) an airline's competitive policy and translating parts of it into an FFP constitute another situation in which the statement was brought to bear. Although the account did not trace in detail the required environment for the statement's proliferation in this setting, it seems clear that the ideas on which FFPs built were extracted from experience from other types of bonus programmes, and that expertise concerning such programmes was actively employed in their construction. While a distinction between the introduction of the first FFP and subsequent mimetic efforts is tempting, the account provides little support for this. In a sense, all the airlines were copycats. Furthermore, altered images of the competitive situation contributed in the process: for American Airlines these images were linked to the US deregulation; for SAS they concerned increased international competition and lost business on specific routes.

A third environmental requirement for FFPs, besides policy decisions and customer participation, becomes evident once customers start to take them into account: in order to reward loyalty, one must also record loyalty. This requires a workable definition of loyalty and a monitoring system for registering member-specific travelling. Hence, the statement carried by the programmes also had to be performed through representational practices. Although airlines anticipated this when designing their programmes, the availability of data storage and processing capacity was an important infrastructural requirement in this third situation in which the statement was brought to bear.

These three observations concerning the process of adjustment between the statement and a required environment seem to be generally applicable to FFPs. But as the account of EuroBonus shows, this was not enough in the Swedish setting where tax regulations interfered with the idea of rewarding loyal customers. Hence, SAS also engaged in normalizing practices to exempt loyalty rewards from taxation. These efforts were directed towards the national political arena, particularly towards the government at the time. In this setting, the statement required other circumstances to prosper: a spokesperson willing to propose a new bill and enough support for it to pass through parliament. To achieve this, SAS elaborated on their need for home market conditions on a par with their international competitors. Through these activities, SAS succeeded in achieving the sought after legislative change, thus making available yet another part of the required environment.

INTERFERENCE BETWEEN TWO PROCESSES OF ADJUSTMENT

The major obstacle against SAS's efforts to realize the market presupposed by EuroBonus resulted from the two complaints filed with the SCA. These complaints questioned the alignment of EuroBonus with the statement about markets performed through normalizing practices associated with competition law. In doing so, the complaints triggered a performance struggle by causing interference between two processes of adjusting statements about markets for air travel and their associated worlds. The decision by the SCA, SAS's appeal to the Market Court, the proceedings, the ruling, SAS's efforts to comply with the ruling, and the SCA's recent invalidation of the ruling, all constitute episodes in this prolonged struggle.

The process of adjustment that now interfered with the efforts of SAS was part of a wider effort to increase competition in Sweden, whose first tangible effect on air travel had been the domestic deregulation in 1992. Through this regulatory change, the SCA was given responsibility for monitoring the market, and for promoting the statement about markets inscribed in the Competition Act. During the EuroBonus controversy, then, the SCA promoted a statement about markets based on the IO theory of markets (e.g. Scherer and Ross 1990), which had been successfully translated into legal code and methods of measurement to support its enforcement well before the controversy (Willig et al. 1991; McChesney 1996; Djelic 2002). Apart from this general link to IO theory, the SCA also employed experts versed in this tradition to evaluate the market in question.

The events following the two complaints clarified that the statement implied by EuroBonus now required a different environment than that needed for its performation as part of on-going exchange practice (discussed above). As part of the process of adjustment in which the SCA was engaged, and with which the current regulatory framework was aligned, EuroBonus was a device carrying a statement not only about individual exchanges of airline tickets but also about the market for air travel. As such, it could only be evaluated in relation to a carefully defined 'relevant market'. Whether or not the statement could continue to be performed thus hinged on establishing its consequences for the functioning of that market (rather than, or in addition to, its consequences for individual exchanges).

The initial evaluation by the SCA, based on standards associated with 'its' market version, suggested that the device hindered the realization of a domestic market for air travel with competition. Whether SAS entertained an alternative market version or not, it did not interfere with this evaluation; its world was not made available in that setting. The result was an attempt by the SCA to interfere directly with the exchange practices of SAS through a captation device of its own: a conditional fine of SEK 100 million. Thus, the SCA sought to impose its market version on ongoing exchange practices concerning air travel in Sweden through a dramatic recalibration of the economic consequences of EuroBonus for SAS (Mol 2002: 85). This attempted interference was diverted by SAS through their appeal to the Market Court, which gave the airline an opportunity to make its market version available, and hence capable of interfering with the SCA version, as part of normalizing practices.

This required SAS to connect EuroBonus to an image of the market for air travel, explicating that the airline was indeed promoting an alternative market version compared to that of the SCA. During the legal process, both parties engaged in representational market practices to depict the consequences of EuroBonus based on their respective conceptions of the relevant market. As should be clear from the case, these representational practices were far from disinterested observations of a market already there, but heated, contentious engagements with what the market for air travel should be. Here, the two sides appear to have pursued different representational strategies, reflecting the character of their respective statements about markets. The SCA relied on theoretical reasoning supported by examples, for example, concerning the loyalty-creating effect of EuroBonus and what was to count as an acceptable means of competition. SAS, on the other hand, emphasized empirically derived representations, for example a survey of travellers' reasons for choosing airlines, and descriptions of how airlines compete.

The court ruling required SAS to cease applying EuroBonus to routes where they faced competition. This partially privileged the process of adjustment championed by the SCA (Sjögren and Helgesson 2007). Equipped with the court ruling, the SCA was now able to produce the required environment for its market version in some of the ongoing exchange practices for air travel in Sweden. Through the penalty fine, the SCA version (national travel for air travel) interfered with the SAS version (international travel market), leading SAS to assist the SCA in producing the required environment for its version of the market by adjusting EuroBonus. SAS now recognized a Swedish market for passenger travel by air on which EuroBonus was not applicable. Although EuroBonus as a whole was out of reach for the SCA, their actions still came to interfere with EuroBonus beyond the Swedish market through SAS's alliance partners. SAS resolved these interferences by establishing time-consuming sorting routines to perform a distinction between the Swedish market for passenger travel by air and its other markets. Rather than decoupling practices, then,

SAS carefully orchestrated their coupling to reduce the number of situations where incompatible versions encountered each other (Kjellberg and Helgesson 2006).

Concluding remarks on the need for precarious engagements with markets

The EuroBonus controversy highlights the roles of both marketing and regulatory efforts in shaping markets. It also illustrates the precarious and shifting character of their influence, not least in the face of competing attempts to control market processes. This brings into question the use of tidy concepts like market institutions to explain how markets are shaped. The arduous and uncertain work required of both SAS and the SCA to associate their ideas about markets with an actual market implies a critique of approaches that explain outcomes with reference to structural traits of various interest groups (Fligstein 2001). If concrete efforts to adjust statements and their environments matter, and interfere with each other, then approaches that ascribe explanatory power to structural preconditions are at best incomplete.[11]

For actors engaging in efforts to shape markets a central lesson from the case concerns the dependence on others. It was SAS—not the SCA—that in the end realized a market for domestic air travel *without* EuroBonus. Similarly, the SCA was instrumental in the recent revival of some markets *with* EuroBonus. But there is more to these contributions of others than a simple programme/anti-programme dichotomy (Latour 1992); the others on which proponents of alternative market versions have to rely have more complex patterns of response than simply aye or nay (Helgesson and Kjellberg 2005). SAS *complied* with the Market Court ruling, that is it adjusted its marketing practices to a direct prescription. But, as company representatives indicated, SAS never became *aligned* with this market version. That is, SAS never accepted the new role ascribed to it by the Market Court, explicitly holding the ruling to be incorrect and reverting to previous practices as soon as the financial consequence of non-compliance was removed. This also applies to the SCA, who may well open a new inquiry into the legality of EuroBonus despite its recent compliance with SAS's request to invalidate the court ruling.

This lack of alignment might seem to suggest that few changes actually took place in the market for air travel and that recent events simply have returned it to *status quo ante bellum*. But this is hardly the case. For those who engage in shaping markets, achieving compliance with the particular statement about markets they propose is arguably the central objective. For a period of time, in those parts of the market where SAS faced competition, the SCA version was indeed being realized. Failing to align relevant others with a particular market version simply makes it difficult to render compliance durable. And this is generally a good thing, contributing to the dynamic quality of markets (Alderson and Cox 1948). As such, it provides for resilience and checks against the totalizing power of economics so feared by some commentators (Mirowski and Nik-Khah 2008). Of course, this check applies equally to marketing, or any other body of expertise employed in shaping markets.

For all the reassurance it provides, the EuroBonus case also underscores the necessity of engagement. Markets are shaped by multiple practices, and while their performance can be neatly separated to produce an image of efficiency, the prospects of producing better markets feeds on actors engaging with this multiplicity. The plasticity of markets calls for a reflexive production, capable of questioning not only how economic exchanges are performed but also how we generate market images and produce normalizing statements about markets. On this count, there is scope for improvement from economics and marketing alike.

■ NOTES

1. The study is based on historical documents from the actors involved. Legal processes are particularly appropriate to study with this method since available documents are remnants from the process rather than retrospective accounts. The document study was complemented with interviews with representatives of SAS and the SCA to provide a more thorough understanding of their respective stances, and with a review of trade journals and literature on the development of the airline industry.

2. These programmes gave consumers coupons relative to their purchases in participating stores. Collected in booklets, the coupons could be traded for goods such as household appliances. The pros and cons of this marketing practice, primarily its effects on price and effectiveness as a competitive measure, was subject to debate among market scholars in the 1950s and 1960s (e.g. Beem 1957; Strotz 1958; Davis 1959; Bell 1967; Sherman 1968).

3. The airline industry in Europe was excluded from the common transport policy in the Treaty of Rome and national airlines were supported by their respective governments. Without a multilateral agreement in place, European liberalization proceeded slowly during the 1980s. Following the liberalization of the UK domestic routes, bilateral negotiations resulted in a handful of 'open skies' agreements. In parallel, deregulation efforts were made within the European Union and a series of regulatory changes in 1987, 1990, and 1992 gradually deregulated the industry (Dearden 1994; Button 2004).

4. e.g. Keetch, Blair 'Collecting Miles' *The Toronto Star*, 5 October 1997.

5. In 1993, the Competition Act was revised in anticipation of Swedish membership in the European Union and legislation patterned on EU-law was introduced.

6. Based on the SCA's decision (1999-11-12).

7. Based on SAS's appeal (1999-12-03).

8. Based on the statements presented to the Market Court by the SCA (1999-12-16; 2000-01-18; 2000-03-01; 2000-05-31; 2000-07-06).

9. Based on statements presented to the Market Court by SAS (1999-12-20; 2000-02-14; 2000-04-28; 2000-06-28).

10. Based on the ruling of the Market Court (Marknadsdomstolen 2001).

11. Of course, my narrative is also incomplete, focusing almost exclusively on SAS and the SCA despite indications of others figuring in the process. There are two important reasons for this. First, awarding a more prominent role to others would have resulted in an even more complex narrative. Second, the legal controversy actually channelled many of these others into either camp, for instance allowing the SCA to become a spokesperson for competitors and travel agents.

10 Trading bads and goods

Market practices in Fair Trade retailing

DANIEL NEYLAND AND ELENA SIMAKOVA

Introduction

This chapter engages with the recent debate on the performativity of economics (Callon 1998*a*; MacKenzie et al. 2007) in the context of market practices. In particular the chapter explores the currency of notions such as market and trade in the construction of Fair Trade clothing. We shall look at the ways in which Fair Trade clothing retailers understand and attempt to build market spaces.[1] We identify and analyse three distinct forms of market making: first, there are Fair Traders who opt to build a market niche within (what they understand as) the clothing industry; second, there are those who seek to compete in (what they understand as) the mainstream clothing market; while the third group display a tendency to opt out of markets altogether, focusing on (what they understand as) charity. The main purpose of the chapter is to examine discourses and practices which frame the 'hybrid forums' (Callon 1998*b*; see below) of Fair Trade through alternate market practices in situations of competing discourses of what counts as 'Fair' and what counts as 'Trade'.

First, the chapter offers an introduction to Fair Trade and how this fits and does not fit with conventional literature on marketing. We give consideration to literature on green marketing and critical consumer studies, and critically engage with debates on the selective applicability of the marketing analogy in order to introduce the idea of variability in Fair Trade discourses. Second, the chapter explores in more depth, using empirical material, the three versions of Fair Trade briefly introduced above. Third, the chapter engages with two complexities—of changing perceptions of markets and the relations of worlds and goods—in order to provide a distinct take on market practices. Finally, the chapter concludes with an assessment of the analytical opportunities offered by 'hybrid forums' for understanding the performativity of markets.

Fair Trading as the creation of 'hybrid forums'

In summary terms, Fair Trade can be defined as attempts at constructing certain forms of economic exchange as a solution to social problems, such as poverty (Neyland and Simakova 2009). These social problems can be framed as a need to redress the disadvantaged status of certain social groups, and/or to change the nature of consumption practices so as to contribute to social justice and sustainable development. Fair Trade is thus about rearranging social–material relations in such a way as to make them accountable as accommodating and solving these societal concerns. In this chapter, we focus specifically on the practical efforts to introduce and sustain Fair Trade arrangements in the form of clothing markets.

What does it mean and what does it take to market Fair Trade and build Fair Trade markets? In line with the overall purpose of this collection to offer a novel analytic approach to the ways in which markets and marketing are interconnected in practice, we will describe Fair Trade marketing practices as *Fair Trading*. This discursive move, we believe, will help us to explore various instances of the application of notions of trade and market in Fair Trade practices.[2] We intend to interrogate the boundaries of Fair Trade as economic activity via analysis of the nuanced crafting of framings of Fair Trade in participants' accounts. Fair Trading allows us to place an emphasis on the active accomplishments of participants and steer away from assumptions that Fair Trade is a single, simple, known entity.

What can the marketing literature tell us about Fair Trade? And the other way round, what can Fair Trading reveal to us about markets, marketing, and trade? We turned to the marketing literature in order to find a place for Fair Trading by trying on different approaches to marketing. Our efforts have been illustrative of the tensions currently experienced by marketing theory which falls short of accounting for the boundaries of marketing and markets (cf. Araujo et al., this volume). Both notions of *green* marketing and *social* marketing that could accommodate Fair Trading are based on the assumption that these types of marketing practices operate with concerns *other* than simply profit making. Such concerns may include the introduction of a sustainability orientation in corporations, assessments of the attractiveness of green strategies for shareholders, and promoting different ways of constructing (capturing, or even 'isolating', as in Peattie and Charter 2002) the 'green' consumer as a different consumer group. The literature highlights that the introduction of these marketing variations in organizations is a *process*: some authors speak of 'greening' the marketing strategy as a kind of managerial practice (Peattie and Charter 2002), or of 're-tooling' marketing for sustainability (Peattie 2007). This requires work to create a space for these marketing strategies and practices in organizations. As suggested by authors working in the stream of critical marketing and in critical consumer studies in particular (Gordon et al. 2007; Kajzer Mitchell 2007), recognition of the societal and environmental contexts in and of marketing practice is a powerful means to explore the limits of normative marketing stances. The kinds of marketing practices that purport to address societal concerns appear at times awkward and in conflict with the corporate profit orientation, opening up opportunities for problematizing the ordinary, taken for granted, aspects of what marketing ought to be focused on. In that sense, both social and green marketing—in theory and in practice—already perform a critique on the generic (Kotlerian) version of marketing as a universal 'discipline of exchange behaviour' (Kotler and Levy 1969; Kotler 1972) and on marketing management as a 'function of universal applicability'.

Studies in anthropology help us to expand this critique, placing Fair Trading into a socio-political-economic context that appears contestable and contentious. As long as forms of political (eco-, green, Fair Trade) consumerism emerge, markets become sites of politics (Micheletti et al. 2004). Fair Trading is thus a highly politicized form of marketing. Corporate efforts to promote (or to refuse to promote) goods seemingly embodying some ethical values via means of economic exchange encounter a variety of forms of individual and collective action, both supportive (consumption, citizen lobbying groups) and critical (boycotts, buycotts, resistance). The close intertwining of and boundary work between political, economic, and individual choice (of e.g. taste) is reflected in the construction of new forms of consumer cultures (Kroen 2004; Schudson 2006). One example of this is the *consumer–citizen* 'in whom economic agency and political goal setting come together' (Mol 2009).

How can we account analytically for Fair Trading without losing the richness of its contexts and practices? Can we avoid fitting these practices into the rigid framework of marketing management categories (of e.g. the '4Ps'[3]) in order to give us space to investigate Fair Trading particularities? Our focus here is on the kind of work which goes into creating and sustaining the political-economic worlds of Fair Trade via engaging in various types of practices. Below we will examine how some ideas found in the area of Science and Technology Studies can help us build a perspective on Fair Trading.

As noted previously (Neyland and Simakova 2009), participants in Fair Trade find themselves acting in multiple worlds of certification, strategizing, identity work, and market building. The production, distribution, and consumption of Fair Trade goods are underpinned by at times very different notions of what counts as 'Fair' and of what counts as 'Trade' (see analysis below). One way of approaching Fair Trading that we will explore in this chapter is to look at these discursive practices as the creation of what Callon (1998b, together with Ari Rip) calls 'the hybrid forum'. The 'hybrid forums' of Fair Trade can be understood in terms of distributed networks of socio-material *actants.*[4] Labels, packaging, and goods all play a role in performing various versions of Fair Trade via offering particular versions of Fair Trade for interpretation. The identities and roles of entities enrolled into Fair Trade and made available via, for example, labels become a matter of interpretation and contestation. We approach Fair Trading as attempts at proposing and achieving *new* forms of relationships between producers and consumers. This suggests thinking of Fair Trading in terms of ongoing participants' efforts to rethink and reconfigure the existing notions and arrangements of economic exchange; to actively engage in constructing new forms of exchange; as well as to articulate the aims, outcomes, and criteria of success of these efforts.

As the introduction to this volume notes, markets can be usefully considered as otherwise heterogeneous interminglings of people and things, which are drawn together into hybrid collectives. What might otherwise be diverse becomes more singular in the figurative space of the market. For our purposes in analysing Fair Trade, we will try to open up what might otherwise be the singular space of the Fair Trade market to trace out some of the contours of hybridity from which singularity might have emerged and to test out the singularity of Fair Trade.

Various worlds of Fair Trade, in other words, struggle to 'hold responsible specific forms of agency' (Dilley 1992: 24) via offering competing versions of what it means to do Fair Trade. As Dubuisson-Quellier and Lamine (2008) show, Fair Trade network building assumes trading distinctions between the individual (choice) and the collective (action); producer–consumer identities emerge in these new forms of engagement *ad hoc* as forms of solidarity, organization of lobbying, and involvement in legal disputes. These authors emphasize the shifting, fluid nature of distribution of roles and identities in Fair Trade networking achieved in various ways for the purposes at hand. Recent studies of Fair Trade and alternative food distribution networks (Whatmore et al. 2003) also draw attention to the multiple and local ways of accomplishing the 'quality' of products and of the nature of trade (Callon et al. 2002).

We continue with a suggestion that in order to build a Fair Trade 'hybrid forum' participants engage in what Michel Callon (1998*b*: 244) termed 'strategies and calculation'. These notions stress the ongoing work of *framing* (fixation of the relationships between entities around an economic transaction, contractual or by agreement) and *overflowing* (an economic transaction spreading out to involve more entities defined as economic outsiders) that make for the fabrics of market making. As Callon argues, entities and the relations between them emerge as the economic actors engage in the work of accounting for their relationships with others in the market arena, or in articulating the *externalities*[5] of their market actions. In the case of Fair Trade, articulation of such externalities may involve deliberations about whether the Fair Trade practices are ethical enough, whether disadvantaged communities receive enough benefit, or, also a form of externality, accounting for relations to other market actors in the form of competition or cooperation. Thus, Callon's approach suggests a productive analytic shift from the conventional marketing notions of producers and consumers as single (or aggregated) fixed entities to appreciation of the dynamic and shifting forms of agency in market relations, or, as Dubuisson-Quellier and Lamine (2008: 63) put it, the 're-locations' of economic exchange and political participation in collective decision making. Hence a crucial question for this chapter is what are these 'other places', hybrid forums, or *heterotopias* (as in Foucault; featured in Mol 2009) where Fair Trade is performed? We will unpack this question below by offering the idea of places as loci for interpretation.

The emphasis on places should not lead one to always think geographically; the 'places' in question are abstract locales where questions of agency, identity, and articulation work[6] between entities come into focus. Illustrating the point about the shifting nature of agency and articulation work in Fair Trade relations, Mol poses a question which captures a feature of these other places or 'hybrid forums': 'How indeed is it possible to add different goods together— like pleasure *and* health; or pleasure *and* fairness?' (Mol 2009). According to Mol, the loci of the accomplishment of these categories as working together to produce a new socio-political reality are *labels* offered to the consumer– citizen to interpret. The 're-location' (as above) of consumer–citizen involvement is accomplished through the material practices of reading, interpreting, feeling, and reacting to Fair Trade goods via consuming labels. Our chapter notes and interrogates another locus of interpretation. We are concerned with understanding, in Mol's terms, how the wor(l)ds get 'fluidly added together' (Mol 2009) via offering an analysis of Fair Traders' deliberations concerning their retailing strategies for clothing.

Our examination of the work that goes into the creation of various 'hybrid forums' of Fair Trade aims to further explore the argument made elsewhere (Neyland and Simakova 2009) that the creation of markets can be interrogated in terms of an inversion of conventional world-product relations. Namely, we suggest, and will illustrate below, that instead of launching a (Fair Trade) product into the world, Fair Traders attempt to launch a world into their products. In other words, the practices of creating Fair Trade 'hybrid forums' hinge on the participants' notions of accomplishing a (fair, healthy, religious, economic, rational) world out there through consumption (in this sense, the 'out there' is putatively 'in here' in this product). The Fair Trade items to be consumed incorporate a world to be accomplished. To connect the discussion to the main aim of the chapter, in what sense exactly are the 'hybrid forums', or worlds to be consumed, accomplished through the negotiation of the externalities of economic transactions?

Fair Trading in theory, and in practice

The ideas of 'goods' and 'bads' as forms of externalities accomplished by Fair Trade are of particular interest to this chapter as an instantiation of the performativity of economic language in the construction of 'hybrid forums'. What deserves more attention, we argue, is the observed uneasy[7] distinction between *positive* and *negative* externalities in Callon's approach. In this chapter we are particularly interested in offering an analysis of the constitution of the positive ('goods') and negative ('bads') externalities in strategizing and calculating forms of economic transactions and modes of consumer engagement. How are these notions defined and made sense of in the processes of constructing and accounting for Fair Trade as ethically superior 'hybrid forums'?

The research for this chapter draws on an extended series of interviews with organizations involved in the production, movement, certification, and retailing of Fair Trade clothing. Twenty organizations took part in semi-structured interviews,[8] many offered tours of their facilities, and many provided objects for analysis (including annual reports, their own research, Fair Trade goods and labels). Their participation was at least partly stimulated by the proposal that the outcomes of this research might provide a basis for addressing some of the challenges they feel Fair Trade involves (see below).

FAIR TRADE AND FAIRTRADE

Prior to getting into the details of the interviews, we first outline some sources of tension between normative approaches to Fair Trade and Fair Traders' discourse. The global textile trade has been a focus of concern over many years. Concerns have been expressed regarding exploitation of workers (low pay, child labour, long hours, hazardous working conditions), pollution of local environments (through crop spraying, leading to health issues for farmers), and the consequences of trading bloc agreements on the movement of goods (particularly for countries whose economies are highly dependent on selling cotton or clothing to developed country markets). These concerns have been expressed in Lesotho (Irin 2006); Macedonia (amongst several places highlighted by the Clean Clothes Campaign 2006); Honduras, Brazil, Guatemala, Dominican Republic, and Bali (all featured in Corpwatch 1996); Australia (The Age 2006); Morocco (UNRISD 1996); and Bangladesh (see WSWS 2006) amongst many other places. The promotion of these concerns has been the responsibility of campaigning organizations (such as the Clean Clothes Campaign).

Fair Trade has provided one response to these concerns. But what counts as Fair Trade? Fair Trade has already been a topic of research in terms of proposing normative prescriptions of Fair Trade. Some of the basic principles of Fair Trade are set out by Nicholls and Opal (2005): moving people in the developing world out of poverty (mostly through market access); connecting producers and consumers into direct trading relationships; introducing beneficial rather than exploitative working conditions; a more equitable distribution of profits across the supply chain; and addressing imbalances of information and power. In order to achieve these aims Fair Trade schemes seek to establish an agreed minimum price for goods above the market minimum; provide development and technical assistance funded by this market premium for Fair Trade goods; introduce direct purchasing from farmers; employ transparent and long-term contracts for goods; work with cooperative not competitive trade; provide credit in the form of advance payments; provide market information to producers; organize farm workers into democratic, participatory decision-making bodies; operate sustainable production; and remove labour abuses.

To what extent and in what sense do the principles of Fair Trade, as formulated in the normative literature, feature in Fair Traders' discourse? Articulating aims, outcomes, and characteristics of Fair Trade was a notable part of the interviews. Some Fair Traders recognized these notions as acceptable descriptions of their practices. Indeed many of the interviewees without prompting articulated detailed versions of these aims and how their business operated in relation to the aims. For many, aims such as 'capacity building', 'transparency', and 'accountability' were a regular feature of describing their Fair Trade practices:

I think [Fair Trade's] in the area of capacity building... In encouraging transparency ... Accountability... In terms of long-term relationships with producers, working on product development... sort of market information skills so that producers can build their own sort of independence and ability to trade on Fair Trade terms and just trade full stop to be honest. (Interviewee 1, mainstream Fair Trade importer)

We should not automatically assume that all involved in Fair Trade found this articulation easy. For many the aims of Fair Trade were a straightforward means to separate the kinds of 'goods' they wished to pursue from 'bads'. 'Goods' could, for example, incorporate transparent supply chain relations, whereas 'bads' often acted as a miscellaneous category for most conventional, unethical items and their associated trading relations. For others the aims were a long-forgotten feature of their initial organizational application to be recognized as Fair Traders. For example, amongst those who were prompted to express what they thought were the aims of Fair Trade, were some Fair Traders who struggled with articulation:

Um... I can't remember what the [Fair Trade] questions were [pause] I'm just seeing if I can find it in um [long pause] in my e-mails [longer pause] der der der Fair-Trade [long pause] importers, importers [pause] let's have a look [pause] no [really long pause, lots of background noise, papers shuffling] Yes [Interviewee then lists Fair Trade questions they had to answer]. (Interviewee 7, niche, small-scale Fair Trade importer and retailer, telephone interview)

We note here that different Fair Trade organizations have different degrees of awareness of what are the aims of Fairness to which they are trying to adhere. This might lead us into assuming that notions of 'good' and 'bad' are always construed and articulated through the language of the aims. We observe, however, that the register employed by the interviewees changes when they discuss what happens *in practice*. How are Fair Trade aims accomplished through the practices of Fair Trading? How are the notions of 'goods' and 'bads' construed in the accounts of Fair Trade practice?

The discourse of Fair Trade offers a number of devices to account for this activity as a form of economic exchange. For instance, an important and oft repeated slogan amongst Fair Traders is 'Trade not Aid'. According to this slogan fairness ought to be accomplished through selling goods which adhere to Fair Trade aims and principles, and the market and marketing for Fair Trade ought to be based on communicating beyond doubt the goodness of Fair Trade goods (see e.g. Fairtrade Foundation 2008). However, Fair Trade is not simply about sticking a Fair Trade label on a good and hoping this communicates notions of goodness. What counts as 'good' is the outcome of a designed, deliberate, lengthy, and expensive process of certification. The Fair Trade label is not solely a piece of design; it is a certificate which stands in for a process.

The Fairtrade Labelling Organizations International (FLO) group has established certification standards. Certification involves sending FLO inspectors to spend a week or two with potential Fair Trade producers, checking their accounts and interviewing a random selection of workers. These inspectors assess the extent to which workers are organized into democratic, participatory groups engaged in decision making, and that production is sustainable. They also audit trade standards. A report is compiled by FLO-cert and sent to FLO's committee which decides whether or not a producer is entitled to be labelled and certified Fair Trade. This process also establishes a base price for the goods to be sold. The term 'Fairtrade' is protected by FLO and refers exclusively to FLO-certified goods. 'Fairtrade' thus stands distinct from other goods labelled Fair Trade.

Once certified, FLO continues to monitor and certify the trading of certificated goods. Certified producers send to FLO six-monthly aggregate data on Fairtrade sales and certified traders also submit aggregate quarterly data. The trader then sells the produce to a certified manufacturer who can then label the goods Fairtrade and sell the goods to retailers. The traders and manufacturers also inform FLO of these sales. FLO then forwards this information on quantities to recognized Fairtrade organizations in the country of the manufacturer who checks for any discrepancy in produce. The amount of Fairtrade premium the producers should have received is then calculated and on the next FLO inspection the producers have to demonstrate how this premium has been invested. Any discrepancies can lead to a loss of certification. Producers, traders, and manufacturers must pay for FLO certifications and renewals (see Nicholls and Opal 2005).

This is one version of a claimed and articulated 'good' (the 'good' might be noted as a hybrid forum drawing together otherwise heterogeneous entities such as a product, the relations built into it, and a fairer world to which it aspires). However, there are other Fair Trade organizations with their own aims, processes, labels, and outcomes; in other words, their own ways of doing 'goods'. For example, the Fair Trade Organization (FTO) mark (run by the International Federation of Alternative Trade—IFAT) relies more on self-reporting and is designed to cover an organization, not a product. IFAT specializes in goods with complex supply chains (including clothing), which go through several production stages prior to retail sales.[9] There are also further labels that can be attached to Fair Trade products.[10] Fair Trade/Fairtrade is hence more complex than a single process with a single certified outcome. Thus attention needs to be paid to the production, certification, and labelling of 'goods'; there is much variety amongst Fair Trade hybrid forums.

Interviewees were keen to express views on these distinctions. For Fair Traders, this was not solely a matter of alternative processes; the forms of certification also embodied the distinct aims and ethos of the certification organization. What counts as 'good' and 'bad' in Fair Trading is hence attributable to the aims of the Fair Traders (those importing and selling 'goods') and the processes and aims of the certification organization to which the Fair Traders are connected (who uses processes of certification to build a particular kind of good into 'goods'):

I think they feel that they've got a different role in that I think that IFAT feels like it's more a support...Because it's helping a lot of kind of small-scale producers, you know, across the world...Whereas FLO is very much kind of an authority; you know, top down. IFAT's very much from the bottom up. You know, trying to help lots of different groups; you know, and help them to be marketed and whatever else. Find customers. (Interviewee 18, niche, small-scale, high-end Fair Trade retailer)

...evaluation for development is the way we would look at it. Rather than evaluation for decapitation!...I mean it's this whole issue right. Once you put a label on something that you actually know what that label means...(Interviewee 4, mainstream, large-scale, 100% Fair Trade organization)

Hence we find within a broad version of Fair Trade, different labels, produced via different modes of certification and also imbuing the distinct, articulated ethos of the organization responsible for certification. What comes to count as 'good' or 'bad' is thus accomplished through distinct practices. However, what do organizations involved in producing, importing, and retailing Fair Trade 'goods' make of these labels and certification processes? How might we draw together and analyse distinct hybrid forums of Fair Trade? We now look in more detail at their practices in order to analyse the ways in which they accomplish versions of Fair Trade.

Fair Traders

Those involved in the manufacturing, importing–exporting, and retailing of Fair Trade clothing noted differences in their particular approaches to Fair Trade. Hence, what counted as Fair Trading and how 'goods' ought to be accomplished, and 'bads' not, differed. In this section we present three distinct communities of Fair Trade and analyse the ways in which their articulations of practice produced particular orientations of 'goods' (which could be understood as hybrid forums for the intermingling of such hetero-geneous features as labels, products, trading relations, and worlds to which products aspired). This categorization of three communities was accom-plished by coding the interviews according to the identities offered by the organizational participants themselves. It does not imply that the views within each community are completely uniform. The first of these three categories were niche retailers.

NICHE RETAILERS

Fair Trade niche retailers (entered into attempts to) build Fair Trade as an ethical alternative or accompaniment to mainstream clothing. Fair Trade became (or was in the process of continually becoming) a small-scale, often artisan, non-industrial, ethical means to offer a Fair corrective to the textile Trade. However, the terms of selling were still trade. That is, nichers were looking to make a profit on top of the amounts they sent back to producers. Furthermore, the relationship with the mainstream was not straightforward. As more and more mainstream retailers sold Fair Trade clothing, nichers were unsure of their market position. Were they trying to sell a different product to the mainstream, were they trying to appeal to a different consumer segment (by offering something Fairer than the mainstream), or were they looking to prove their ability to trade in order to move from a niche into the main-stream? These tensions and difficulties were articulated by nichers.

Nichers found a tension in their relationship with producers. Although nichers wanted ethical relations with producers, they also wanted to be able to tell producers what kinds of product-design would sell. This generated a tension between neocolonial concerns with developed country nichers imposing views on developing country producers and the need to sell something to somebody in a developed country. Some nichers felt that allowing producers the freedom to manufacture 'goods' would provide the unique (niche) selling points they were seeking; others sought products which had the potential to sell well and be simultaneously 'good'. This latter view is expressed by the following interviewee:

So they [the producers] sort of sent me stuff and I thought oh, my God . . . Some of the stuff they sent I thought—oh no, this is awful! (Interviewee 2, niche, small-scale Fair Trade retailer)

Other nichers have looked to use what they perceive to be good design to increase sales. However, as the following nicher explains, this was not all about making a niche into the mainstream, it could instead be about building a niche through 'goods' which might sit alongside the mainstream:

There's real design involved in the process as well now. So . . . I think the idea was that we were just going to obviously not only meet our existing customer but broaden it out because we know that there's people within the mainstream that are becoming more and more interested in green issues and ethical issues. But they're not willing to sacrifice their style for that. (Interviewee 6, niche, ethical clothing retailer and campaigner)

Yet other nichers found that their direct trading with producers, their long-standing relations and their aim to remain a niche, did limit processes such as the speed with which goods could move through manufacture to retail and consumption. The following nicher found this to be an acceptable aspect of operating in a niche:

You know, we started to realise that actually there were companies who were offering Fair Trade clothes; you know, kind of actual proper clothes as opposed to just you know, from the kind of hand loomed kind of just smocks . . . So that in a way does kind of limit kind of capabilities in terms of being able to produce things very, very quickly. But my aim of the company is not produce clothes which are very, very fast fashion because I think that that's a slightly—it's a kind of a slightly silly view. If you're trying to produce something which has all of its processes that are very sustainable . . . But to produce something which is only actually kind of wearable for a few months, is not the right aspiration. (Interviewee 18, niche, small-scale, high-end Fair Trade retailer)

For this nicher, speed operates in two areas of clothing production: the manufacture and the lifespan of goods. The emphasis is placed on the 'goods' of slow manufacture and slow consumption (see also below in our analysis of environmental concerns). Alongside discussion of the design and speed of 'goods', price was articulated as a point of tension around which nichers oriented notions of 'goods' and 'bads'. For example, small-scale, direct, slow trading relations could lead to expensive products. However, some nichers thought this a reasonable aspect of operating in a niche, and perhaps providing a commentary on the mainstream:

Well, I think there should be an extra price involved [for Fair Trade goods] but that's only when you directly relate it to how ridiculously cheap clothes are now...I mean three T shirts for £5, what—Where's the value in that? There's no value. (Interviewee 6, niche, ethical clothing retailer and campaigner)

Still other nichers sought to use their trading position as an opportunity to also pass strong comment on the actions of mainstreamers:

I mean [mainstream retailers] are in an interesting position because they, and they are sort of typical of the sort of schizophrenia of the market at the moment but they, on the one hand they are slashing prices left, right and centre because that's the way the industry is going....And on the other hand they are promoting themselves as an ethical retailer and it is quite ironic and the way they are doing it is...that they can say, 'well we are rolling out Fairtrade cotton across as much of our supply chain as we can' but you know if they are cutting their prices like that we know that that's going to translate into workers losing out sort of in other bits of the supply chain, other than the cotton bit. (Interviewee 10, niche, ethical clothing retailer and campaigner)

This last excerpt offers an articulation of nichers' views on the 'goods' and 'bads' of Fair Trading. The mainstream was cutting prices, squeezing margins, and reducing income for the producers of Fair Trade products (aside from cotton farmers whose pay was guaranteed by Fair Trade certification). The products being sold in this way were not 'goods'. Instead they were to be understood as 'bads'. The worlds built into these products (of low pay, squeezed margins, Fair Trade bargains for developed country consumers) were what accomplished the 'bad'. On the other hand, nichers felt they were in a better position to retail 'goods' which built a different world into the product (a small-scale world of close relations between retailers and producers, where retailers know that all involved producers are getting paid a fair price). These 'goods' were not of sufficient scale to alter the entire world of the mainstream, but were instead a comment on it. At the least they were a better 'good' than the mainstream, or at times a 'good' to contrast with the mainstream 'bad'.

A second group of Fair Traders sought instead to enter the mainstream, in order to do business on a larger scale. Instead of correcting or acting as a commentary on the mainstream, the aim was to alter the mainstream from within, to scale up Fair Trading practices, and to reach mass markets for ethical goods.

MAINSTREAMERS

Mainstreamers often sought to demarcate their market from that of either nichers or those involved in charitable work (see below). This work was done to both justify their mainstream identity and to note that it could sit alongside other Fair Trade markets. Mainstreamers seemed keen to emphasize that they were not trying to push nichers or charities out of Fair Trade. This comparative positioning is emphasized by the following interviewee:

... you know a lot of [Fair Trade] it's based on the Christian work in this country as well. You know the Christian bookshops will go and they will sell Fair Trade gifts and that is really the image I wanted to get away from. I have absolutely no issue with what they are doing but I just want to try and bring it to the mainstream. (Interviewee 19, mainstream Fair Trade retailer)

Others involved in Fair Trade (e.g. in the certification organizations) were keen to highlight the importance of scaled-up Fair Trade. For the following interviewee scaling up mainstream involvement was not just important, it was essential:

Well, empowerment is the—this is the issue. I mean I think this is—if you're talking about Fair Trade in terms of empowering the poor and the marginalised, if you were to go to I would say, [a mainstream retailer's] best factory in wherever; let's say Indonesia, I would ... say that it's probably one of the best places to work.... You know, they are the most skilled, they are the best paid. They've got the best working conditions. Okay. It is—you know, it's great ... the supply chain work they're doing and I think it's totally important. It's totally essential. (Interviewee 12, mainstream Fair Trade organization)

Simultaneously, mainstreamers recognized that this scaling up would be a problematic issue for many traditional Fair Trade producers. However, mainstreamers viewed this as an inevitable feature of the moves Fair Trade goods were making into popular retail:

The proposals for pushing Fair Trade values down the supply chain seem to be moving towards criteria that can be fulfilled by larger producing units ... Small factories ... This has made very small-scale artisan based units who have previously seen themselves as being right at the heart of the Fair Trade movement suddenly thinking, well actually we wouldn't be able to fulfil Fairtrade foundation criteria ... we are going to be marginalised from this particular definition of Fairtrade and that makes them feel uncomfortable because that Fairtrade Foundation trademark is regarded by the public as some kind of absolute benchmark. (Interviewee 1, mainstream, medium-scale Fair Trade importer)

Several of the niche retailers also sought to comment on the viability of these mainstream moves. Although some nichers felt they could continue quite comfortably alongside the mainstream, others noted that mainstreaming in one form or another might become inevitable for those involved with the Fairtrade Foundation, due to costs, scale of certification, and need to connect with certified traders/retailers:

I think one of the biggest challenges that you know, Fair Trade fashion has faced in the past is it's been very difficult to up scale these small co-operatives into something you know, sort of can they deliver on the time to the right quality... the Fairtrade Foundation it does, you know, whether you like it or not it does favour bigger customers... —they have to go through the SA8000 or some form of ethical process. And if you're a very small spinning or dying unit or weaving... You're not going to be able to get SA8000. IFAT can take three years. So there are real challenges to everything... (Interviewee 6, niche, ethical clothing retailer and campaigner)

For mainstreamers, the 'goods' they promoted were intertwined with a politics of scale. The only way to introduce the kind of world to which Fair Trade aspired (in this case, for the mainstreamers, a world of reduced exploitation in trade) was to build a Fair world into goods on a mass scale. This was not focused on commenting on the mainstream, but shifting the mainstream from historical 'bads' to contemporary 'goods'.

CHARITABLE NON-TRADERS

A third group sought to position themselves outside the conventions of markets. For (often religious) charitable Fair Traders, God (rather than the devil) was in the detail. In place of a mass market orientation towards large-scale, mainstream business, there was a focus on long-term relationships, understanding the needs of developing country producers, and forsaking profit in return for local community development projects. In other words, Fair Trade was about getting close to the needs, practices, and problems of producers and communicating that closeness in opportunities for consumption.

Several Fair Traders who identified themselves as outside conventional market practices, sought to change entire supply chain relations to operate on a more equitable or 'fair' basis. This was noted as beyond the aims of mainstreamers who at the same time were criticized for their narrow supply chain focus. Concerns were expressed amongst the charitable group that mainstreamers were selling, for example, Fair Trade t-shirts where only the cotton farming had been certified (not the weaving, sewing, stitching, dyeing, or importing processes). The charitable group instead sought to extend equity throughout the supply chain. This was thought to represent too great a cost for mainstreamers since certifying every part of a supply chain would produce a very costly t-shirt. For the charitable group, however, profit was not a motivation. This enabled them to express their (self-proclaimed) view that they were doing the most 'good(s)'. The following interviewee articulated one version of altering the entire supply chain for clothing goods:

...there's a very interesting suggestion that we should ensure that the price a consumer pays is not inconsistent with what is happening on the ground. This means that if the producer is selling their cotton at 15% profit the last person in the chain should not be getting more than that in profit. Not irrespective of overheads. (Interviewee 8, religious Fair Trade charity)

Others sought to stay outside the mainstream for their own ethical and personal happiness. They disputed the necessity and importance of large-scale retail and sought to do Fair Trading on a (just about, most of the time) subsistence basis:

I wouldn't touch it [mainstream business] because you see this is another thing that comes because mainstreaming seems to be the only good word these days and the lovely old idea that small is beautiful seems to have gone for a Burton [laughing]. (Interviewee 15, charitable Fair Trader)

In sum, the articulations of these three alternative communities raise questions about the ways in which (in this case, retail) practices actively constitute markets as (what we have termed) hybrid forums. Specifically, how do Fair Traders' attempts to build a distinction between 'bads' (what they perceived as normal market practices) and 'goods' (a particular version of Fair Trade modifications of markets) intertwine with their understanding of the aims of Fair Trade? The 'goods' of niche Fair Trade were noted as markedly better than the 'bads' of mainstream retailing they sat alongside. However, these 'goods' were not to be understood as a threat to the 'bads' and even those involved in niche Fair Trade clothing 'confessed' to consuming 'bads' while being committed to their 'goods'. Instead the 'goods' offered a commentary on the 'bads'. Niche Fair Trade goods mostly occupied a position as gifts, noted by Fair Traders as opportunities for one to demonstrate their 'good'-ness to others in moments of gift giving, and providing a commentary on the 'bads' of excessive, scaled-up, exploitative consumerism that such gift-giving occasions encouraged.

Mainstreamers disavowed these arguments over ethical disjunctures of scale and attempted to position 'goods' in the midst of (rather than in a niche alongside) 'bads'. Away from nichers' hybrid forums of artisan, community-based, craft skills, came alternate heterogeneous assemblies of factory units, codes of conduct, inspection processes, independent, verified, audited, and certified 'goods' on a mass scale. Within the heart of mainstream 'bads' (even supermarkets, gasp) came 'goods', which carried with them their authenticated provenance of Fair-ness.

But this does nothing to change the terms of Trade, came the litany of charitable Fair (more or less) non-Traders. For the latter, commitment to 'goods' came through dismantling the terms of Trade. In place of a focus on maximizing Fair-ness through scale, came a dedicated, relentless, and (often) non-profit making pursuit of charity. Not just a traditional charity of donations and gift giving, but charity through consumption of 'goods'. The 'goods' were managed, coordinated, and marshalled by, not figures of industry or figures in accounting columns, but figurative gestures of poverty. It was through charity, that the genuine authenticity of poverty was to be made available for (charitable) consumption. It was through close relationships that a particular and (for charitable Fair Traders) poignant hybrid forum of poverty was made available for purchase. But this was not availability through certification and audit; availability here appeared closer to the achievement of anthropological kinship systems than bureaucratic account-ability regimes. It was through articulating the heterogeneity of charitable sacrifice (non-profitability, small-scale, lack of market presence, business insecurity) and ability to replay the close relations of these hybrid trades in a kind of singular detail that the authenticity of poverty was made clear.

Although the picture of distinct Fair Trade communities offers us detail on the nature and accomplishment of 'goods' and 'bads' and market relations, it tells us little of the future. Fair Trade 'goods' and 'bads' were not noted as static by interviewees. The next section will chart views on where the market(s) for Fair Trade might be heading.

FAIR TRADE FUTURES?

Fair Traders (particularly niche and charitable) speculated on whether forms of Fair Trade marketing and consumption had any future at all. Concerns were raised that the mainstreamers were insufficiently committed to Fair Trade and might pull out once it was noted that profit margins were not necessarily higher than other premium-rate goods or if they noted a decline in consumers' interest in these particular 'goods':

I think there's a big risk ... It will be interesting to see what happens with [mainstream retailers] because they've all gone into it in a way that limits their exposure and maximises their publicity. For them it's not that much money and it's a way to see if there is take up and if there's not, they'll drop it. (Interviewee 9, niche importer)

Concerns were also raised that Fair Trade itself might get overtaken by other issues. This Fair Trader raised concerns that the kind of 'good' world sought by consumers might in the future be oriented towards the environment, rather than trade concerns:

Well I have a nasty feeling that it is a fashion. They are all interested in it, it is the thing this year and particularly with clothing that's fashion orientated it's the thing and next year I think, and rightly they will be more worried about the climate change. (Interviewee 15, charitable Fair Trader)

This particular articulation of what would count as the best kind of 'good(s)' was mirrored across Fair Trading. All three Fair Trade communities were aware of (attempts to mobilize) the looming presence in the market of 'green' concerns and the 'credit-crunch'. But building 'green' concerns into the particular hybrid forums of Fair Trade required even more articulation work, reconsidering delineations between 'goods' and 'bads', and the potential for these delineations to mobilize consumer response. What kind of 'good' contained this many non-green air miles? Should t-shirts be measured in cotton-miles? What kind of 'good' ignored the hardships of the credit-crunched consumer? When premium prices became 'bads', what remained for high cost 'goods'? During the research these concerns were articulated, but never resolved. The hybrid world of 'goods' was not about to be accomplished in a single, simple, and definitive fashion any time soon.

Conclusion: hybrid forums and performativity

The relationship between market identities, the 'goods' on sale, and the worlds to which they attest is complex. Building Fair Trade products, labels, and markets, akin to many branding practices, is about offering something more than a product to wear (adhering to those contemporary conventions that brands are about lifestyles, identities, etc.). Yet, where is the world beyond Fair Trade which is offered for consumption? And to whom is this world being offered? It appears that the world of 'Fair'-ness is only available within and through the 'goods' themselves. This suggests that market practices in Fair Trade are focused on building worlds as hybrid forums (markets, consumers, producers, supply chain relations, community developments, poverty alleviation) into the product. This inversion of conventional marketing ideas—that instead of a product being launched into the world, a world is launched into a product—is a notable aspect of establishing the authentic provenance of Fair Trade 'goods' (Neyland and Simakova 2009). But what does this inversion enable us to do? To what extent does the inversion provide us with a means to adequately grasp Fair Trade marketing practice?

Our initial proposal was to analyse heuristically the practices of Fair Trade as the construction of 'hybrid forums'. The 'hybrid forums' of Fair Trade appear to be not so much the worlds out there *per se*, but constructs articulated (with more or less certainty) by participants engaged in 'strategizing and calculation'. What kind of Fair Trade world is to be made available, and to whom? These are the questions continually asked and to some extent never answered in practice. One feature of deliberations upon the versions of Fair Trade on offer is the articulation work within and between Fair Trade communities. Within each community, Fair Traders operated to build hybridity and heterogeneity into more singular forms. Simultaneously, however, it is a notable feature of the interviews that the participants were also well aware of alternate market practices. Hence, alongside building hybridity-as-singularity within each community, interviewees' versions of Fair Trade, and hence notions of 'goods' and 'bads', were also closely intertwined with assessing and dismissing *other* Fair Traders' interpretations of 'goods' and 'bads' (for instance, by offering a commentary on these other communities). Attempts to stabilize the future of Fair Trade were also a feature of ongoing articulation work by each of the communities. However, this work was characterized by a deep uncertainty over the nature, direction, and future security of Fair Trade.

The working suggestion for this chapter was to approach the hybrid forums of Fair Trade as ongoing articulations of heterogeneous collections of Fair Traders, beneficiaries of Fair Trade, acts of Fair Trading, labels, certificates, assessment processes, figurative notions of poverty, and 'goods'. There is not just one kind of Fair Trade, however, and this chapter has outlined the contours of three distinct Fair Trade communities. Further, the 'goods' of Fair Trade are not simply made to be launched into the world. Instead, the relations of world and product, producer, and consumer are complex, and require discursive work to be sustained.

In conclusion, in what ways do our empirical observations speak to the discussion of the performativity of economics? As we discussed throughout, building hybrid forums involves ongoing work of (re)configuration and re-articulation of entities and the relations between them. Articulation work attempts to build into the products the Fair world to which the Trading relations aspire. However, the kind of hybrid forum they are to perform and the extent to which their 'good'-ness is realized are construed as depending on consumers. A notional consumer is one feature of the hybridity articulated into the world of the product.

Unlike the disputable yet manageable boundaries between the communities of Fair Traders themselves, in the accounts above 'consumers' is a category that congeals the voluntary in the relations of exchange aspiring to a fairer world. As such, consumers serve in the practitioners' discourse as a contested terrain for the attribution of successes and failures in Fair Trade efforts. Consumers are articulated as an evasive but powerful constituent performing Fair Trade in an unpredictable manner against attempts to 'shape markets according to particular templates' (Araujo et al., this volume). The 'dependence' of Fair Trade discourses on notions of the consumer can thus be seen as a practical means to manage the tension between more or less straightforward normative ways of achieving 'fairness' and the contingencies of assessing and representing the efforts to accomplish 'fairness' (be it through audit and certification or in everyday communication strategies). In constructing worlds where particular terms of trade may make more (ethical) sense than others, Fair Trade is performed through keeping the uncertainties over the nature of consumption alive. Articulating the unruly consumer into the Fair Trade hybrid forums allows for a creative open-endedness of the terms of trade as opposed to being performed by the predefined representations of exchange.

Since Fair Trade is perceived as possibly a transient concern by retail trade organizations, will hybrid forums of Fair Trade be rearticulated one day as green hybrid forums? What kind of work will be required to achieve the transition and relocation of practices and to construct new concepts of 'goods' by building a 'green' world into the products as opposed to the world struggling against poverty? Will these wor(l)ds be 'fluidly added together' (as in Mol 2009), or will the reconstruction of the hybrid forums allow for even more diverse practices and readings? The conclusion of many Fair Traders is that consumers will make poverty history, not through heroic acts of consumption, but through switching their attention to other issues. Fair Traders worry that poverty will become last year's concern, due to the tentative and perhaps unreliable articulation of the hybrid forums of Fair Trade. The utility of hybrid forums as a means to represent and analyse this diverse array of people, things, relations, and issues is that they help us to capture both the security and uncertainty of these attempts to build (Fair Trade) markets.

■ NOTES

1. 'Space' is used in the abstract figurative sense (see Araujo et al., this volume).
2. We draw on Wensley's observation (1990) that the marketing analogy, due to its recognized reliance on certain sets of expectations, responsibilities, and power relations between (active, strategy-minded, or even aggressive) producers and (passive) consumers, does not suit certain groups (like charities, or lawyers) wishing not to associate themselves with the image of a powerful producer. In a similar vein, we shall look at the applications of the *trade* and *market* analogies to Fair Trading.
3. Critiqued by Brownlie and Saren (1992) who suggest moving from understanding marketing as a set of prescriptive rules and norms to its *use* in organizations, drawing on ethno-methodology (Garfinkel 1967) to look at marketing as part of the reflexive activities of participants in the organizations.
4. Our proposition here builds on the ideas developed within actor-network theory (ANT). For some examples of recent anthropological research on markets, marketing, and financial institutions inspired by ANT, see Callon (1998) and MacKenzie et al. (2007).
5. This notion initially coming from the discourse of economics thus acquires the sense of ongoing accomplishment: markets never cease 'to emerge and re-emerge' (Callon 1998*b*: 266).
6. See Dilley (1999) for more on articulation.
7. As Callon observes, while the distinction seems obvious to the economists, it becomes rather problematic from a Science and Technology Studies perspective looking at the construction of externalities (of e.g. Fair Trade) in practice.

8. The interviews used a loosely structured, accumulative, and investigative empiricist approach developed in Neyland (2007).

9. Further Fair Trade alternatives include membership schemes such as the British Association of Fair Trade Shops (BAFTS); the Ethical Trading Initiative (ETI); and organic certification by the Soil Association.

10. Such as organic (Skal and AGRECO/IFOAM), recycled (Mobius triangular loop), reduced environmental impact (Oeko-Tex Standard 1000 and ISO 14001), charitable, and ethical (SA8000) labels.

Marketing as an art and science of market framing: Commentary

MICHEL CALLON

'Marketing is the activity, set of institutions, and processes for creating, communicating, delivering, and exchanging offerings that have value for customers, clients, partners, and society at large.'[1] What is striking about this definition, officially approved by the American Marketing Association, is the absence of the term market. And there is nothing accidental about this omission. In their introduction to this book, Araujo, Finch, and Kjellberg confirm that marketing, as an academic discipline that develops discourses and designs, and prescribes practices and tools, has gradually turned away from markets and focused, typically from a one-sided (seller) perspective, on exchange behaviours and their management.[2] Considering markets only marginally, this approach reduces them to little more than 'collections of actual and potential buyers' (Araujo et al., this volume).

This conception and practice of marketing does not deny the existence of markets. But, rather than considering them as collective socio-technical organizations that impose certain regularities, it conceives them as a sort of ether in which economic agents are steeped.[3] The focus is on market behaviours. A well-organized and efficient market is one in which individual agencies have been adequately formatted or, if you prefer, disciplined. It is the outcome of competition between these agencies, and not the mechanism itself, that organizes and frames markets.

Marketing is inside not outside markets

We could be content just to take note of this orientation of marketing in order to study what it does and to assess the extent to which it manages (or not) to carry out the programme it has set for itself, and with what consequences. Why dream of another form of marketing? Why raise the question, as the editors of this book do, of reconnecting marketing to markets? Why not accept this narrow but legitimate and potentially fertile focus on market transactions and agencies?

The first answer that naturally comes to mind revolves around the plurality of possible definitions of marketing. Professional societies are indeed entitled to set the limits and content of these definitions, but that is no reason to follow them. Despite their attempts at standardization, the term marketing is a label with an increasingly fuzzy meaning, denoting a set of extraordinarily diverse occupations, knowledge, and sites. Even academic specialists are unable to agree (assuming they so wish) on what it refers to and what its goals and methods are, or under which conditions it is effective. It is therefore perfectly legitimate to join in the debate with a view to steering marketing, its discourses, and its practices in new directions deemed to be more promising, fertile, or legitimate. 'Reconnecting marketing to markets' can therefore be understood as both a statement and a programme. It is a statement about a change in trajectory, for marketing is not close enough to the reality of markets. And it is a programme aimed at remedying that situation, for if marketing wants to remain in touch with reality, it has to turn its attention back to markets.

This aim of remaining in touch with real markets is significant. But the authors of the contributions to this book explore another way that, in my opinion, is more promising in the long run. Here, the slogan 'reconnecting marketing to markets' is not (only) a call for more realism, addressed to a discipline that is thought to have narrowed down its ambitions as it departed from its real subject. It is also a loud and clear affirmation that marketing is an integral part of markets, within and not outside of them, irrespective of how they are defined.

One way of clarifying this point is by starting with the explanation given by some economists to account for the emergence of markets and the gradual elaboration, throughout history, of the rules of their organization and functioning.[4] The organization of exchanges in which agents engage to optimize the use of their own resources and competencies is seen as both critical and strategic. Markets as we know them, with sophisticated rules governing their functioning, are the outcome of a long process of trial and error, mostly conducted by the agents themselves. This process has required a great deal of imagination, ingenuity, and creativity, as well as heavy investment. It has contributed to the constant improvement of real markets, progressively rendering their functioning more satisfactory, if not more efficient. Thus, over time, by paying attention to their own interests, economic agents not only invented markets but also set their rules and forms of organization (North 1990).

Hence, it is not so much the—probably debatable—genealogy of market institutions that is so relevant here as the simple and hardly questionable idea that even, and especially, from the point of view of individual economic agents and the optimization of their situation, the organization of markets has undoubtedly constituted (and still does) a constant and major preoccupation. What we can add to this history is that, as markets have diversified and become more complex, as their importance and role have grown, and as the issue of new markets deliberately created from scratch has become more urgent,[5] new competencies have been added to the more traditional ones of the agents directly involved in market exchanges. Designing markets, devising and adjusting their operating rules, and experimenting with new forms of organization and devices are now increasingly entrusted to full-time specialists. These specialists naturally include economists, as well as the growing and active population of those whom we call marketers. 'Reconnecting marketing to markets' means recognizing the work accomplished not only by traditional economic agents (who continue to format markets) but also by all those professionals who, in a more or less coordinated and collaborative way and with diverse ambitions and objectives, imagine and transform what Koray Caliskan and I (Caliskan and Callon 2010) have called market socio-technical *agencements* (mSTAs). If we agree that marketing is this work of design, experimentation, and implementation of mSTAs (with the different framings that it involves), and that marketing collectives are the multiple actors who carry it out, we could simply say that we can no longer describe and analyse markets without including all those who endeavour to format and transform them. Reconnecting marketing to markets! This is clearly not (only) a matter of bringing marketing closer to market realities (from which it is accused of moving away), but of plunging it, or rather of plunging marketing collectives, into markets; in short, of endogenizing them.

This approach leads us to study marketing collectives, somewhat like the sociology of science and techniques has studied research collectives (Latour 1987; Knorr-Cetina 1999). The morphology of the networks structuring them, their forms of organization, the types of competencies they encompass, the modalities of training and recruitment of their members, the subjects they study, and the forms of transposition/translation/transport of knowledge and techniques that they prefer are some of the subjects that merit detailed research. Recently, we have started to see efforts to address these issues at the intersection of the sociology of science and techniques, economic sociology, and marketing (e.g. Cochoy 2002; Kjellberg and Helgesson 2006, 2007*a, b*; Callon et al. 2007; Araujo et al. 2008). As the reader will see, the chapters of this book all contribute decisively to this research programme. They further our understanding of the functioning, role, and evolution of these marketing collectives and thereby of markets themselves.

Marketing, markets, and dynamics of innovation

Including marketing collectives in markets, that is considering all those who work on the design, organization, and formatting of markets as economic actors in their own right, produces a view of markets that has much in common with the approach of evolutionary economics (Nelson and Winter 1982). A rapid comparison of these two lines of analysis can highlight the originality and specific contribution of the research presented in this book.

The first common point concerns the definition of markets. Evolutionary economics goes beyond regular descriptions limited essentially to the actors of supply and demand—generally, firms and consumers—by including in its conception of markets all the actors who participate in their functioning and dynamics. We find the usual suspects and also, for example, the research laboratories, mainly public sector and including academic ones, involved in designing new products or production techniques; governments and their industrial policies; regulatory authorities (that deal with competition, sanitary or environmental security, intellectual property rights, etc.); professional societies; employers' or workers' unions; international organizations; consultancy firms; NGOs; and so on. The list varies depending on the sector and domain. It might for instance, include hospitals and medical professionals in the case of health markets. All these forces, which maintain relations of competition and cooperation with one another, constitute markets as described by evolutionary economics. This book fits perfectly with this approach and provides numerous examples of the important role of these others. However, it refrains from using the dangerous repertoire of evolutionism when it proposes to reconnect marketing to markets, that is, as I have emphasized, to include marketing collectives in markets.

At the heart of market dynamics we find innovation, the cornerstone of evolutionary economics. Innovation, the competitive strategy aimed at getting rid of competition, is the source of the variations subjected to selection. And these variations, as studies of innovation have shown, affect and structure markets, their organization, and the competencies that they mobilize (what Caliskan and I have called the framing of mSTAs).[6] Innovation is simply another name for the process of transformation and reconfiguration of markets, of re-*agencements* of mSTAs (reframing products, agencies, encounters, etc.). Here too—and this is the second common point—the similarity with the contributions to this book is striking. Studying the work of marketing means putting oneself in the place where innovations take shape, where their successes or failures are decided; it means plunging to the heart of this dynamic, the wellspring of the constantly renewed tension, described thousands of times, that it generates between the exploration of new configurations and the exploitation of existing architectures.[7] In the cases of both evolutionary economics and the study of marketing collectives, as conducted in this book, markets are defined in terms of their dynamics, that is, the mechanisms of their transformation and not the competitive balance that they are supposed to strike between supply and demand.

Yet, apart from these fundamental convergences, there are significant differences that I would now like to emphasize. The following observations will, I hope, clarify some of the issues that are closely linked to the study of marketing and the role played by marketing collectives in the dynamics and evolution of markets.

Because of the importance granted to innovation in the dynamic reconfiguration of markets, evolutionary economics emphasizes the central and strategic character of knowledge, know-how, and competencies, as well as the many devices (human bodies, rules, routines, conventions, artefacts, texts, etc.) in which they are embedded and which determine the conditions of their mobilization and transportation. This type of approach excludes no form of expertise, technical competency, or knowledge. Yet, despite this ecumenism, evolutionary economics rarely takes into consideration the knowledge and competencies of marketing or economics. Until now, most of the effort in analysis and empirical investigation has focused on the natural and life sciences, or on the so-called hard technologies.[8] Competencies in organization, management science, financial and accounting techniques, marketing, and human resource management may not have been excluded, but nor have they received any particular attention or treatment. Hence, for evolutionary economics the work of reconnecting marketing to markets remains largely to be done!

This silence explains, at least partially, the relevance of certain criticisms levelled at evolutionary economics by orthodox economics.[9] The most serious criticism in this respect challenges the legitimacy of a direct transposition of evolutionary theory to economic life. Pointing out the imprecision surrounding both the delimitation of the population engaged in the struggle for survival, and the definition of the entities that are subject to selection, this critique highlights the difficulty of applying the notions of variation and selection to economic life without profoundly altering them. In my opinion, this difficulty would at least partially be resolved if, instead of ignoring them, evolutionary economics explicitly took into account the knowledge, competencies, and equipment that are elaborated and mobilized by marketing collectives to develop the innovation dynamics that reconfigure markets. The activity of these collectives consists primarily in defining and creating not only the units subject to selection but also the populations within which the mechanisms of variation-selection develop.

Take the case of the consumer, of such keen interest to modern marketing. We know that, depending on the market configuration, consumers can be active to varying degrees in the elaboration of the (product) innovations intended for them (see chapter 1 by Shove and Araujo). In some cases they are an important source of variations;[10] in others they passively follow (or not) the novelties proposed by firms or research laboratories. A market will veer more towards one or the other, depending largely on how the marketing collective secures the consumers' collaboration (or not) in the innovation process. Likewise, the delimitations of populations and sub-populations of potential customers, which determine the scope of application of selection mechanisms, are almost exclusively a matter of marketing. In other words, to understand the conditions and modalities of consumers' involvement in the production of variations and in the mechanisms of their selection, one has to analyse the marketing collectives and their role in the innovation dynamic (as do, for instance, Cochoy and Hagberg in this volume). This reasoning can also be applied to other market agencies apart from consumers (as in chapters 5 and 7 by Azimont and Araujo, and Fries, respectively), thus showing the massive involvement of marketing collectives in the shaping and framing of the evolutionary process itself.

As long as it refuses to explicitly integrate marketing knowledge into its analysis of the dynamics of innovation and markets, evolutionary economics will prevent itself from being able to identify—at least empirically—the units that produce variations and that are therefore targets for the processes of selection. If, on the other hand, it accepted this integration, it would also be answering a second criticism, one which is essential and closely related to the preceding one: the absence of a theory of agency in evolutionary economics. To the question 'What are the drivers of innovation or (in other words) the mechanisms of variation-selection?', evolutionary economics can only reply awkwardly and metaphorically. Chance occurrences in the tinkering process of reproduction (genetic mutations with the variations they introduce into genetic heritage) may be able to explain the evolution of living beings, but chance does not explain much in the case of markets, irrespective of the entity to which it is applied. Innovations, sources of variations that result in the reconfiguration of mSTAs, are obviously the fruit of complex strategic calculations in which marketing collectives play a decisive role. No innovation without agency and, more precisely, no innovation without the qualculative agencies of marketing.[11] Evolutionary economics, which has never sought to endow itself with such a theory of agency,[12] is now paying the price. By ignoring the equipment, competencies, and networks of know-how that enable the different assemblages of economic agents (firms, routines, etc.) to work progressively, thoughtfully, and reactively towards their own transformation and that of the environments in which they are embedded, evolutionary economists paradoxically preclude their own in-depth under-standing of the mechanisms of variation-selection, that is, *in fine*, the dynamics of innovation and markets. It is only by focusing the analysis on marketing collectives that we can further our understanding of market mechanisms; that is, an understanding of the singular dynamics that makes markets nothing more than the series of their transformations, as new architectures constantly extend and prey on existing markets or, in some extreme cases, are built on their ruins (see for instance chapters 8 and 9 by Reverdy and Kjellberg, respectively).

Understanding marketing in action to be able to act on markets

The endogenization of marketing collectives in markets makes it possible to renew the understanding of market dynamics, that is, processes of innovation or, as I would put it, of qualification–requalification of goods (Callon et al. 2002; see also chapter 4 by Dubuisson-Quellier). It also contributes—and this is no secondary benefit—to the renewal of many questions about the place occupied by markets in our contemporary societies and about the issues that their functioning raises. The following are but a few examples.

Marketing, the practices that it inspires, and the tools that it helps to design or implement are accused by some of facilitating the growing manipulation of consumers. These critics see marketing as the new opium of the masses! Their critique denounces the unbridled, endless growth of needs and highlights their artificialization (consumers are encouraged to want more and more things which are less and less necessary to their existence and well-being). It stigmatizes the creation of a model in which individuals are constantly summoned to identify, through systematic introspection, the problems that they encounter so that they can determine their needs and then participate in designing the products or services that meet those needs and that they will eventually have to pay for to obtain.

This critique is in no way unfounded, since in its own definition of itself, academic marketing explicitly assigns itself this task and ambition (see above, the definition approved by the AMA). Yet, whether marketing collectives are entirely oriented towards this single goal remains an open question that would need empirical investigation. This statement is probably true in some fields. It is nevertheless probable that, in others, marketing plays different cards and endeavours to format the market agencies and transactions in which they engage based on other models.[13] Above all, once it has been endogenized, marketing is much the same as all the other forces contributing to the design, establishment, and formatting of mSTAs, and which can trigger resistances and oppositions, even counter-proposals (as illustrated in chapters 6 and 10 by Finch and Geiger, and Neyland and Simakova, respectively). As we know, the involvement of certain collectives like those working on the design and diffusion of GMOs, nanotechnologies, or nuclear power causes the emergence of matters of concern and issues that generate controversies and debates. These lead to proposals aimed at reorienting the dynamics of innovation and consequently reorganizing markets (Barthe et al. 2009; Bonneuil and Thomas 2009). Why not envisage that certain versions of marketing, like those that forget to take into account essential dimensions of mSTAs, trigger the same type of opposition and lead to the design of other definitions and other practices of marketing? One of the ambitions of mSTA studies could be to examine these debates and to push further the investigation of the issues and practices around which they are structured. I am convinced that it is by penetrating to the heart of these controversies and the conflicting programmes and counter-programmes concerned, that is by plunging into the dynamics of the knowledge and competencies that marketing collectives develop and mobilize, that we will be able to act in a thoughtful and informed manner on the organization of markets.

This investigative work should free itself of disciplinary boundaries. It is striking to see, for instance, that one of the essential formattings of mSTAs, that of the organization of encounters between goods, suppliers, and consumers (Caliskan and Callon 2010), has been neglected by 'official' marketing (as defined by the AMA, for example). This does not mean that it has not been studied or worked on in practice. The conditions of competition that are a key element in this formatting are, for example, a major preoccupation in economics and law, as are all the studies which, following those of Roth (2008), analyse and experiment with various mechanisms of matching supply and demand. Nevertheless, although legitimate, this division of work has the unfortunate consequence of dissociating problems that are actually interdependent. The approach outlined in this book, with the broad definition of marketing that it proposes, will enable us to transcend these disciplinary barriers. Marketing collectives, as defined above, include for example economics and its work on competition or market engineering, as well as the agencies that implement its recommendations (as illustrated in chapter 9 by Kjellberg).

Marketing is often vilified, not only because it contributes powerfully and deliberately to consumers' alienation (see above) but also because it is an ideal vehicle for extending markets; in short, for the commodification of contemporary societies. It is accused of dynamically imposing the law of the market in such diverse fields as public services, health, art, science, and even religion, the family and charity. It is anti-humanist and destroys the social link by promoting, through many costly investments, a selfish, greedy, narcissistic, and eternally unsatisfied individual. This type of analysis, which captures important aspects of marketing, is nonetheless based on a narrow and therefore partial definition of the term. As a result, it could lead to the indiscriminate jettisoning of marketing as a set of knowledge and practices, which are actually necessary in the conception of mSTAs. This would also deprive us of powerful means of acting on markets.

The point of view of the performativity programme is that the forms of organization of markets are multiple because their formatting is also multiple. The only valid question is not on the existence or not of markets, and their extension or containment, but on their design and consequently the constitution and composition of marketing collectives and the modalities of their intervention. The main message of this book is that we might do well to forget markets, at least for a while, and to focus rather on the marketing collectives that format them. That is paradoxically the challenge of reconnecting marketing to markets.

■ NOTES

1. Zwick and Cayla (2010) cite this definition in their introduction to a book that should be read in parallel to this one.
2. The following definition, also proposed by the AMA, emphasizes this point: 'Marketing research is the function that links the consumer, customer, and public to the marketer through information—information used to identify and define marketing opportunities and problems; generate, refine, and evaluate marketing actions; monitor marketing performance; and improve understanding of marketing as a process. Marketing research specifies the information required to address these issues, designs the method for collecting information, manages and implements the data collection process, analyzes the results, and communicates the findings and their implications' (Approved October 2004).
3. Sometimes this denial is explicit: market transactions do not need markets to exist. See for example the conference organized by Aggeri et al. (2008) in Cerisy on market activities without markets.
4. For a clear presentation of this approach see McMillan (2002).
5. As in carbon markets or spectrum auctions, where we can observe explicit efforts of market engineering.
6. The seminal article by Abernathy and Clark (1985) draws a direct link between the different forms of innovation and the various elements comprising a market.
7. On the notions of exploration and exploitation applied to research and innovation, see Doganova (2010).
8. For example, to my knowledge there is nothing on communities of practice or epistemic communities, on the exploration of knowledge and marketing tools, or on economics.
9. For a clear presentation of these issues, see Coyle (2007).

10. There is an abundant literature on consumers' and users' involvement in the design of the products intended for them (see in particular Von Hippel 2005). Consumers are invited to participate directly and formally in the process of value creation.

11. On the notion of qualculation see Cochoy (2002).

12. Probably for fear of reverting to the model that it does its utmost to escape from: the optimizing agency of neoclassical models.

13. An ethnographic study of the uses of marketing in charities or NGOs would be highly instructive from this point of view (see chapter 10 by Neyland and Simakova).

Connecting to markets

Conclusion

LUIS ARAUJO, JOHN FINCH, AND HANS KJELLBERG

This book gathers a collection of empirical studies about how a variety of actors, especially marketers, are involved in making and shaping markets. Despite the omnipresence of markets in marketing discourse, the academic discipline of marketing has barely been concerned with understanding markets (Venkatesh et al. 2006; Araujo and Kjellberg 2009). In part, this side-stepping has resulted from defining marketing as the '. . . science, art and practice of exchange' (Bagozzi 2009: 262). Marketers are advised to focus their activities on understanding buyer behaviour, often represented as categories of demand and buyer profiles, and to view markets as collections of actual and potential customers of more or less substitutable offers. Marketers then 'market' by sending representatives such as offers, promises, brands, packaging, and communications to perform 'out there' (in the marketplace) or 'in there' (addressing the customers' cognitive schemas). In either case, markets are typically not regarded as sites of intervention in themselves. As a result, neither concrete markets nor the considerable work involved in organizing them has received much attention.

Our aim in this book has been to address these deficiencies through detailed, empirical studies of concrete markets and to examine the roles played by marketers, broadly defined, in markets. Muniesa et al. (2007) described the coalition of human and non-human actors that becomes organized in markets as an *agencement*, which we expect to be shifting and contested as entities try and act, try and acquire agency, through recruiting others to their causes. The *agencement* is important because it implies that actors, human and non-human, can join in and so shape and reshape the market, or break bits off one arrangement to build a new assemblage. A capacity to calculate, itself an activity requiring some combination of calculative devices and means of assembling an array of entities deemed to be interesting, and an ability to address others' attempts at calculating, characterizes the ways in which actors can join in markets. And, following Callon (1998b, 2007), calculating necessarily involves framing; marking out insiders and outsiders, variables and residuals, and heat and noise. We contend that professional and amateur marketers, and their colleagues in sales, design, advertising, packaging, and logistics, to name but a few, are heavily involved in shaping markets. In other words, they are not simply involved in describing the world they inhabit but also in shaping that world, which in effect is how others—for example, clients, senior managers, regulators—hold marketers and their colleagues accountable for their activities.

As academic marketers, we join in the activities of shaping markets, perhaps by contributing some reflexivity and a broadened outlook, and also by proposing new models, concepts, and metrics, which become available to practitioners of various denominations (Tucker 1974). Academic research involves the diffusion of concepts, experimental results, and empirical accounts, allowing those who practice marketing (including academics acting as consultants) to convert or translate ideas into practices to be tried out in markets. For example, the translations can include the creation of new or modified market actors (e.g. the self-service consumer), material devices (e.g. shopping carts), and metrics (e.g. total category margins). In seeking to enhance the reflexive capacities of market actors, we also assume parts of the significant responsibility of reshaping markets in ways we can neither articulate nor anticipate. We can thus conclude that marketing is a performative discipline involved in framing market exchanges, and in producing the objects, material devices, and metrics that a variety of market professionals deploy in their everyday practices (Marion 2009).

In this closing comment, we seek to bring together the results of the individual studies reported above. We do this by reflecting on four themes emerging from our editing of this book. First, we consider how marketing efforts have consequences beyond the individual exchange. Second, we discuss the plasticity of market actors and the active attempts made to shape them according to various templates for action. Third, we address the issue of values in markets, observing how many efforts to engage with markets are related to the introduction and/or determination of novel values. Finally, we discuss the inherent instability of markets evident from many of the empirical studies reported here. We conclude with a future-oriented reflection on implications for studying marketization processes.

Formatting large numbers of exchanges

If we follow conventional marketing theory, we are advised to concentrate on exchanges under the assumption that '... the market is the arena within which exchanges take place' (Buzzell 1999: 61). But the empirical studies of exchange presented in this volume highlight that many efforts to format exchange are—for the lack of a better word—totalizing in their ambition. That is, practical marketing efforts are often directed at formatting exchange in large numbers and over long periods of time. Thus, although one may argue that the form and content of exchange in principle is determined anew for each individual exchange, we observe that much of this formatting in practice has already been performed elsewhere. What specific observations do the accounts offer concerning this process of upscaling the formatting of exchange?

The empirical studies provide ample illustration of how exchanges may become subject to large-scale formatting via efforts to shape the objects, modes, and agents of exchange. The qualification of exchange objects is a recurrent theme in several chapters, including the routine testing of product qualities detailed by Dubuisson-Quellier (chapter 4) and the efforts to label Fair Trade goods described by Neyland and Simakova (chapter 10). These efforts concern both the make-up of exchange objects, as in the literal alteration of a recipe for a cured-meat product, and how a made-up object is to be qualified, as in the creation of auditing procedures for Fair Trade products. The standardization of such processes of qualification involving multiple trials of both exchange objects and intended targets is central to large-scale formatting of exchange. It allows moving beyond individual exchanges to generic types, which can be classified and represented through the scenarios, metrics, and instruments that result from the work of mediators (e.g. market research agencies). Without these attempts at qualifying and classifying, growth in scale is difficult to achieve.

Another aspect of exchange that is subject to large-scale formatting is the exchange situation, as illustrated by Cochoy (chapter 2), Hagberg (chapter 3), and Kjellberg (chapter 9). Both Cochoy and Hagberg draw attention to the material framing of exchanges. In the case of Cochoy's grocery stores, a complementary strategy of signalling (e.g. brands, commercial signs) and fencing (e.g. shelves, checkout counters), assembled by grocery retailers and their suppliers, defined new spaces for exchange and promoted new behavioural patterns. In Hagberg's study of NetOnNet a new, mediated exchange situation was designed (the web store) with an 'e-commerce literate' customer-type in mind. Kjellberg's study of the frequent flyer programme controversy highlights another form that these formatting efforts can take, namely, the putting in place of incentive systems to promote a certain type of exchange behaviour. This latter type of formatting has received considerable attention in connection with deregulatory efforts, but can be employed by others than regulators.

Finally, several of the studies illustrate how exchange agents become subject to formatting efforts. This work is evident in the attempts to make up the 'grocery retail self-service' customer (Cochoy, chapter 2), the 'e-commerce literate' customer of NetOnNet (Hagberg, chapter 3), and the 'consumer-on-the go' (Azimont and Araujo, chapter 5). The 'the's' in these accounts are telling, with categories and types standing in for many buyers, whom marketers seek to typify. Due both to its prevalence and theoretical import, we will return to this aspect of market shaping in the second theme below.

A second issue related to large-scale formatting concerns what it is that allows formatting beyond the individual exchange; that is, how are increases in scale achieved? Here, the studies provide examples of large-scale formatting being achieved through expansion both in time and space. The challenge of large-scale formatting over time lies in realizing formats that last beyond the execution of an individual exchange. Whatever formatting is achieved, it needs to remain in place also after the exchange is completed. Several studies suggest that material devices are an important vehicle for achieving this, illustrated by the fencing and branding strategies of grocery retailers detailed by Cochoy (chapter 2), and the arrangements of Ryanair to herd their travellers as described by Finch and Geiger (chapter 6). In both cases, grocery retailing and low-cost air travel, the work of mediators is crucial in categorizing, anticipating, and framing customers' behaviours.[1]

Large-scale formatting can also be achieved through replication of formats across space. Here, the central challenge is to make the formatting portable, so that it can travel to new locations through the use of various technologies of replication. But achieving scale is not enough in itself; typically it is the growth of a very specific type of formatting that is sought. Hence, the issue of control comes to the fore. What allows for action at a distance? The setting up of metrological systems, such as the performance dashboards described by Azimont and Araujo (chapter 5), offers one way in which remote control can be attempted and the replication of exchange formats can be achieved. Most of the studies suggest that efforts at enacting exchanges on a wider scale rely on distal representations of exchange situations through a host of instruments and metrics that abbreviate, summarize, and condense aggregate information.

Although the reliance on material devices and metrological systems appear important for large-scale formatting, several of the chapters point towards complementary ways of achieving scale. In Dubuisson-Quellier's study (chapter 4) of the qualification of cured-meat products, it is the recurrent work of testing both products and consumers that produce a space of circulation and exchange. But relying purely on your own efforts at controlling from afar is not always a very effective way of increasing the scale of exchange formatting. Better then to co-opt others' efforts to scale up. Finch and Geiger (chapter 6) exemplify this in what they call interlanguage trading zones, where growth in scale comes from the enrolment of others in co-formatting the exchanges. A more insidious version of this is observed in the subversive trading zone, where Starbucks attempt to co-opt their customers' into learning their language to facilitate exchanges. Another example is provided by Shove and Araujo (chapter 1) who document how DIY can be expanded through the subtle design of tools and the ensuing dynamics of practitioner careers and projects. Finally, Fries' study (chapter 7) of a federation of trade associations highlights the import of assembling new collectives on behalf of which large-scale formatting can be attempted. But these examples also illustrate the difficulty of achieving growth of a particular form of exchange through collective action. The more large-scale formatting of exchanges relies on the efforts of others, the more difficult it will be to control; the others may have their own views as to the kind of formatting to be achieved.

Formatting market agencies

Our second theme considers how agencies become equipped with devices, models, stories, and other guides allowing them to strike some compromise, however uncomfortable, between the heterogeneity of their intended uses of an offer and the large-scale, standardizing, even totalizing, carrying capacity of some markets' devices. As we saw above, the issue of increasing the scale of exchange formatting is often closely linked to how actors acquire agency to join in and make exchanges. In several of the examples, the work of mediators was linked to the make-up of particular types of agents, such as the self-serving grocery customer (chapter 2). Indeed, putting in place certain devices allowed these agencies to be assembled and successful exchange to take place according to a certain template, as in the frequent flyer programme devised by SAS (chapter 9).

But equipping agencies is hardly confined to the devices that frame inter-actions at the point of sale. In the case of DIY, as Shove and Araujo (chapter 1) illustrate, equipping agencies is a matter of embedding, or compensating for the absence of, user skills through product design. Non-drip varnish, for example, enables amateur DIY enthusiasts to undertake tasks with a realistic expectation of a quality of outcome only previously attainable by employing a professional craftsman. The relationship between practitioners and their tools evolves over time, allowing practitioners to become ever more competent agents in the DIY market and taking a chunk off the professional painter and decorator market. This suggests a link between agential capacities outside of exchange situations proper and the formatting of those exchange situations.

Other attempts at shaping market agencies involve the intervention of third parties such as regulators and business associations. In Fries' study (chapter 7), a federation of trade associations acts as mediator between individual members' interests and political actors, providing expertise where required and enhancing the reflexivity of its members about the possibilities of shaping the market for public service outsourcing in Sweden. In Reverdy's study (chapter 8) of the natural gas market, deregulation led to the proliferation of market devices, calculative practices, and new forms of mediation between buyers and sellers. In Finch and Geiger's study (chapter 6), regulators attempted to detach intermediaries in the UK market for personal financial services from their dependency on providers and reconfigure them as effective mediators between the complex offers of finance companies and buyers' often-complex personal circumstances. These studies illustrate how attempts at enacting particular market templates (e.g. a perfectly competitive market) require matching calculative capabilities from buyers and sellers that may not easily obtain without external assistance.

Attempts at equipping market agencies and performing markets in particular ways are not always successful. In Hagberg's study (chapter 3) of NetOnNet some customers refused to subscribe to the initial format proposed by the seller who had little choice but to cater for multiple modes of exchange through multiple retail formats. In the gas market (Reverdy, chapter 8), the regulatory ambition to realize an ideal buyer of gas was hindered by the industrial customers' continued reliance on calculative devices linked to a previous market form. Finally, Finch and Geiger's study (chapter 6) draws attention to instances of outright resistance to proposed agential configurations in two otherwise successful coercive trading zones (Ryanair and Starbucks). These examples of resistance against attempted exchange formats bring us to our third theme: the issue of values.

Shaping market values

What kinds of values are associated with markets and market exchanges, and how are these values determined? Several of the chapters illustrate the richness of practices and tools related to determining (economic) values. Shove and Araujo (chapter 1) show how acts of consumption contribute to the realization of things that are valued, thus highlighting the poverty of seeing value as realized exclusively through exchange or as relying solely on symbolic underpinnings. From a practice perspective, both the values that are sought by engaging in markets and the specific ways in which they are realized vary considerably. Instead of carving a sharp distinction between economic value and other values, a practice approach focuses on ongoing processes of valuation (Stark 2009). At the same time, Dubuisson-Quellier's study (chapter 4) shows that the determination of value remains important for exchanges to take place. She portrays the process of qualification (establishing valued features of exchange objects) as a never-ending quest involving multiple stages and professionals mobilizing a variety of market devices. In this process, market feedback, expert opinions, test results, production considerations, and internal debates around tastings are all combined, with great difficulty at times, to produce multiple and always provisional qualifications of products.

Other chapters illustrate that what is to be valued in a market is itself subject to contention and change. Azimont and Araujo (chapter 5) illustrate how metrological systems produce value-laden images of exchange that have consequences for markets. Finch and Geiger (chapter 6) demonstrate several different strategies for introducing values into markets, ranging from 'putting things out there' to more complex negotiations over meaning. Reverdy (chapter 8) shows how different actors pursue different values on the gas market with industrial customers opting for stable exchange relations, while regulators promote transparent transactions on a commodity market. These studies underscore that many engagements with markets are specifically linked to ongoing processes of valuation and competing orders of worth (Stark 2009).

Valuations that actors develop without reference to a commercial calculus may appear antithetical to markets, but we witness increasing attempts to link moral values and social and political causes to exchanges. The study of Fair Trade clothing by Neyland and Simakova (chapter 10) illustrates both the attempted introduction of novel values into markets and how values and political causes might be pursued through both market and non-market exchange (e.g. mainstream clothing retailers vs. charity shops). There is no one way of performing Fair Trade but rather a multiplicity of ways of strategizing and calculating about the best ways to pursue the construction of 'Fair Trade'.

A final observation on the introduction and realization of values in markets concerns the link between the pursuit of values and efforts to format exchange on a large scale. The rigid and totalizing formatting of exchange pursued by Ryanair (chapter 6) is linked to their promise of realizing one specific value in travelling: low cost. Either you value this, and agree to the proposed format, or you are directed elsewhere. Similarly, in the case of the fuel retailer described by Azimont and Araujo (chapter 5), the unified formatting of exchange throughout the retail chain was made possible through the alignment of different economic values (e.g. up-front margins, promotional support, and kick-backs) into a single value (total margin).

In other cases, the inability to align multiple values appears to have negatively affected the achievement of a unified, large-scale exchange formatting. Thus, although Hagberg's study (chapter 3) suggests that NetOnNet started with a totalizing ambition concerning exchange formatting, the company's formatting multiplied in response to recognition of customers pursuing multiple values (low prices, short waiting time, low delivery costs). An even more telling example of this multiplication of formatting is Finch and Geiger's (chapter 6) discussion of Starbucks' recently introduced stealth shops. These shops represent an attempt by the global chain to recover a local character valued by some, but considered incompatible with its widely successful global exchange format. As Dubuisson-Quellier reminds us (chapter 4), no consensual agreement or settlement of differences is required for exchanges to take place; it is the scale of formatting that is affected. Our tentative suggestion, based on these observations, is that the pursuit of multiple, non-aligned, or radically different values in a market renders the upscaling of techniques to format exchange both difficult and contestable.

Destabilizing markets

Our fourth theme emerges when combining the observations of efforts to format exchanges on a large scale, reconstitute agencies, and promote different values, with the observations of failure, incompatibility, and contestation also reported in the cases. Rather than observing how markets stabilize exchanges and benefit from stable exchanges, we are led to examine the extent to which markets produce and tolerate instability. The thread that runs across all the chapters in this book is that the multiple and distributed work of performing market exchanges is never finished, and never allows for more than temporary and provisional stabilizations. Here, Kjellberg's study (chapter 9) of the prolonged controversy concerning SAS's frequent flyer programme provides a striking example of the repeated efforts made to organize markets, of the proposition that market forms are never settled once and for all. But as exemplified by the recurrent efforts to qualify goods described by Dubuisson-Quellier (chapter 4), markets are also momentarily unstable and exchanges fluid in character.

A second common feature of the empirical studies included in this volume is the long and often tortuous chains of translations that different actors enact in their efforts to bridge production and consumption. These seem incredibly complex in their own right, with a myriad of mediating devices, calculations, and representations being employed to help the process along, for instance, defining product formulations, packaging, product assortment in stores, logistics, training, and so on. As expected, we find buyers and sellers involved in defining market boundaries, collecting data and generating metrics about consumer preferences or seller capabilities, socio-demographics, product characteristics, and so on. But we also note how other types of actors, such as market regulators (e.g. competition authorities) and market educators (e.g. consultants), provide templates for organizing markets. If we look at the combined efforts of these various market professionals we arrive at a more comprehensive but also more complex image of how markets are shaped. The long and diverse chains of translation now intersect and interlink to form a web of associations that provides multiple opportunities for destabilizing existing arrangements. To exemplify, Kjellberg's study of SAS's frequent flyer programme (chapter 9) suggests that to contest EuroBonus, an actor could choose to target any combination of travellers, company customers, travel agencies, politicians and competition authorities.

As expected, some of these opportunities to undermine and destabilize chains of translation play out as competition amongst sellers in a market. But even among these efforts, the variation in scope and form is substantial. Some of these efforts largely exploit existing chains of translation and only propose to replace some limited but central aspect, for instance by offering a product improvement along an established dimension. Others propose more encompassing changes, establishing new translations as in the Fair Trade firms venturing to launch a fair(er) world into their goods (chapter 10). Yet others are more similar to Palamountain's notion (1955) of intertype competition, representing an extensive dismissal of established chains of translation, such as the grocers proposing to replace over-the-counter service with self-service (chapter 2).

Other opportunities to destabilize markets are exploited, more or less strategically, by buyers. Hagberg's account (chapter 3) of how consumer electronics customers put up their own website in order to exploit the price guarantees offered by large electronics retailers is a good example of an effort that destabilized current arrangements in a market. Another potential source of instability is the unintended uses of objects that Shove and Araujo bring attention to in their discussion of consumption (chapter 1). Finally, Finch and Geiger (chapter 6) highlight the role of outright contestation of current exchange practices by consumers through boycotts and protests.

But, as several of the studies in this volume illustrate, actors that are not directly involved in exchanges, or in some cases position themselves as alternatives to markets, can also undertake efforts to undermine current chains of translations. Regulators can play a key role in dismantling established chains of translations and encouraging the build-up of others as the studies by Reverdy and Kjellberg show (chapters 8 and 9). Business associations can speak and act on behalf of their members in political and regulatory arenas, as Fries' study demonstrates (chapter 7). Media attention can challenge current exchange practices, as exemplified by Finch and Geiger's discussion of Ryanair (chapter 6). Markets can also be reformed from within or pushed aside by alternative modes of exchange, as Neyland and Simakova's study of Fair Trade demonstrates (chapter 10). In this sense, markets are but one way of organizing exchanges, of matching heterogeneous supply and demand as Alderson (1957) put it.

Future connections?

Our final task in this chapter is to anticipate and tentatively suggest where to go next with market studies, with a special reference to marketing. Recently, Caliskan and Callon (2009) sketched a project for 'economization', to include 'the processes that constitute the behaviours, organizations, institutions and...

the objects in a particular society which are tentatively and often controversially qualified, by scholars and/or lay people, as "economic"'. Marketization is one form of 'economization' and our interest in understanding where marketers and marketing fit in this process could thus warrant the pursuit of a 'marketization' project.[2]

The starting point for a marketization project is that markets are not passive, institutional backdrops of human actors' exchanges' and calculations, nor elaborate systems of customs and norms by which actors perform exchanges to fulfil social objectives. Rather, markets are socio-technical assemblages, or *agencements*, which set in motion chains of translation amongst entities and situations, such as designing, producing, and using, and which the actors involved may choose to reconfigure. Markets can thus neither be 'designed' in the experimental economics sense of formulating rules and allocation algorithms—as in (Roth 2008)—nor should they be seen as the '. . . cold, implacable, impersonal monster which imposes its laws and procedures while extending them even further' (Callon 1998a: 51).

The view of markets as constituted by complex chains of translation, involving collective and distributed performances, and a multiplicity of agencies engaged in enrolling, configuring, and assembling other agencies, presents a challenge to marketing academics. We can no longer proceed on the basis that we are here to close the gap between theory and practice, to learn from practitioner experiments, and '. . . bring rigour to the process of learning from these experiments, develop new tools, and testing the generality of the findings' (Reibstein et al. 2009: 2). To paraphrase Law and Urry (2004), to the extent that marketing conceals its performativity from itself, it assumes a position of innocence and neutrality that it neither deserves nor can credibly sustain.

When turning attention to the process of marketization, the central question becomes what kinds of markets the academic marketing discipline proposes to perform, rather than how to help practitioners generalize and validate the findings of their experiments. This is decidedly not a call for further exporting of marketing techniques and for marketizing new domains. On the contrary, it is a plea for reflection concerning the objects, models, representations, and tools we are helping to set up and propagate, and concerning the templates and values that underpin those instruments. An often-justifiable critique of marketing is that, in its quest to broaden its domain and legitimize its practices, it ends up treating the virtues of the perfectly competitive, neoclassical market as a marketing exercise in itself.

Callon (2009) reminds us that the process of creating a market—qualifying goods, developing modes of exchange, configuring market agencies—is a huge collective undertaking that cannot be delegated to experts alone. The studies in this book illustrate that the shaping of markets accommodates a much larger variety of voices, deconstructing, appropriating, and deploying expert discourses and tools, including marketing, to help perform their preferred versions of markets. In other words, the performance of markets is a political struggle over what constitutes appropriate values and modes of valuation (Caliskan and Callon 2009; Kjellberg and Helgesson 2010 (forthcoming)).

When 'reality' becomes the effect rather than a mirror of our knowledge, we open up new vistas for the construction of economic orders that both encompass and go beyond markets, especially of the idealized kind promoted in public discourse. This raises issues both about the scope and the moral limits of markets—issues that are being explored in situ through various resistances to markets, such as anti-consumption movements (see e.g. Kozinets 2002; Arnould 2007), and the production, distribution, and marketing of open source software (Benkler 2002).[3] It leads us to examine critically the capacity of markets to perform the matching of supply and demand in challenging new domains such as blood or organ donation (Healy 2006; Roth 2007, 2008), or the invasion of hitherto untainted areas of social life by market-based incentives. But it also raises issues about the performing of alternative market schemes such as Fair Trade (Neyland and Simakova, chapter 10) and alternatives to traditional markets such as local exchange trading systems (see McLoughlin 2002).

Reconnecting marketing to markets requires scholars to abandon their safe haven of professional expertise, and become full members of the crowded, vibrant, and confusing world of markets as collective, distributed, and ever-changing accomplishments. Markets change, but not necessarily for the better via some natural automatism. To initiate discussions in society about preferred directions of change in markets, while recognizing that there is more than one option, and to provide ideas on how such changes can be and are being realized, constitute two worthwhile tasks for marketing scholars. Pursuing them will not only further strengthen the connection of marketing to markets but may also provide a useful corrective concerning their own relevance to marketers of various denominations.

■ NOTES

1. Latour (2005: 39) makes a crucial distinction between mediators and intermediaries. Mediators 'transform, translate, distort and modify the meaning or the elements they are supposed to carry'. By contrast, an intermediary 'transports meaning without transformation' (Ibid.). We can speculate, following Latour, that much marketing theory attributes intermediation to what those myriads of market professionals consider to be mediators, transforming what is supposed to be merely transported into something else.

2. The use of the term 'marketization' in this context is not to be confused with the penetration of market principles into diverse spheres of social life (cf. Slater and Tonkiss, 2001) or the spread of neoliberal ideas (cf. Wensley, 2009).

3. Open source software is one salient example of the boundary between gift-giving and market exchange being blurred, with effects on software development, specification, and protection of intellectual property rights, and the future of software firms and markets. In these cases, the goal is to reshape or shrink markets from the outside-in, through refusals to engage in market exchanges and promote alternative modes of organizing production and exchange (Benkler 2002).

■ BIBLIOGRAPHY

Abernathy, W. and Clark, K. (1985) Innovation: Mapping the Winds of Creative Destruction, *Research Policy*, 14(1): 3–22.

Ackroyd, S. and Hughes, J. (1992) *Data Collection in Context*, London: Longman.

The Age (2006) Available from: http://www.theage.com.au/news/National/Action-targets-Aussie-textile-industry/2006/03/02/9780199578061.html.

Aggeri, F., Favereau, O., and Hatchuel, A. (2008) *L'activité Marchande sans le Marché?*, http://www.ccic-cerisy.asso.fr/activitemarchande08.html.

Ählström, J. and Egels-Zandén, N. (2008) The Processes of Defining Corporate Responsibility: A Study of Swedish Garment Retailers' Responsibility, *Business Strategy and the Environment*, 17(4): 230–44.

Ahrens, T. and Chapman, C. (2007) Management Accounting as Practice, *Accounting, Organizations and Society*, 32(1–2): 1–27.

Ahrne, G. and Brunsson, N. (2008) *Meta-Organizations*, Cheltenham: Edward Elgar.

Akrich, M. (1992) The De-Scription of Technical Objects, in W.E. Bijker and J. Law (eds), *Shaping Technology/Building Society: Studies in Sociotechnical Change*, Cambridge, MA: MIT Press, pp. 205–24.

—— (1995) User Representations: Practices, Methods and Sociology, in A. Rip, T.J. Misa, and J. Schot (eds), *Managing Technology in Society: The Approach of Constructive Technology Assessment*, London: Pinter, pp. 167–84.

—— and Latour, B. (1992) A Summary of a Convenient Vocabulary for the Semiotics of Human and Non-Human Assemblies, in W.E. Bijker and J. Law (eds), *Shaping Technology/Building Society: Studies in Sociotechnical Change*, Cambridge, MA: MIT Press, pp. 259–64.

—— Callon, M., and Latour, B. (2002) The Key to Success in Innovation, *International Journal of Innovation Management*, 6(2): 187–206.

Alderson, W. (1957) *Marketing Behavior and Executive Action: A Functionalist Approach to Marketing*, Homewood, IL: Richard D. Irwin.

—— (1965) *Dynamic Marketing Behavior: A Functionalist Theory of Marketing*, Homewood, IL: Richard D. Irwin.

—— and Cox, R. (1948) Towards a Theory of Marketing, *Journal of Marketing*, 13(2): 137–52.

—— and Green, P.E. (1964) *Planning and Problem-Solving in Marketing*, Homewood, IL: Richard D. Irwin.

Andersson, P., Aspenberg, K., and Kjellberg, H. (2008) The Configuration of Actors in Market Practice, *Marketing Theory*, 8(1): 67–90.

Appadurai, A. (1986) Introduction: Commodities and the Politics of Value, in A. Appadurai (ed.), *The Social Life of Things: Commodities in Cultural Perspective*, Cambridge: Cambridge University Press, pp. 3–63.

Araujo, L. (2007) Markets, Market-Making and Marketing, *Marketing Theory*, 7(3): 211–26.

—— and Kjellberg, H. (2009) Shaping Exchanges, Performing Markets: The Study of Marketing Practices, in P. Maclaran, M. Saren, B. Stern, and M. Tadajewski (eds), *The Sage Handbook of Marketing Theory*, London: Sage, pp. 195–218.

—— and Spring, M. (2006) Services, Products, and the Institutional Structure of Production, *Industrial Marketing Management*, 35(7): 797–805.

—— Kjellberg, H., and Spencer, R. (2008) Market Practices and Forms: Introduction to the Special Issue, *Marketing Theory*, 8(1): 5–14.

Arndt, J. (1979) Toward a Concept of Domesticated Markets, *Journal of Marketing*, 43(4): 69–75.

Arnesen, D.W., Fleenor, C.P., and Toh, R.S. (1997) The Ethical Dimensions of Airline Frequent Flier Programs, *Business Horizons*, 40(1): 47–56.

Arnould, E.J. (2007) Should Consumer Citizens Escape the Market?, *The Annals of the American Academy of Political and Social Science*, 611(1): 96–111.

—— and Thompson, C.J. (2005) Consumer Culture Theory (CCT): Twenty Years of Research, *Journal of Consumer Research*, 31(4): 868–82.

Atkinson, P. (1990) *The Ethnographic Imagination: Textual Constructions of Reality*, London: Routledge.

—— and Hammersley, M. (2007) *Ethnography. Principles in Practice*, 3rd ed., London: Routledge.

Austin, J.L. (1961) *Philosophical Papers*, London: Oxford University Press.

Azimont, F. and Araujo, L. (2007) Category Reviews as Market-Shaping Events, *Industrial Marketing Management*, 36(7): 849–60.

Bagozzi, R.P. (1974) Marketing as an Organized Behavioral System of Exchange, *Journal of Marketing*, 38(4): 77–81.

—— (1975) Marketing as Exchange, *Journal of Marketing*, 39(4): 32–9.

—— (2000) On the Concept of Intentional Social Action in Consumer Behavior, *Journal of Consumer Research*, 27(3): 388–96.

—— (2009) The Evolution of Marketing Thought: from Economic to Social Exchange Theory and Beyond, in P. Maclaran, M. Saren, B. Stern, and M. Tadajewski (eds), *The Sage Handbook of Marketing Theory*, London: Sage, pp. 244–65.

Baird, D. and Cohen, M.S. (1999) Why Trade? *Perspectives on Science*, 7(2): 231–54.

Barnhill, J.A. and Lawson, W.M. (1980) Toward a Theory of Modern Markets, *European Journal of Marketing*, 14(1): 50–60.

Barrey, S. (2007) Struggling to be Displayed at the Point of Purchase: The Emergence of Merchandising in French Supermarkets, in M. Callon, Y. Millo, and F. Muniesa (eds), *Market Devices*, Oxford: Blackwell, pp. 92–108.

—— Cochoy, F. and Dubuisson-Quellier, S. (2000) Designer, Packager, Merchandiser: Trois Professionnels Pour une Même Scène Marchande, *Sociologie du Travail*, 42(3): 457–82.

Barry, A. (2002) The Anti-political Economy, *Economy and Society*, 31(2): 268–84.

—— and Slater, D. (2002) Introduction: The Technological Economy, *Economy and Society*, 31(2): 175–93.

Bartels, R. (1962) *The Development of Marketing Thought*, Homewood, IL: Richard D. Irwin.

Barthe, Y., Callon, M., and Lascoumes, P. (2009) La Decisione Politica Reversibile. Storia di un Inatteso Contributo l'Instaurazione della Democrazia Dialogica, *Italian Journal of Social Policy*, 3: 47–69.

Bartle, I. and Vass, P. (2007) Self-regulation within the Regulatory State: Towards a New Regulatory Paradigm?, *Public Administration*, 85(4): 885–905.

Bauman, Z. (1992) *Intimations of Postmodernity*, London: Routledge.

BBC (2009) Why Hate Ryanair? *Panorama*, BBC One, 12 October, accessible at http://news. bbc.co.uk/2/hi/8297211.stm.

Beckert, J. (1996) What is Sociological About Economic Sociology? Uncertainty and the Embeddedness of Economic Action, *Theory and Society*, 25(6): 803–40.

—— (2002) *Beyond the Market: The Social Foundations of Economic Efficiency*. Princeton, NJ: Princeton University Press.

—— (2009) The Social Order of Markets, *Theory and Society*, 38(3): 245–69.

Beem, E.R. (1957) Who Profits from Trading Stamps? *Harvard Business Review*, 35(6): 123–36.

Belk, R.W. (1988) Possessions and the Extended Self, *Journal of Consumer Research*, 15(2): 139–68.

—— (2009) Representing Global Consumers: Desire, Possession and Identity, in P. Maclaran, M. Saren, B. Stern, and M. Tadajewski (eds), *The SAGE Handbook of Marketing Theory*, London: Sage, pp. 283–98.

Bell, C.S. (1967) Liberty and Property, and No Stamps, *The Journal of Business*, 40(2): 194–202.

Benkler, Y. (2002) *The Wealth of Networks: How Social Production Transforms Markets and Freedom*, New Haven, CT: Yale University Press.

Bennett, R.J. and Ramsden, M. (2007) The Contribution of Business Associations to SMEs: Strategy, Bundling or Reassurance, *International Small Business Journal*, 25(1): 49–76.

Bergman, M. (1996) *Avregleringen av Inrikesflyget*, Konkurrensverkets Rapportserie, Stockholm: Konkurrensverket.

Berk, G. and Schneiberg, M. (2005) Varieties in Capitalism, Varieties of Association: Collaborative Learning in American Industry, 1900 to 1925, *Politics and Society*, 33(1): 46–86.

Biggart, N.W. and Castanias, R.P. (2001) Collateralized Social Relations: The Social in Economic Calculation, *American Journal of Economics & Sociology*, 60(2): 471–500.

Bijker, W. (1995) *Of Bicycles, Bakelites, and Bulbs. Studies in Sociotechnical Change*, Cambridge, MA: MIT Press.

Bonneuil, C. and Thomas, F. (2009) *Gènes, Pouvoirs et Profits, Recherche Publique et Régimes de Production des Savoirs de Mendel aux OGM*, Versaille, Fph Quae.

Bourdieu, P. (1992) Thinking About Limits, *Theory, Culture & Society*, 9(1): 37–49.

Bowker, G.C. and Star, S.L. (2000) *Sorting Things Out: Classification and Its Consequences*, Cambridge, MA: MIT Press.

Bowlby, R. (2001) *Carried Away: The Invention of Modern Shopping*, New York: Columbia University Press.

Boyer, R. (1997) The Variety and Unequal Performance of Really Existing Markets: Farewell to Dr. Pangloss? in J.R. Hollingsworth and R. Boyer (eds), *Contemporary Capitalism: The Embeddedness of Institutions*, Cambridge: Cambridge University Press, pp. 55–93.

Brown, S. (2006) Ambi-Brand Culture: On a Wing and a Swear with Ryanair, in J.E. Schroeder and M. Salzer-Möhrling (eds), *Brand Culture*, Oxford and New York: Routledge, pp. 50–66.

—— (2007) Are We Nearly There Yet? On the Retro-Dominant Logic of Marketing, *Marketing Theory*, 7(3): 291–300.

Brownlie, D. and Saren, M. (1992) The Four Ps of the Marketing Concept: Prescriptive, Polemical, Permanent and Problematical, *European Journal of Marketing*, 26(4): 34–47.

—— Saren, M., Wensley, R., and Whittington, R. (eds) (1999) *Rethinking Marketing. Towards Critical Marketing Accountings*, London: Sage.

Butler, J. (2010) Performative Agency, *Journal of Cultural Economy* 3(2): 147–61.

Button, K. (2004) *Wings Across Europe: Towards an Efficient European Air Transport System*, Aldershot: Ashgate.

Buzzell, R.D. (1999) Market Functions and Market Evolution, *Journal of Marketing*, 63(SISI), 61–3.

Calder, S. (2003) *No Frills: The Truth Behind the Low-Cost Revolution in the Skies*, London: Virgin Press.

Caldwell, N., Walker, H., Harland, C., Knight, L., Zheng, J., and Wakeley, T. (2005) Promoting Competitive Markets: The Role of Public Procurement, *Journal of Purchasing & Supply Management*, 11(5): 242–51.

Caliskan, K. (2007) Price as a Market Device: Cotton Trading in Izmir Mercantile Exchange, in M. Callon, Y. Millo, and F. Muniesa (eds), *Market Devices*, Oxford: Blackwell, pp. 241–60.

—— and Callon, M. (2009) Economization, Part 1: Shifting Attention from the Economy Towards Processes of Economization, *Economy and Society*, 38(3): 369–98.

—— —— (2010) Economization, Part 2: A Research Programme for the Study of Markets, *Economy and Society*, 39(1): 1–32.

Callon, M. (1986) Some Elements of a Sociology of Translation: Domestication of the Scallops and the Fishermen of St. Brieuc Bay, in J. Law (ed.), *Power, Action and Belief: A New Sociology of Knowledge?* London: Routledge & Kegan Paul, pp. 196–229.

—— (ed.) (1998) *The Laws of the Markets*, Oxford: Blackwell.

—— (1998a) Introduction: The Embeddedness of Economic Markets in Economics, in M. Callon (ed.), *The Laws of the Markets*, Oxford: Blackwell, pp. 1–57.

—— (1998b) An Essay on Framing and Overflowing: Economic Externalities Revisited by Sociology, in M. Callon (ed.), *The Laws of the Markets*, Oxford: Blackwell, pp. 244–69.

—— (1999) Actor-Network Theory: The Market Test, in J. Law and J. Hassard (eds), *Actor Network Theory and After*, Oxford: Blackwell, pp. 181–95.

—— (2005) Why Virtualism Paves the Way to Political Impotence: A Reply to Daniel Miller's Critique of *The Laws of the Markets*, *Economic Sociology: European Electronic Newsletter*, 6(2) (February): 3–20 (available online at: http://econsoc.mpifg.de/archive/esfeb05.pdf).

—— (2007a) What Does it Mean to Say that Economics is Performative?, in D. MacKenzie, F. Muniesa, and L. Siu (eds), *Do Economists Make Markets? On the Performativity of Economics*, Princeton, NJ: Princeton University Press, pp. 311–57.

—— (2007b) An Essay on the Growing Contribution of Economic Markets to the Proliferation of the Social, *Theory, Culture & Society*, 24(7–8): 139–63.

—— (2008) Economic Markets and the Rise of Interactive Agencements: From Prosthetic Agencies to Habilitated Agencies, in T. Pinch and R. Swedberg (eds), *Living in a Material World: Economic Sociology Meets Science and Technology Studies*, Cambridge, MA: MIT Press, pp. 29–56.

—— (2009a) Civilizing Markets: Carbon Trading between *In Vitro* and *In Vivo* Experiments, *Accounting, Organizations and Society*, 34(3–4): 535–48.

Callon, M. (2009b) Elaborating the Notion of Performativity, *Le Libellio d'Aegis*, 5(1): 18–29.

—— (2010) Performativity, Misfires and Politics, *Journal of Cultural Economy* 3(2) 163–9.

—— and Law, J. (1995) Agency and the Hybrid Collectif, *South Atlantic Quarterly*, 94(2): 481–507.

—— and Muniesa, F. (2005) Economic Markets as Calculative Collective Devices, *Organization Studies*, 26(8): 1229–50.

—— Méadel, C., and Rabeharisoa, V. (2002) The Economy of Qualities, *Economy and Society*, 31(2): 194–217.

—— Millo, Y., and Muniesa, F. (eds) (2007) *Market Devices:* Oxford: Blackwell.

—— Lascoumes, P., and Barthe, Y. (2009) *Acting in an Uncertain World. An Essay on Technical Democracy*, Cambridge, MA: MIT Press.

Carruthers, B.G. and Espeland, W.N. (1991) Accounting for Rationality: Double-Entry Bookkeeping and the Rhetoric of Economic Rationality, *American Journal of Sociology*, 97(1): 31–69.

Chamberlin, E.W. (1933) *The Theory of Monopolistic Competition*, Cambridge, MA: Harvard University Press.

Chan, C.S.C. (2009) Creating a Market in the Presence of Cultural Resistance: The Case of Life Insurance in China, *Theory and Society*, 38(3): 271–305.

Clark, T. (2007) *Starbucked*. New York: Little, Brown and Company.

Clarkson, R. (1991) Motion 1991/92:Sk13 med anledning av prop. 1991/92:48 Justeringar i beskattningen av inkomstslaget tjänst, m.m. *1991/92:Sk13*. Sveriges Riksdag.

Clean Clothes Campaign (2006) Available from: http://www.cleanclothes.org/news/03-05-20.htm.

Cochoy, F. (1998) Another Discipline for the Market Economy: Marketing as a Performative Knowledge and Know-how for Capitalism, in M. Callon (ed.), *The Laws of the Markets*, Oxford: Blackwell, pp. 194–221.

—— (2002) *Une Sociologie du Packaging ou l'âne du Buridan Face au Marché*, Paris: Presses Universitaires de France.

—— (2007a) A Brief Theory of the 'Captation' of Publics: Understanding the Market with Little Red Riding Hood, *Theory, Culture & Society*, 24(7–8): 213–33.

—— (2007b) A Sociology of Market-Things: On Tending the Garden of Choices in Mass Retailing, in M. Callon, Y. Millo, and F. Muniesa (eds), *Market Devices*, Oxford: Blackwell, pp. 109–29.

—— (2008a) Calculation, Qualculation, Calqulation: Shopping Cart Arithmetic, Equipped Cognition and the Clustered Consumer, *Marketing Theory*, 8(1): 15–44.

—— (2008b) Parquer et Marquer les Produits, ou Comment Gérer le Territoire du Petit Commerce (États Unis, 1929–1959), *Entreprises et Histoire*, 53(4): 34–53.

—— (2009) Driving a Shopping Cart from STS to Business, and the Other Way Round: On the Introduction of Shopping Carts in American Grocery Stores (1936–1959), *Organization*, 16(1): 31–55.

—— (2010) 'Market-things' Inside: Insights from *Progressive Grocer* (1929–1959), in D. Zwick and J. Cayla (eds), *Inside Marketing*, Oxford: Oxford University Press (forthcoming).

—— and Dubuisson-Quellier, S. (2000) Les Professionnels du Marché: Vers une Sociologie du Travail Marchand, *Sociologie du Travail*, 42(3): 359–68.

Collins, H., Evans, R., and Gorman, M. (2007) Trading Zones and Interactional Expertise, *Studies in History and Philosophy of Science*, 38(4): 657–66.

Cooper, R. (1992) Formal Organization as Representation: Remote Control, Displacement and Abbreviation, in M. Reed and M. Hughes (eds), *Rethinking Organization: New Directions in Organization Theory and Analysis*, London: Sage, pp. 254–72.

Corpwatch (1996) Available from: http://www.corpwatch.org/article.php?id=3034.

Cova, B. and Cova, V. (2009) Les Figures du Nouveau Consommateur: Une Genèse de la Gouvernementalité du Consommateur, *Recherche et Applications en Marketing*, 24(3): 81–100.

—— and Salle, R. (2008) Marketing Solutions in Accordance with the S-D Logic: Co-creating Value with Customer Network Actors, *Industrial Marketing Management*, 37(3): 270–7.

Coviello, N.E., Brodie, R.J., Danaher, P.J., and Johnston, W.J. (2002) How Firms Relate to Their Markets: An Empirical Examination of Contemporary Marketing Practices, *Journal of Marketing*, 66(3): 33–46.

Coyle, D. (2007) *The Soulful Science: What Economists Really Do and Why it Matters*, Princeton, NJ: Princeton University Press.

Cranz, G. (2000) *The Chair: Rethinking Culture, Body and Design*, New York: W.W. Norton.

Creaton, S. (2004) *Ryanair: How a Small Irish Airline Conquered Europe*, London: Aurum Press.

—— (2007) *Ryanair: The Full Story of the Controversial Low-Cost Airline*, London: Aurum Press.

Crew, M.A. and Kleindorfer, P.R. (2002) Regulatory Economics: Twenty Years of Progress?, *Journal of Regulatory Economics*, 21(1): 5–22.

Cromie, J.G. and Ewing, M.T. (2009) The Rejection of Brand Hegemony, *Journal of Business Research*, 62(2): 218–30.

Csíkszentmihályi, M. and Rochberg-Halton, E. (1981) *The Meaning of Things: Domestic Symbols and the Self*, New York: Cambridge University Press.

Cumbo, J. (2009) Swinton Fined for Sales Rule Breaches, *Financial Times*, 28 October, http://www.ft.com/cms/s/0/ad380f04-c3c2-11de-a290-00144feab49a.html.

Czarniawska, B. (2004) On Time, Space and Action Nets, *Organization*, 11(6): 773–91.

—— (2007) *Shadowing and Other Techniques for Doing Fieldwork in Modern Societies*, Malmö: Liber.

—— (2008) *A Theory of Organizing*, Cheltenham, UK: Edward Elgar.

—— (2010) *Cyberfactories: How News Agencies Produce News*, unpublished manuscript (forthcoming).

—— and Mouritsen, J. (2009) What is the Object of Management? in C.S. Chapman, D.J. Cooper, and P. Miller (eds), *Accounting, Organizations, and Institutions: Essays in Honour of Anthony Hopwood*, Oxford: Oxford University Press, pp. 157–74.

D'Adderio, L. (2008) The Performativity of Routines: Theorising the Influence of Artefacts and Distributed Agencies on Routine Dynamics, *Research Policy*, 37(5): 769–89.

Davis, O.A. (1959) The Economics of Trading Stamps, *The Journal of Business*, 32(5): 141–50.

Dearden, S.J.H. (1994) Air Transport Regulation in the European Union, *European Business Review*, 94: 15–19.

de Certeau, M. (1984) *The Practice of Everyday Life*, Translated by S. Rendall, Berkeley, CA: University of California Press.

Deleuze, G. and Guattari, F. (2004) *A Thousand Plateaus: Capitalism and Schizophrenia*, London: Continuum.

Deutsch, T.A. (2001) *Making Change at the Grocery Store: Government, Grocers, and the Problem of Women's Autonomy in the Creation of Chicago's Supermarkets, 1920–1950*, PhD thesis, Madison: University of Wisconsin-Madison.

Devlin, J.F. (2003) Monitoring the Success of Policy Initiatives to Increase Consumer Understanding of Financial Services, *Journal of Financial Regulation and Compliance*, 11(2): 151–63.

De Wit, O., Van den Ende, J., Schot, J., and van Oost, E. (2002) Innovation Junctions—Office Technologies in the Netherlands, 1880–1980, *Technology and Culture*, 43(1): 50–72.

Dilley, R. (1992) Contesting Markets: A General Introduction to Market Ideology, Imagery and Discourse, in R. Dilley (ed.), *Contesting Markets: Analyses of Ideology, Discourse and Practice*, Edinburgh: Edinburgh University Press, pp. 1–37.

—— (1999) Introduction: The Problem of Context, in R. Dilley (ed.), *The Problem of Context*, New York and Oxford: Berghahn Books, pp. 1–47.

DiMaggio, P. and Louch, H. (1998) Socially Embedded Consumer Transactions: For What Kinds of Purchases Do People Most Often Use Networks?, *American Sociological Review*, 63(5): 619–37.

Djelic, M.-L. (2002) Does Europe Mean Americanization? The Case of Competition, *Competition and Change*, 6(3): 233–50.

Doganova, L. (2010) *Faire valoir l'exploration collective. Dynamiques, instruments et résultats des partenariats avec des spin-off académiques* PhD thesis, Paris: École des Mines de Paris.

Doner, R.F. and Schneider, B.R. (2000a) Business Associations and Economic Development: Why Some Associations Contribute More than Others, *Business and Politics*, 2(3): 261–88.

—— —— (2000b) *The New Institutional Economics, Business Associations and Development (No. DP 110/2000)*, Geneva: ILO and International Institute for Labour Studies.

Dubuisson-Quellier, S. (2006) Routine et Délibération: Les Arbitrages des Consommateurs en Situation d'Achat, *Réseaux*, 24(135–136): 253–84.

—— (2007) The Shop as Market Space: The Commercial Qualities of Retail Architecture, in D. Vernet and L. de Wit (eds), *Boutiques and Other Retail Spaces: The Architecture of Seduction*, London: Routledge, pp. 16–33.

—— and Lamine, C. (2008) Consumer Involvement in Fair Trade and Local Food Systems: Delegation and Empowerment Regimes, *GeoJournal*, 73(1): 55–65.

—— and Neuville, J.-P. (eds) (2003) *Juger pour échanger: La construction sociale de l'accord sur la qualité dans une économie des jugements individuels*, Paris: Editions INRA.

du Gay, P. (2004) Self-Service: Retail, Shopping and Personhood, *Consumption, Markets and Culture*, 7(2): 149–63.

—— (2008) Organising Conduct, Making up People, in L. McFall, P. du Gay, and S. Carter (eds), *Conduct: Sociology and Social Worlds*, Manchester: Manchester University Press, pp. 21–53.

Edwards, P.N. (2003) Infrastructure and Modernity: Force, Time, and Social Organization in the History of Sociotechnical Systems, in T.J. Misa, P. Brey, and A. Feenberg (eds), *Modernity and Technology*, Cambridge, MA: MIT Press, pp. 185–226.

Espeland, W.N. and Stevens, M.L. (1998) Commensuration as a Social Process, *Annual Review of Sociology*, 24(1): 313–43.

Fairtrade Foundation (2008) Core Standards and Practice behind Fairtrade Labelling, available from: http://www.fairtrade.org.uk/includes/documents/cm_docs/2008/F/1_Five%20Key%20Fairtrade%20Benefits.pdf.

Finch, J. and Geiger, S. (2010) Positioning and Relating: Market Boundaries and the Slippery Identity of the Marketing object, *Marketing Theory*, 10(3): 237–51.

Firat, A.F. and Venkatesh, A. (1995) Liberatory Postmodernism and the Reenchantment of Consumption, *Journal of Consumer Research*, 22(3): 239–67.

Fischler, C. (1990) *L'Hominivore: le goût, la cuisine et le corps*, Paris: Éditions Odile Jacob.

Fisher, A. (2009a) Why Commission had to be Banned, *Financial Times*, 26 June, http://www.ft.com/cms/s/2/d2c98efc-626d-11de-b1c9-00144feabdc0.html.

—— (2009b) Do We Really Need a Change to the Way Financial Advisers Operate? *Observer*, 21 June, http://www.guardian.co.uk/money/2009/jun/21/financial-advisers-fsa-reform.

Fligstein, N. (1996) Markets as Politics: A Political-Cultural Approach to Market Institutions, *American Sociological Review*, 61(4): 656–73.

—— (2001) *The Architecture of Markets: An Economic Sociology of Twenty-First-Century Capitalist Societies*, Princeton, NJ: Princeton University Press.

Foucault, M. (1991) Governmentality, in G. Burchell, C. Gordon, and P. Miller (eds), *The Foucault Effect: Studies in Governmentality*, Hemel Hempstead: Harvester Wheatsheaf, pp. 87–104.

Fourcade, M. (2007) Theories of Markets, Theories of Society, *American Behavioral Scientist*, 50(8): 1015–34.

Franke, N. and Shah, S. (2003) How Communities Support Innovative Activities: An Exploration of Assistance and Sharing Among End-Users, *Research Policy*, 32(1): 157–78.

Fulton Suri, J. (2005) *Thoughtless Acts? Observations on Intuitive Design*, New York: Chronicle Books.

Galison, P. (1997) *Image and Logic: A Material Culture of Microphysics*, Chicago, IL: University of Chicago Press.

—— (1999) Trading Zone: Coordinating Action and Belief, in M. Biagioli (ed.), *The Science Studies Reader*, London and New York: Routledge, pp. 137–60.

Garcia, M.-F. (1986) La Construction Social d'un Marché Parfait: Le Marché au Cadran de Fontaines-en-Sologne, *Actes de la Recherche en Sciences Sociales*, 65: 2–13.

Garcia-Parpet, M.-F. (2007) The Social Construction of a Perfect Market: The Strawberry Auction at Fontaines-en-Sologne, in D. Mackenzie, F. Muniesa, and L. Siu (eds), *Do Economists Make Markets? On the Performativity of Economics*, Princeton, NJ: Princeton University Press, pp. 20–53.

Garfinkel, H. (1967) *Studies in Ethnomethodology*, Englewood Cliffs, NJ: Prentice-Hall.

Geels, F.W. (2006) Major System Change Through Stepwise Reconfiguration: A Multi-level Analysis of the Transformation of American Factory Production (1850–1930), *Technology in Society*, 28(4): 445–76.

Giddens, A. (1984) *The Constitution of Society*, Cambridge: Polity Press.

Gjøen, H. and Hård, M. (2002) Cultural Politics in Action: Developing User Scripts in Relation to the Electric Vehicle, *Science Technology & Human Values*, 27(2): 262–81.

Glaser, B.G. and Strauss, A.L. (1967) *The Discovery of Grounded Theory: Strategies for Qualitative Research*, New York: Aldine de Gruyter.

Goffman, E. (1959) *The Presentation of Self in Everyday Life*, Garden City, NY: Doubleday.

Gordon, R., Hastings, G., McDermott, L., and Siquier, P. (2007) The Critical Role of Social Marketing, in M. Saren, P. Maclaran, C. Goulding, R. Elliott, A. Shankar, and M. Catterall (eds), *Critical Marketing: Defining the Field*, Oxford: Butterworth-Heinemann, pp. 159–77.

Gorman, M. (2002) Levels of Expertise and Trading Zones: A Framework for Multidisciplinary Collaboration, *Social Studies of Science*, 32(5–6): 933–8.

—— (2005) Levels of Expertise and Trading Zones: Combining Cognitive and Social Approaches to Technology Studies, in M.E. Gorman, R.D. Tweney, D.C. Gooding, and A.P. Kincannon (eds), *Scientific and Technological Thinking*, London and New York: Routledge, pp. 287–302.

—— and Mehalik, M.M. (2002) Turning Good into Gold: A Comparative Study of Two Environmental Invention Networks, *Science, Technology & Human Values*, 27(4): 499–529.

Grandclément, C. (2006) Wheeling Food Products Around the Store . . . and Away: The Invention of the Shopping Cart, 1936–1953, Paper presented at the Food Chains Conference: Provisioning, Technology, and Science, Hagley Museum and Library, Wilmington, Delaware, November 2–4. Available at: http://www.csi.ensmp.fr/Items/WorkingPapers/Download/DLWP.php?wp=WP_CSI_006.pdf.

—— (2008) *Vendre sans Vendeurs: Sociologie des Dispositifs d'Achalandage en Supermarché*, PhD thesis, Paris: École des Mines de Paris.

Granovetter, M. (1985) Economic Action and Social Structure: The Problem of Embeddedness, *American Journal of Sociology*, 91(3) 481–510.

—— (2005) The Impact of Social Structure on Economic Outcomes, *Journal of Economic Perspectives*, 19(1): 33–50.

—— and McGuire, P. (1998) The Making of an Industry: Electricity in the United States, in M. Callon (ed.), *The Laws of the Markets*, Oxford: Blackwell, pp. 147–73.

Greenwood, J. (2002) *Inside the EU Business Associations*, New York: Palgrave.

Gronow, J. and Warde, A. (2001) Introduction, in J. Gronow and A. Warde (eds), *Ordinary Consumption*, London: Routledge, pp. 1–8.

Grönroos, C. (2006) Adopting a Service Logic for Marketing, *Marketing Theory*, 6(3): 317–33.

Gummesson, E. (2002) *Total Relationship Marketing: Marketing Strategy Moving from the 4Ps—Product, Price, Promotion, Place—of Traditional Marketing Management to the 30Rs—the Thirty Relationships: of a New Marketing Paradigm*, Oxford: Butterworth-Heinemann.

Haas, H.M. (1979) *Social and Economic Aspects of the Chain Store Movement*, New York: Arno Press.

Hagberg, J. (2008) *Flytande identitet: NetOnNet och e-handelns återkomst*, Borås: Högskolan i Borås.

Håkansson, H. and Lind, J. (2004) Accounting and Network Coordination, *Accounting Organizations and Society*, 29(1): 51–72.

—— and Prenkert, F. (2004) Exploring the Exchange Concept in Marketing, in H. Håkansson, D. Harrison, and A. Waluszewski (eds), *Rethinking Marketing: Developing a New Understanding of Markets*, Chichester: Wiley, pp. 75–94.

—— Harrison, D. and Waluszewski, A. (eds) (2004) *Rethinking Marketing: Developing a New Understanding of Markets*, Chichester: Wiley.

Hall, P.A. and Soskice, D. (eds) (2001) *Varieties of Capitalism: The Institutional Foundations of Comparative Advantage*, Oxford and New York: Oxford University Press.

Hand, M. and Shove, E. (2004) Orchestrating Concepts: Kitchen Dynamics and Regime Change in *Good Housekeeping* and *Ideal Home*, 1922–2002, *Home Cultures*, 1(3): 235–56.

Harré, R. (2002) Material Objects in Social Worlds, *Theory, Culture & Society*, 19(5–6): 23–33.

Healy, K. (2006) *Last Best Gifts: Altruism and the Market for Human Blood and Organs*, Chicago: Chicago University Press.

Helgesson, C.-F. and Kjellberg, H. (2005) Macro-actors and the Sounds of the Silenced, in B. Czarniawska and T. Hernes (eds), *Actor Network Theory and Organizing*, Malmö and Copenhagen: Liber and Copenhagen Business School Press, pp. 175–98.

Hess, D.J. (2001) Ethnography and the Development of Science and Technology Studies, in P. Atkinson, A. Coffey, S. Delamont, J. Lofland, and L. Lofland (eds), *Sage Handbook of Ethnography*, Thousand Oaks, CA: Sage, pp. 234–45.

HI Europe (1999) *AirTrack, The Survey of European Frequent Flyers*, London: HI Europe.

Hine, C. (2007) Multi-sited Ethnography as a Middle Range Methodology for Contemporary STS, *Science, Technology & Human Values*, 32(6): 652–71.

Hoffman, D.L., Novak, T.P., and Peralta, M.A. (1999) Information Privacy in the Marketspace: Implications for the Commercial Uses of Anonymity on the Web, *Information Society*, 15(2): 129–39.

Hoffman, K. (1984) An American Revolution, *Advertising Age*, 7: (May 16) M17.

Holt, D.B. (1995) How Consumers Consume: A Typology of Consumption Practices, *Journal of Consumer Research*, 22(1): 1–16.

—— (2002) Why Do Brands Cause Trouble? A Dialectical Theory of Consumer Culture and Branding, *Journal of Consumer Research*, 29(1): 70–90.

Hunt, S.D. (1976) The Nature and Scope of Marketing, *Journal of Marketing*, 40(3): 17–28.

Hutchins, E. (1995) *Cognition in the Wild*, Cambridge, MA: MIT Press.

Irin (2006) Available from: http://www.irinnews.org/report.asp?ReportID=27897&SelectRegion=Southern_Africa&SelectCountry=LESOTHO.

Jackson, W.A. (2007) On the Social Structure of Markets, *Cambridge Journal of Economics*, 31(2): 235–53.

Jeppesen, L.B. and Frederiksen, L. (2006) Why Do Users Contribute to Firm-Hosted User Communities? The Case of Computer-Controlled Music Instruments, *Organization Science*, 17(1): 45–63.

Juliusson, A.E., Gamble, A., and Gärling, T. (2007) Loss Aversion and Price Volatility as Determinants of Attitude Towards and Preference for Variable Price in the Swedish Electricity Market, *Energy Policy*, 35(11): 5953–7.

Kajzer Mitchell, I. (2007) Journeying Beyond Marketing's Collective Consciousness, in M. Saren, P. Maclaran, C. Goulding, R. Elliott, A. Shankar, and M. Catterall (eds), *Critical Marketing: Defining the Field*, Oxford: Butterworth Heinemann, pp. 211–32.

Karpik, L. (2007) *L'Économie des Singularités*, Paris: Gallimard.

Karpik, L. (2010) *Valuing the Unique: The Economics of Singularities*, Princeton, NJ: Princeton University Press.

Kellogg, K., Orlikowski, W., and Yates, J.A. (2006) Life in the Trading Zone: Structuring Coordination Across Boundaries in Postbureaucratic Organizations, *Organization Science*, 17(1): 22–44.

Kerrigan, G. (2006) Ryanair Case Crash Lands Spectacularly in the High Court, *Irish Independent (Sunday Edition)*, 16 July.

Kjärstad, J. and Johnsson, F. (2007) Prospects of the European Gas Market, *Energy Policy*, 35(2): 869–88.

Kjellberg, H. (2001) *Organising Distribution: Hakonbolaget and the Efforts to Rationalise Food Distribution, 1940–1960*, Stockholm: Economic Research Institute, Stockholm School of Economics [Ekonomiska forskningsinstitutet vid Handelshögsk.] (EFI).

—— (2007). The Death of a Salesman? Reconfiguring Economic Exchange in Swedish Post-war Food Distribution, in M. Callon, Y. Millo and F. Muniesa (eds), *Market Devices*, Oxford, Basil Blackwell. pp. 65–91.

—— (2008) Market Practices and Over-consumption, *Consumption, Markets & Culture*, 11(2): 151–67.

—— and Helgesson, C.-F. (2006) Multiple Versions of Markets: Multiplicity and Performativity in Market Practice, *Industrial Marketing Management*, 35(7): 839–55.

—— —— (2007a) On the Nature of Markets and Their Practices, *Marketing Theory*, 7(2): 137–62.

—— —— (2007b) The Mode of Exchange and Shaping of Markets: Distributor Influence in the Swedish Post-war Food Industry, *Industrial Marketing Management*, 36(7): 861–78.

—— —— (2010), Political Marketing: Multiple Values, Performativities and Modes of Engaging, *Journal of Cultural Economy*, 3(2), 279–97.

Klein, N. (2001) *No Logo*, London: Flamingo.

Knorr-Cetina, K. (1999) *Epistemic Cultures: How Scientists Make Sense*, Cambridge, MA: Harvard University Press.

—— (2001) Laboratory Studies. The Cultural Approach to the Study of Science, in S. Jasanoff (ed.), *Handbook of Science and Technology Studies*, Thousand Oaks, CA: Sage, pp. 140–66.

Korkman, O. (2006) *Customer Value Formation in Practice. A Practice-Theoretical Approach*, PhD thesis, Helsinki: Hanken School of Economics.

Kotler, P. (1972) A Generic Concept of Marketing, *Journal of Marketing*, 36(2): 46–54.

—— (1980) *Marketing Management: Analysis, Planning and Control*, 4th edn, Englewood Cliffs, NJ: Prentice-Hall.

—— and Keller, K. (2008) *Marketing Management*, New York: Prentice-Hall.

—— and Levy, S.J. (1969) Broadening the Concept of Marketing, *Journal of Marketing*, 33(1): 10–15.

—— —— (1973) Buying is Marketing Too!, *Journal of Marketing*, 37(1): 54–9.

Kozinets, R.V. (2002) Can Consumers Escape the Market? Emancipatory Illuminations from Burning Man, *Journal of Consumer Research*, 29(1): 20–38.

Krippner, G.R. (2002) The Elusive Market: Embeddedness and the Paradigm of Economic Sociology, *Theory and Society*, 30(6): 775–810.

Kroen, S. (2004) A Political History of the Consumer, *The Historical Journal*, 47(3): 709–36.

Kunda, G. (1992) *Engineering Culture: Control and Commitment in a High-Tech Corporation*, Philadelphia: Temple University Press.

Kurunmäki, L. (2004) A Hybrid Profession: The Acquisition of Management Accounting Expertise by Medical Professionals, *Accounting, Organizations and Society*, 29(3–4): 327–47.

Langlois, R.N. and Cosgel, M.M. (1999) The Organization of Consumption, in M. Bianchi (ed.), *The Active Consumer: Novelty and Surprise in Consumer Choice*, London: Routledge, pp. 107–121.

Lascoumes, P. and le Galès, P. (2004) *Gouverner par les Instruments*, Paris: Sciences Po les Presses.

Latour, B. (1986) The Powers of Association, in J. Law (ed.), *Power, Action and Belief: A New Sociology of Knowledge*, London: Routledge and Kegan Paul, pp. 264–80.

—— (1987) *Science in Action: How to Follow Scientists and Engineers Through Society*, Cambridge, MA: Harvard University Press.

—— (1991) Technology is Society Made Durable, in J. Law (ed.), *A Sociology of Monsters: Essays on Power, Technology, and Domination*, London: Routledge, pp. 103–31.

—— (1992) Where are the Missing Masses? The Sociology of a Few Mundane Artefacts, in W.E. Bijker and J. Law (eds), *Shaping Technology/Building Society: Studies in Sociotechnical Change*, Cambridge, MA: The MIT Press, pp. 225–58.

—— (1993) *We Have Never Been Modern*, Cambridge, MA: Harvard University Press.

—— (1995) The 'Pedofil' of Boa Vista: A Photo-Philosophical Montage, *Common Knowledge*, 4(1): 145–87.

—— (1996) On Interobjectivity, *Mind, Culture & Activity*, 3(4): 228–45.

—— (1999) *Pandora's Hope: Essays on the Reality of Science Studies*, Cambridge, MA: Harvard University Press.

—— (2005) *Reassembling the Social: An Introduction to Actor-Network Theory*, Clarendon Lectures in Management Studies, Oxford: Oxford University Press.

—— and Woolgar, S. (1979) *Laboratory Life: The Social Construction of Scientific Facts*, Beverly Hills, CA: Sage.

Lave, J. and Wenger, E. (1991) *Situated Learning: Legitimate Peripheral Participation*, Cambridge: Cambridge University Press.

Law, J. (1994) *Organizing Modernity*, Oxford: Blackwell.

—— and Akrich, M. (1996) On Customers and Costs: A Story from Public Sector Science, in M. Power (ed.), *Accounting and Science: Natural Inquiry and Commercial Reason*, Cambridge: Cambridge University Press, pp. 195–218.

—— and Urry, J. (2004) Enacting the Social, *Economy and Society*, 33(3): 390–410.

Lenox, M.J. and Nash, J. (2003) Industry Self-regulation and Adverse Selection: A Comparison Across Four Trade Association Programs, *Business Strategy and the Environment*, 12(6): 343–56.

Lépinay, V.A. (2007) Parasitic Formulae: The Case of Capital Guarantee Products, in M. Callon, Y. Millo, and F. Muniesa (eds), *Market Devices*, Oxford: Blackwell, pp. 261–83.

Levy, S.J. (1959) Symbols for Sale, *Harvard Business Review*, 37(4): 117–24.

Levy, D.T. (1994) Guaranteed Pricing in Industrial Purchases: Making Use of Markets in Contractual Relations, *Industrial Marketing Management*, 23(4): 307–13.

Leymonerie, C. (2006) La vitrine d'Appareils Ménagers. Reflet des Structures Commerciales dans la France des Années 1950, *Réseaux*, 24(135–136): 93–124.

Lezaun, J. (2007) A Market of Opinions: The Political Epistemology of Focus Groups, in M. Callon, Y. Millo, and F. Muniesa (eds), *Market Devices*, Oxford: Blackwell, pp. 130–51.

Lie, J. (1992) The Concept of Mode of Exchange, *American Sociological Review*, 57(4): 508–23.

Lie, M., and Sørensen, K.H. (1996) Making Technology Our Own? Domesticating Technology into Everyday Life, in M. Lie and K.H. Sørensen (eds), *Making Technology Our Own? Domesticating Technology into Everyday Life*, Oslo: Scandinavian University Press, pp. 1–30.

Lindberg, N. and Nordin, F. (2008) From Products to Services and Back Again: Towards a New Service Procurement Logic, *Industrial Marketing Management*, 37(3): 292–300.

Lindblom, C.E. (2001) *The Market System: What it is, How it Works, and What to Make of it*, New Haven, CT: Yale University Press.

Loasby, B.J. (1999) *Knowledge, Institutions and Evolution in Economics*, London: Routledge.

Longstreth, R.W. (1999) *The Drive-in, the Supermarket, and the Transformation of Commercial Space in Los Angeles, 1914–1941*, Cambridge, MA: MIT Press.

Lusch, R.F. and Vargo, S.L. (2006) Service-Dominant Logic: Reactions, Reflections and Refinements, *Marketing Theory*, 6(3): 281–8.

—— —— (2006) Service-Dominant Logic as a Foundation for a General Theory, in R.F. Lusch and S.L. Vargo (eds), *The Service-Dominant Logic of Marketing*: Dialog, Debate, and Directions, Armonk, NY: M.E. Sharpe pp. 406–20.

—— —— and O'Brien, M. (2007) Competing Through Service: Insights from Service-Dominant Logic, *Journal of Retailing*, 83(1): 5–18.

McChesney, F.S. (1996) The Role of Economists in Modern Antitrust: An Overview and Summary, *Managerial and Decision Economics*, 17(2): 119–26.

McCracken, G. (1986) Culture and Consumption: A Theoretical Account of the Structure and Movement of the Cultural Meaning of Consumer Goods, *Journal of Consumer Research*, 13(1): 71–84.

McGinnis, L.P. and Gentry, J.G. (2009) Underdog Consumption: An Exploration into Meanings and Motives, *Journal of Business Research*, 62(2): 191–9.

MacInnis, D. and Folkes, V. (2010) The Disciplinary Status of Consumer Behaviour: A Sociology of Science Perspective on Key Controversies, *Journal of Consumer Research*, 36(6): 899–914.

McInnes, W. (1964) A Conceptual Approach to Marketing, in R. Cox, W. Alderson, and S.J. Shapiro (eds), *Theory in Marketing*, Homewood, IL: Richard D. Irwin, pp. 51–67.

MacKenzie, D. (2003) An Equation and its Worlds: Bricolage, Exemplars, Disunity and Performativity in Financial Economics, *Social Studies of Science*, 33(6): 831–68.

—— (2006) *An Engine, Not a Camera: How Financial Models Shape Markets*, Cambridge, MA: MIT Press.

—— (2009) *Material Markets: How Economic Agents Are Constructed*. Oxford: Oxford University Press.

—— and Millo, Y. (2003) Constructing a Market, Performing a Theory: The Historical Sociology of a Financial Derivatives Exchange, *American Journal of Sociology*, 109(1): 107–45.

—— Muniesa, F. and Siu, L. (eds) (2007) *Do Economists Make Markets? On the Performativity of Economics*, Princeton, NJ: Princeton University Press.

McLoughlin, D. (2002) *Towards an Expanded Understanding of Exchange in Marketing: A Case Study of a New Exchange Movement*, PhD thesis, Lancaster: Lancaster University.

McMillan, J. (2002) *Reinventing the Bazaar: A Natural History of Markets*, New York: W.W. Norton and Company.

March, J.G. (1988) *Decisions and Organizations*, New York: Blackwell.

—— and Olsen, J.P. (2004) *The Logic of Appropriateness*, Oslo: ARENA, Centre for European Studies.

Marion, G. (2009) Une Relance de la Critique en Marketing; Science et Performation, *Économies et Sociétés. Série: "Économie de l'Entreprise"*, 12(1): 2115–52.

Marknadsdomstolen (2000) *Protokoll Dnr A14/99, Aktbilaga 129A*, Stockholm: Marknadsdomstolen.

—— (2001) *Konsortiet Scandinavian Airlines Systems vs Konkurrensverket*, Stockholm: Marknadsdomstolen.

Micheletti, M., Follesdal, A., and Stolle, D. (2004) *Politics, Products and Markets. Exploring Political Consumerism Past and Present*, New Brunswick NJ: Transaction Publishers.

Miller, D. (1997) *Material Cultures: Why Some Things Matter*, London: Routledge.

—— (2002) Turning Callon the Right Way Up, *Economy and Society*, 31(2): 218–33.

—— (2008a) The Uses of Value, *Geoforum*, 39(3): 1122–32.

—— (2008b) *The Comfort of Things*, Cambridge: Polity Press.

Miller, P. (2001) Governing by Numbers: Why Calculative Practices Matter, *Social Research*, 68(2): 379–96.

—— (2008) Calculating Economic Life, *Journal of Cultural Economy*, 1(1): 51–64.

—— and O'Leary, T. (1994) The Factory as a Laboratory, in M. Power (ed.), *Accounting and Science: Natural Inquiry and Commercial Reason*, Cambridge: Cambridge University Press, pp. 120–51.

—— —— (2007) Mediating Instruments and Making Markets: Capital Budgeting, Science and the Economy, *Accounting, Organizations and Society*, 32(7–8): 701–34.

—— and Rose, N. (1990) Governing Economic Life, *Economy and Society*, 19(1): 1–31.

Milward, D. (2008) Ryanair Sued by Passengers over Cancelled Flights, *Daily Telegraph*, 2 October, Accessed on 6 May 2009 at: http://www.telegraph.co.uk/travel/travelnews/3118107/Ryanair-sued-by-passengers-over-cancelled-flights.html.

Mirowski, P. and Nik-Khah, E. (2008) Command Performance: Exploring What STS Thinks it Takes to Build a Market, in T. Pinch and R. Swedberg (eds), *Living in a Material World*, Cambridge, MA: MIT Press, pp. 89–128.

Mitchell, T. (2008) Rethinking Economy, *Geoforum*, 39(13): 1116–21.

Mol, A. (2002) *The Body Multiple: Ontology in Medical Practice*, Durham NC: Duke University Press.

—— (2009) Good Taste. The Embodied Normativity of Consumer-Citizen, *Journal of Cultural Economy*, 2(3): 269–83.

Molotch, H. (2005) *Where Stuff Comes From: How Toasters, Toilets, Cars, Computers, and Many Other Things Come to Be As They Are*, New York: Routledge.

Monod, D. (1996) *Store Wars: Shopkeepers and the Culture of Mass Marketing, 1890–1939*, Toronto: University of Toronto Press.

Moor, L. (2010) Neoliberal Experiments: Social Marketing and the Governance of Populations, in D. Zwick and J. Cayla (eds), *Inside Marketing*, Oxford: Oxford University Press (forthcoming).

Mouritsen, J. and Thrane, S. (2006) Accounting, Network Complementarities and the Development of Inter-Organisational Relations, *Accounting, Organizations and Society*, 31(3): 241–75.

Muniesa, F., Callon, M., and Millo, Y. (2007) An Introduction to Market Devices, in M. Callon, Y. Millo, and F. Muniesa (eds), *Market Devices*, Oxford: Blackwell, pp. 1–12.

Nelson, R.R. (2002) The Problem of Market Bias in Modern Capitalist Economies, *Industrial and Corporate Change*, 11(2): 207–44.

—— and Winter, S. (1982) *An Evolutionary Theory of Economic Change*, Cambridge, MA: Harvard University Press.

Neyland, D. (2007) *Organizational Ethnography*, London: Sage.

—— and Simakova, E. (2009) How Far can We Push Sceptical Reflexivity? An Analysis of Marketing Ethics and the Certification of Poverty, *Journal of Marketing Management*, 25(7–8): 777–94.

Nicholls, A. and Opal, C. (2005) *Fair Trade: Market Driven Ethical Consumption*, London: Sage.

Normann, R. (2001) *Reframing Business: When the Map Changes the Landscape*, Chichester: Wiley.

North, D.C. (1977) Markets and Other Allocation Systems in History: The Challenge of Karl Polanyi, *Journal of European Economic History*, 6(3): 703–16.

—— (1990) *Institutions, Institutional Change and Economic Performance*, Cambridge: Cambridge University Press.

Oldenburg, R. (1989) *The Great Good Place: Cafes, Coffee Shops, Community Centers, Beauty Parlors, General Stores, Bars, Hangouts and How They Get You Through the Day*, New York: Paragon House.

Oliver, D. and Roos, J. (2003) Dealing with the Unexpected: Critical Incidents in the LEGO Mindstorms Team, *Human Relations*, 56(6): 1057–82.

Oudshoorn, N. and Pinch, T.J. (2003) How Users and Non-Users Matter, in N. Oudshoorn and T.J. Pinch (eds), *How Users Matter: The Co-construction of Users and Technology*, Cambridge, MA: MIT Press, pp. 1–25.

Palamountain, J.C. (1955) *The Politics of Distribution*, Cambridge, MA: Harvard University Press.

Pantzar, M. (1997) Domestication of Everyday Life Technology: Dynamic Views on the Social Histories of Artifacts, *Design Issues*, 13(3): 52–65.

Parsons, T. and Smelser, N.J. (1956) *Economy and Society*, London: Routledge and Kegan Paul.

Payne, A., Storbacka, K., and Frow, P. (2008) Managing the Co-creation of Value, *Journal of the Academy of Marketing Science*, 36(1): 83–96.

Peattie, K. (2007) Sustainable Marketing: Marketing Re-thought, Re-mixed and Re-tooled, in M. Saren, P. Maclaran, C. Goulding, R. Elliott, A. Shankar, and M. Catterall (eds), *Critical Marketing: Defining the Field*, Oxford: Butterworth-Heinemann, pp. 193–210.

—— and Charter, M. (2002) Green Marketing, in M.J. Baker (ed.), *The Marketing Book*, 5th edn, Oxford: Butterworth-Heinemann.

Peñaloza, L. (2000) The Commodification of the American West: Marketers' Production of Cultural Meanings at the Trade Show, *Journal of Marketing*, 64(4): 82–109.

Pettinger, L. (2005) Representing Shop Work: A Dual Ethnography, *Qualitative Research*, 5(3): 347–64.

Piller, F., Schubert, P., Koch, M., and Möslein, K. (2006) Overcoming Mass Confusion: Collaborative Customer Co-design in Online Communites, *Journal of Computer-Mediated Communication*, 10(4): article 8 http://jcmc.indiana.edu/vol10/issue4/piller.html.

Pinch, T. and Swedberg, R. (2008) Introduction, in T. Pinch and R. Swedberg (eds), *Living in a Material World: Economic Sociology Meets Science and Technology Studies*, Cambridge, MA: MIT Press, pp. 1–26.

Ponte, S. (2002) The "Latte Revolution"? Regulation, Markets and Consumption in the Global Coffee Chain, *World Development*, 30(7): 1099–122.

Porter, T.M. (2008) Locating the Domain of Calculation, *Journal of Cultural Economy*, 1(1): 39–50.

Power, M. (2004) Counting, Control and Calculation: Reflections on Measuring and Management, *Human Relations*, 57(6): 765–83.

Prahalad, C.K. and Ramaswamy, V. (2000) Co-opting Customer Competence, *Harvard Business Review*, 78(1): 79–88.

—— (2004) Co-creation Experiences: The Next Practice in Value Creation, *Journal of Interactive Marketing*, 18(3): 5–14.

Pred, A. (1977) Choreography of Existence—Comments on Hagerstrand's Time-Geography and Its Usefulness, *Economic Geography*, 53(2): 207–21.

—— (1981) Social Reproduction and the Time-Geography of Everyday Life, *Geografiska Annaler Series B—Human Geography*, 63(1): 5–22.

—— (1983) Structuration and Place—On the Becoming of Sense of Place and Structure of Feeling, *Journal for the Theory of Social Behaviour*, 13(1): 45–68.

Preda, A. (1999) The Turn to Things: Arguments for a Sociological Theory of Things, *Sociological Quarterly*, 40(2): 347–66.

Ramírez, R. (1999) Value Co-production: Intellectual Origins and Implications for Practice and Research, *Strategic Management Journal*, 20(1): 49–65.

Razac, O. (2000) *Histoire Politique du Barbelé: La Prairie, la Tranchée, le Camp*, Paris: La Fabrique.

Reckwitz, A. (2002a) The Status of the "Material" in Theories of Culture: From "Social Structure" to "Artefacts", *Journal for the Theory of Social Behaviour*, 32(2): 195–218.

—— (2002b) Toward a Theory of Social Practices: A Development in Culturalist Theorizing, *European Journal of Social Theory*, 5(2): 243–63.

Reibstein, D.J., Day, G.S., and Wind, J. (2009) Guest Editorial: Is Marketing Academia Losing its Way?, *Journal of Marketing*, 73(4): 1–3.

Ribeiro, R. (2007) The Language Barrier as an Aid to Communication, *Social Studies of Science*, 37(4): 561–84.

Rinallo, D. and Golfetto, F. (2006) Representing Markets: The Shaping of Fashion Trends by French and Italian Fabric Companies, *Industrial Marketing Management*, 35(7): 856–69.

Roberts, J. (2006) Limits to Communities of Practice, *Journal of Management Studies*, 43(3): 623–39.

Ronit, K. (2006) International Governance by Organized Business: The Shifting Roles of Firms, Associations and Inter-governmental Organizations in Self-regulation, in W. Streeck, J.R. Grote, V. Schneider, and J. Visser (eds), *Governing Interests: Business Associations Facing Internationalization*, London and New York: Routledge, pp. 219–41.

Rosa, J.A., Porac, J.F., Runser-Spanjol, J., and Saxon, M.S. (1999) Sociocognitive Dynamics in a Product Market, *Journal of Marketing*, 63(SISI): 64–77.

Rose, N. (1999) *Powers of Freedom: Reframing Political Thought*, Cambridge: Cambridge University Press.

—— and Miller, P. (1992) Political Power Beyond the State: Problematics of Government, *British Journal of Sociology*, 43(2): 173–205.

Ross, A. (2009a) Industry Revamp to Hit Advisers, *Financial Times*, 25 July, http://cachef.ft.com/cms/s/0/9461e0de-61c2-11de-9e03-00144feabdc0.html.

—— (2009b) Financial Advisers Fear Impact of New Rule, *Financial Times*, 19 September, http://www.ft.com/cms/s/0/1b13d7b2-a4b3-11de-92d4-00144feabdc0.html,

Roth, A. (2007) The Art of Designing Markets, *Harvard Business Review*, 85(10): 118–26.

—— (2008) What have We Learned from Market Design?, *Economic Journal*, 118(527): 285–310.

Ryanair (2008) Annual Report http://www.ryanair.com/en/investor/download/2008.

Ryanair (not dated) *Customer Charter* http://www.ryanair.com/en/about/passenger-charter. (current, 8th September 2010).

Samli, A.C. and Bahn, K.D. (1992) The Market Phenomenon: An Alternative Theory and Some Metatheoretical Research Considerations, *Journal of the Academy of Marketing Science*, 20(2): 143–53.

SAS (1997–2008) *SAS Group Annual Reports*, Stockholm: SAS.

—— (1999) *SAS EuroBonus Membership guide*, Stockholm: SAS.

—— (2005) *Earning Points on Swedish Domestic Routes*, http://www.sas.se/en/.

Sawhney, M. and Prandelli, E. (2000) Communities of Creation: Managing Distributed Innovation in Turbulent Markets, *California Management Review*, 42(2): 24–54.

Schatzki, T.R. (2001) Introduction. Practice Theory, in T.R. Schatzki, K. Knorr-Cetina, and E.V. Savigny (eds), *The Practice Turn in Contemporary Theory*, London: Routledge, pp. 1–14.

Scherer, F.M. (1970) *Industrial Market Structure and Economic Performance*, Chicago: Rand McNally.

—— and Ross, D. (1990) *Industrial Market Structure and Economic Performance*, 3rd ed., Boston: Houghton Mifflin.

Schmitter, P.C. and Streeck, W. (1999 [1981]) *The Organization of Business Interests: Studying the Associative Action of Business in Advanced Industrial Societies*, Discussion Paper 99/1, Cologne: Max Planck Institute for the Study of Societies.

Schudson, M. (2006) The Troubling Equivalence of Citizen and Consumer, *The Annals of the American Society of Political and Social Science*, 608(1): 193–204.

Seidl, D. (2005) *Organizational Identities and Self-Transformation: An Autopoietic Perspective*, Aldershot: Ashgate.

Seth, A. (2001) *The Grocers: The Rise and Rise of the Supermarket Chains*, Dover, NH: Kogan Page.

Shaw, E.H. and Jones, D.G.B. (2005) A History of Schools of Marketing Thought, *Marketing Theory*, 5(3): 239–81.

Sherman, R. (1968) Trading Stamps and Consumer Welfare, *The Journal of Industrial Economics*, 17(1): 29–40.

Sheth, J.N., Gardner, D.M., and Garrett, D.E. (1988) *Marketing Theory: Evolution and Evaluation*, New York: Wiley.

Shove, E. and Pantzar, M., (2005) Consumers, Producers and Practices: Understanding the Invention and Reinvention of Nordic Walking, *Journal of Consumer Culture*, 5(1): 43–64.

—— Watson, M., Hand, M., and Ingram, J. (2007) *The Design of Everyday Life*: Oxford: Berg.

—— Trentmann, F., and Wilk, R. (eds) (2009) *Time, Consumption and Everyday Life: Practice, Materiality and Culture*, Oxford: Berg.

Silverstone, R. (1994) *Television and Everyday Life*, London: Routledge.

—— Hirsch, E., and Morley, D. (1992) The Moral Economy of the Household, in E. Hirsch and R. Silverstone (eds), *Consuming Technologies: Media and Information in Domestic Spaces*, London: Routledge, pp. 15–31.

Simakova, E. and Neyland, D. (2008) Marketing Mobile Futures: Assembling Constituencies and Creating Compelling Stories for an Emerging Technology, *Marketing Theory*, 8(1): 91–116.

Sissors, J.Z. (1966) What Is a Market?, *Journal of Marketing*, 30(3): 17–21.

Sjögren, E. and Helgesson, C.-F. (2007) The Q(u)ALYfying Hand: Health Economics and Medicine in the Shaping of Swedish Markets for Subsidised Pharmaceuticals, in M. Callon, Y. Millo, and F. Muniesa (eds), *Market Devices*, Oxford: Blackwell, pp. 215–40.

Skålén, P., Fougère, M., and Fellesson, M. (2008) *Marketing Discourse: A Critical Perspective*, London: Routledge.

Slater, D. (2002a) Markets, Materiality and the "New Economy", in J.S. Metcalfe and A. Warde (eds), *Market Relations and the Competitive Process*, Manchester: Manchester University Press, pp. 95–113.

—— (2002b) Capturing Markets from the Economists, in P. du Gay and M. Pryke (eds), *Cultural Economy: Cultural Analysis and Commercial Life*, London: Sage, pp. 59–77.

—— and Tonkiss, F. (2001) *Market Society: Markets and Modern Social Theory*, Cambridge: Polity Press.

Slattery, L. (2009) Planet Business, *Irish Times*, 24 July.

Snehota, I. (2004) Perspectives and Theories of Market, in H. Håkansson, D. Harrison, and A. Waluszewski (eds), *Rethinking Marketing: Developing a New Understanding of Markets*, Chichester, Wiley pp. 15–32.

Starbucks (2008) *Company Fact Street* http://www.starbucks.com/assets/company-factsheet.pdf.

Stark, D. (2009) *The Sense of Dissonance: Accounts of Worth in Economic Life*, Princeton, NJ: Princeton University Press.

Stern, B.B. (2006) What does Brand Mean? Historical Analysis, Method and Construct Definition, *Journal of the Academy of Marketing Science*, 34(2): 216–23.

Stern, J.P. (1997) The British Gas Market 10 Years After Privatisation: A Model or a Warning for the Rest of Europe?, *Energy Policy*, 25(4): 387–92.

Stidsen, B. (1979) [Toward a Concept of Domesticated Markets]: Comment, *Journal of Marketing*, 43(4): 76–9.

Strasser, S. (1989) *Satisfaction Guaranteed: The Making of the American Mass Market*, New York: Pantheon Books.

—— (2000) *Waste and Want: A Social History of Trash*, New York: Holt.

Streeck, W. Grote, J., Schneider, V., and Visser, J. (eds) (2006) *Governing Interests: Business Associations Facing Internationalization*, New York: Routledge.

Strotz, R.H. (1958) On Being Fooled by Figures: The Case of Trading Stamps, *The Journal of Business*, 31(4): 304–10.

Sunderland, P. and Denny, R. (2010) Consumer Segmentation in Practice: An Ethnographic Account of Slippage, in D. Zwick and J. Cayla (eds), *Inside Marketing*, Oxford: Oxford University Press (forthcoming).

Tamilia, R.D. (2005) *The Wonderful World of the Department Store in Historical Perspective: A Comprehensive International Bibliography Partially Annotated*, École des Sciences de la Gestion, University of Quebec at Montreal.

Tedlow, R.S. (1990) *New and Improved: The Story of Mass Marketing in America*, New York: Basic Books.

Tharp, B. (2002) Value: Anthropological and Design Perspectives, in NEC Proceedings, Virginia: IDSA.

Thoenig, J.-C. and Waldman, C. (2005) *De l'Entreprise Marchande à l'Entreprise Marquante*, Paris: les Éditions d'Organisation.

Thomas, N. (1991) *Entangled Objects: Exchange, Material Culture and Colonialism in the Pacific*, Cambridge, MA: Harvard University Press.

Thompson, C.J. and Arsel, Z. (2004) The Starbucks Brandscape and Consumers' (Anticorporate) Experiences of Glocalization, *Journal of Consumer Research*, 31(3): 631–42.

Toh, R.S., Fleenor, C.P. and Arnesen, D.W. (1993) Frequent-Flier Games: The Problem of Employee Abuse, *Academy of Management Executive*, 7(1): 60–72.

Trentmann, F. (2009) Materiality in the Future of History: Things, Practices and Politics, *Journal of British Studies*, 48(2): 283–307.

Tucker, W.T. (1974) Future Directions in Marketing Theory, *Journal of Marketing*, 38(2): 30–5.

UNRISD (1996) Available from: http://www.unrisd.org/unrisd/website/newsview.nsf/ (httpNews)/4E6D8E48AE83011380256B7B003F94FC?OpenDocument.

Uzzi, B. (1997) Social Structure and Competition in Interfirm Networks: The Paradox of Embeddedness, *Administrative Science Quarterly*, 42(1): 35–67.

Vargo, S.L. and Lusch, R.F. (2004) Evolving to a New Dominant Logic for Marketing, *Journal of Marketing*, 68(1): 1–17.

—— —— (2006) Service-Dominant Logic: What It Is, What It Is Not, What It Might Be, in R.F. Lusch and S.L. Vargo (eds), *The Service-Dominant Logic of Marketing: Dialog, Debate, and Directions*, Armonk, NY: M.E. Sharpe, pp. 43–56.

Venkatesh, A., Peñaloza, L. and Firat, A.F. (2006) The Market as a Sign System and the Logic of the Market, in R.F. Lusch and S.L. Vargo (eds), *The Service-Dominant Logic of Marketing: Dialog, Debate, and Directions*, Armonk, NY: M.E. Sharpe, pp. 251–65.

Vietor, R.H.K. (1990) Contrived Competition: Airline Regulation and Deregulation, 1925–1988, *Business History Review*, 64(1): 61–108.

Von Hippel, E. (1986) Lead Users—A Source of Novel Product Concepts, *Management Science*, 32(7): 791–805.

—— (1988) *The Sources of Innovation*, New York: Oxford University Press.

—— (2001) Perspective: User Toolkits for Innovation, *Journal of Product Innovation Management*, 18(4): 247–57.

—— (2005) *Democratizing Innovation*, Cambridge, MA: The MIT Press.

—— and Katz, R. (2002) Shifting Innovation to Users via Toolkits, *Management Science*, 48(7): 821–33.

Wallich, P. (2001) Mindstorms: Not Just a Kid's Toy, *IEEE Spectrum*, 38(9): 52–7.

Warde, A. (2005) Consumption and Theories of Practice, *Journal of Consumer Culture*, 5(2): 131–53.

Watson, M. (2008) Introduction. The Materials of Consumption, *Journal of Consumer Culture*, 8(1): 5–10.

—— and Shove, E. (2008) Product, Competence, Project and Practice: DIY and the Dynamics of Craft Consumption, *Journal of Consumer Culture*, 8(1): 69–89.

Watson, T.J. (1994) *In Search of Management: Culture, Control and Chaos in Managerial Work*, London: International Thomson Business Press.

Wensley, R. (1990) The Voice of the Consumer? Speculations on the Limits to Marketing Analogy, *European Journal of Marketing*, 24(7): 49–60.

—— (2009) Market Ideology, Globalization and NeoLiberalism, in P. Maclaran, M. Saren, B. Stern, and M. Tadajewski (eds), *The Sage Handbook of Marketing Theory*, London: Sage, pp. 235–43.

Whatmore, S., Stassart, P., and Renting, H. (2003) What's Alternative About Alternative Food Networks?, *Environment and Planning A*, 35(3): 389–91.

Williams, C.C. (2004) The Myth of Marketization: An Evaluation of the Persistence of Non-Market Activities in Advanced Economies, *International Sociology*, 19(4): 437–49.

Willig, R.D., Salop, S.C., and Scherer, F.M. (1991) Merger Analysis, Industrial Organization Theory, and Merger Guidelines, *Brookings Papers on Economic Activity, Microeconomics*, 281–332.

Wilson, P.I. (1997) Deregulation and Natural Gas Trade Relationships: Lessons from the Alberta-California Experience, *Energy Policy*, 25(10): 861–9.

Woolgar, S. (1991) Configuring the User: The Case of Usability Trials, in J. Law (ed.), *A Sociology of Monsters: Essays on Power, Technology and Domination*, London: Routledge, pp. 58–99.

Wooliscroft, B., Tamilia, R.D., and Shapiro, S.J. (eds) (2006) *A Twenty-First Century Guide to Aldersonian Marketing Thought*, New York, Springer-Verlag.

WSWS (2006) Available from: http://www.wsws.org/articles/2006/mar2006/bang-m02.shtml.

Yates, J. (2006) How Business Enterprises Use Technology: Extending the Demand-Side Turn, *Enterprise & Society*, 7(3): 422–55.

Zeitlyn, D. (2003) Gift Economies in the Development of Open Source Software: Anthropological Reflections, *Research Policy*, 32(7): 1287–91.

Zelizer, V. (1978) Human Values and the Market: The Case of Life Insurance and Death in 19th-Century America, *American Journal of Sociology*, 84(3): 591–610.

Zwick, D. and Cayla, J. (2010) Introduction, in D. Zwick and J. Cayla (eds), *Inside Marketing: Practices, Ideologies, Devices*, Oxford: Oxford University Press, (forthcoming).

■ INDEX